THE LUXURY
of
SKEPTICISM

THE LUXURY
of
SKEPTICISM

Politics, Philosophy, and
Dialogue in the
English Public Sphere
1660–1740

TIMOTHY DYKSTAL

UNIVERSITY PRESS OF VIRGINIA
Charlottesville and London

The University Press of Virginia
© 2001 by the Rector and Visitors of the University of Virginia
All rights reserved
Printed in the United States of America
First published 2001

⊚ The paper used in this publication meets the minimum requirements of
the American National Standard for Information Sciences—Permanence of Paper
for Printed Library Materials, ANSI Z39.48-1984.

Library of Congress Cataloging-in-Publication Data

Dykstal, Timothy.
     The luxury of skepticism : politics, philosophy, and dialogue in the English public
sphere, 1660–1740 / Timothy Dykstal.
        p. cm.
     Based on the author's doctoral dissertation (University of Chicago).
     Includes bibliographical references and index.
     ISBN 0-8139-2003-5 (alk. paper)
     1. Political science—Great Britain—History—17th century. 2. Political science—Great
Britain—History—18th century. 3. Great Britain—Politics and government—1660–1714.
4. Great Britain—Politics and government—1714–1760. 5. Dialogues, English—History
and criticism. 6. Skepticism—History. I. Title.

JA84.G7 D85 2001
320'.01—dc21

                                                                              00-060021

For my parents

CONTENTS

CONTENTS

ACKNOWLEDGMENTS

THE LIFE of the mind has many pleasures. The length of time that it can take to see an idea through to its completion is not, to my mind, one of them. It does give me great pleasure, however, to acknowledge the many friends, acquaintances, and intellectual debts that I have acquired during the lengthy composition of this book. It first took life as a doctoral dissertation at the University of Chicago, where I benefited from the perceptive comments and moral support of my fellow students Rebecca Chung, Kevin Gilmartin, Shef Rogers, Craig M. Rustici, and Cynthia Wall. Individual chapters were tempered in the fire of the eighteenth-century and history and literature graduate workshops. The members of the former were gracious enough to invite me back to campus in 1997 to present an entirely new version of the introduction. Also at Chicago, Professors Bruce Redford and Stuart Sherman read the dissertation insightfully and generously, asking critical questions that have stayed with me ever since.

At Auburn University, many colleagues both in and out of the eighteenth century have demonstrated their support of my work. I wish in particular to thank David P. Haney and Harry M. Solomon for sharing their expertise in philosophy and literature. The book began to take its final form during a year of revision at the Institute for Research in the Humanities at my undergraduate institution, the University of Wisconsin, Madison, where critical yet sympathetic listeners and readers included Lloyd F. Bitzer, Phillip Harth, Gordon Hutner, Mark L. Kleinman, Laura Weigert, and George Wright. Special thanks are due to the institute's director, Paul S. Boyer, for lending me a clean, well-lighted place in which to work; to its executive secretary, Loretta Freiling, for supplying the other necessities; and to Heather Dubrow for giving crucial advice. Lawrence E. Klein's work first showed me the way on Shaftesbury, and he provided much-needed guidance toward the end of the project. I want also to thank the two anonymous readers assigned by the University Press of Virginia, whose comments improved the book immensely; the humanities editor there, Cathie Brettschneider, who acquired the book and has shepherded it through the editorial process with great care; and Joanne Allen, for her splendid copyediting.

My research was supported materially by a Dissertation-Year Fellowship from the University of Chicago; by a Competitive Research Grant and a Humanities Development Grant from Auburn University; by a Huntington Library Fellowship; by a visiting fellowship from the Institute for Research in the Humanities, University of Wisconsin, Madison; and by an American Council of Learned Societies Fellowship.

An earlier, abbreviated version of chapter 4 was originally published as "Commerce, Conversation, and Contradiction in Mandeville's *Fable"* in *Studies in Eighteenth-Century Culture,* vol. 23, ed. Carla H. Hay and Syndy M. Conger (East Lansing, Mich.: Colleagues Press for the American Society for Eighteenth-Century Studies, 1994), 93–110. I thank the Johns Hopkins University Press for the permission to reprint.

My deepest appreciation goes out to my teachers Wayne C. Booth and J. Paul Hunter, who prodded when necessary and inspired, both by word and by example, always; and to my colleague Paula R. Backscheider, who has stretched my thinking about the book—and practically everything else.

Finally, I would like to thank my family: my wife, Caroline Burke, who was there from the beginning; my son Henry, who bolstered the middle; and my son Charles, who brightened the end.

THE LUXURY
of
SKEPTICISM

INTRODUCTION
Conversation and Political Controversy

IN THE EPISTLE dedicatory to *Dramatic Poesie, An Essay* (1668), before he asserts that he intended his "whole discourse" to be "skeptical," John Dryden expresses to his friend Lord Buckhurst the hope that his dialogue has placed him in the company not of those "pedants" who have "prosecuted" controversy "with violence of words" but of those "gentlemen" who have "managed" it "with candour and civility."[1] In *The Moralists* (1709), a dialogue by the third earl of Shaftesbury, the narrator Philocles contrasts his "constant way in all Debates"—to be "as well pleas'd with the Reason on one side, as on the other" and never to be "troubl'd . . . about the Success of the Argument"—to the "painful and laborious" process by which some "hold precisely" to what they "at a venture call'd THE TRUTH" and declares his "Sceptical" kind of philosophy to be "the prettiest, agreeablest, roving Exercise of the Mind, possible to be imagin'd."[2] In the prefatory letter to David Hume's *Dialogues Concerning Natural Religion* (1779), Pamphilus, the reporter of the conversation between the orthodox Demea, the deist Cleanthes, and the skeptic Philo, explains why he has chosen to convey the content of this conversation by reproducing its form:

> Any question of philosophy . . . which is so *obscure* and *uncertain* that human reason can reach no fixed determination with regard to it; . . . seems to lead us naturally into the style of dialogue and conversation. Reasonable men may be allowed to differ, where no one can reasonably be positive: Opposite sentiments, even without any decision, afford an agreeable amusement: And if the subject be curious and interesting, the book carries us, in a manner, into company; and unites the two greatest and purest pleasures of human life, study and society.[3]

1

These prefatory remarks to the three best-known dialogues written in English during the long eighteenth century all associate the form with something called "skepticism," and they all define skepticism, at least here, not as a disagreeable condition of epistemological doubt —what Shaftesbury elsewhere calls "a total Uncertainty of what Reason had seemingly so well establish'd" (*Characteristicks*, 1:42)—but as an especially "civil" exercise in ethical restraint. Paradoxically, it is the ability of the participants in these dialogues to suspend agreement— to, as Dryden says, "sustain" their conversations "of several opinions" and yet leave "all of them . . . doubtful" (124)—that makes the dialogues themselves so "agreeable."

But compare this vision of polite conversation among men with the sexual politics conducted in *The Ladies Defence* (1701) by Mary Chudleigh, a dialogue poem written in reply to the attack on women launched in a 1699 wedding sermon by the clergyman John Sprint. There, even as her antagonists exhort her to assume the modest and diffident air of the obedient wife, Chudleigh's protagonist, Melissa, demolishes the alternative futures for women represented by the husband Sir John Brute and the rake Sir Richard Loveall with her impolite, even impolitic wit. Chudleigh, like so many of her lesser-known contemporaries during the late seventeenth and early eighteenth centuries, uses the dialogue form not to cultivate a skeptical unconcern in philosophy but to further her own political agenda.

This book asks how it is that a controversy about politics becomes a conversation about philosophy. In the passages above, Dryden is debating the superiority of English to French drama, and Hume is discussing the possibility of rational religious belief, but Shaftesbury intends his polite, Neoplatonic philosophy to counter the obstinacies of Thomas Hobbes, who argued that human beings' interest in self-preservation would lead them to submit to the authority of an absolute sovereign. Just as Chudleigh pursues her particular controversy when others would caution her to remain "conversable" and polite (or even silent), Hobbes presses for an answer to the political problem of controversy itself, the plethora of opinions that threatened to dissolve the commonwealth. In the middle decades of the seventeenth century Hobbes, like most of the philosophers and polemicists concerned with such matters, would not have described that problem as anything like a "conversation" in which "Reasonable men may be allowed to differ." The stakes were too high to be skeptical about the possibility of settling differences of opinion or to be so disinterested about one's own.

The stakes were too high because the sorts of controversies that Hume later characterized as "agreeable amusement" had resulted in civil war. Differences of opinion in religion were practically indistinguishable from differences of opinion in politics, and both, when pressed, had produced the violent rejection of the sovereign authority that had been thought to transcend such differences. The regicide of Charles I, however much it was deplored after the Restoration, legitimated disagreement in both the theory and the practice of politics: it became possible for ordinary citizens to have an opinion about how society should be constituted, and it became probable that in the attempt to gather popular support their differences would be aired in public. Yet, while pluralism may have been a new fact in the nation's political life, as Stephen N. Zwicker states, "The Restoration did not begin with an open acknowledgment" of it; "it began, in fact, with strenuous efforts to deny faction and dissent."[4] The lament of George Lawson, a clergyman and political theorist who accommodated himself to the various regimes that came and went until his death in 1678, is typical: "Our form of Government is confounded by the different opinions of common Lawyers, Civilians and Divines, who neither agree with one another, nor amongst themselves."[5] Near the end of the Interregnum, Lawson—whose treatise *Politica Sacra et Civilis* is said to anticipate the contract theory of John Locke[6]—notably does not say that the form of government is confounded by the lack of tolerance for different opinions. Rather, he insists that it is confounded by the differences of opinion themselves. Diversity was seen not as something that invigorated politics but as a problem that needed to be solved.

The journalist Leon Wieseltier, criticizing the fashionable talk about dialogue in contemporary politics, describes it as "a weapon against urgency."[7] A longer view of the public function of dialogue, however—specifically, one that takes into account its fashion in late-seventeenth- and early-eighteenth-century political controversy— can only describe it as a weapon *for* urgency. Situated between skepticism and dogmatism, and dedicated to pursuing a solution to the problem of diversity, dialogue exemplifies the "great revolution in human thought" that Christopher Hill dates from the decades of the

civil war: "the general realisation . . . that solutions to political problems might be reached by discussion and argument."[8] In this book I
argue that as a literary form dialogue helped to develop and subse-
quently transform the public sphere in late-seventeenth- and early-
eighteenth-century England. At the beginning of this period the dialogue gained popularity by representing an answer to the controversies that beset the commonwealth, but by the end philosophers were
setting their dialogues against the practical world of political media-
tion and defining a speculative realm that was increasingly private
and apolitical. It was in this sense that what was originally a controversy
about politics among many dialogue writers—a controversy in search
of answers to the questions that plagued civil society—became a "conversation" among a few philosophers that sought to be civil by asking
more questions. By thickly describing a period in history when the
dialogue was both philosophically speculative and politically engaged,
I intend to restore it to its place in the public sphere.

The Efflorescence of the Public Sphere

According to Jürgen Habermas, whose book *The Structural Transformation of the Public Sphere* revived the concept, the public sphere is a
discursive space that arose between the state and the private realm in
early modern Europe. In the institutions of this public sphere—clubs,
coffeehouses, and voluntary associations—the European bourgeoisie
gained the confidence to challenge the authority of the ruling elite by
freely exchanging opinions about cultural and political matters. The
institutions provided the readership for the products of an active
press, which, despite the Licensing Act (first passed in 1662 and renewed intermittently until 1695), expanded the number of printed
pieces in circulation tenfold from the early Stuart years.[9] "In the
course of the 17th century," says Rüdiger Ahrens, controversial literature thus "came to assume the characteristics of a mass phenomenon,
formatively influencing public political opinion."[10] The connection
between the society of the coffeehouses and the world of print is
made in the anonymous *Dialogue between Tom and Dick, Over a Dish of
Coffee* (1680), in which two obvious commoners gather in "a Corner
of this *Coffee-house*" to talk about "matters of *Religion* and *Government*,"
and "Tom," employed as a polemicist, complains that "I have writ my
self half *purblind* already, I *write* commonly in my *sleep*, and *Dream* out

politick Discourses: & *Further Discoveries*." He is only writing to meet the demand, for such matters are "all the Discourse now, from the *Lord* to the *Fidler*, all are grown *States-men*."[11] Controversial literature like the *Dialogue between Tom and Dick*, written to the moment, conveying news as well as ideas, and published to generate even more discussion and argument, depicted for the first time in English literary history ordinary citizens calling their superiors to account.

That they did so in dialogue, and in vast quantities, has been well documented. According to one tabulation, 2,000 works proclaiming or revealing themselves to be dialogues were published between the years 1660 and 1725; another survey counts a mere 1,500 between 1550 and 1750. Whatever the figure, the production of dialogues predictably surged during years of "political excitement." During the height of the Exclusion Crisis, for example, at least 65 dialogues were published, 25 in 1680 and 40 in 1681.[12] Dialogue addressed every conceivable subject, from the antiquity of the English constitution to landscape gardening, and represented, though not necessarily well, every conceivable interest—Tory, Whig, Conformist, Dissenter, country, city, and more. Even Roger L'Estrange, who as "surveyor of the imprimery" was charged with enforcing the Licensing Act and who as early as *Toleration Discuss'd* (1663) had stated that "When *Subjects* come once to dispute *Laws*, The *War* is already *Declar'd* against the *Government*," found himself exploiting the dialogue form to dispute the disputers.[13] The sheer popularity of the dialogue in the late seventeenth and early eighteenth centuries already implies the major premise of my study: that this supply reflects a newfound demand for dialogue in the public sphere. This is not to say that dialogue reproduced, in some transparent fashion, the more immediate conversations actually taking place *in* public. Print, like any medium, changes what it represents, and dialogues idealized or, conversely, satirized how debates were being conducted as often as they tried to reproduce them. But the dialogue is unique among literary forms in imitating, however fairly or well, what it itself facilitated, that is, the exchange of opinions among a variety of interests that distinguishes the Restoration period from what came before. This is why it has to be considered the prototypical organ of the public sphere.

The dialogue was such a popular form for the exercise of reason in the Restoration, in fact, that I have been constrained to convey my conclusions about it in this introduction through a relatively small sample of individual dialogues. Even that sample, however, can prove the overwhelming demand for dialogue in the period, and I have tried to make it as representative as possible by concentrating on a particularly vigorous period of controversy, that of the Exclusion Crisis, from 1679 to 1681. When Parliament and the public considered the question whether the Catholic James should succeed his brother Charles to the throne, according to Mark Knights, it "reinjected life into an older debate that stretched back at least to the 1640s about the nature of government and the allegiance of the subject."[14] But even that does not encompass the entire prehistory of the Exclusion controversy, for it also extended the two-centuries-old debate about the nature of sovereignty that, although it had been conducted in the specialized area of constitutional law, established the tradition of questioning authority that caused the public sphere to develop first in England rather than on the Continent.[15]

Given the complexity of those constitutional issues and the alacrity with which writers often had to engage them, there is a tendency now (as then) to dismiss the literature of this or any other controversy as inferior in substance to those works (such as Locke's *Two Treatises of Government*) that step back from their immediate context to engage the issues in a more measured fashion. Indeed, this critical distance is one measure of the difference between strictly "political" writings and theoretical or "philosophical" ones. But historical research has confirmed that even Locke's *Two Treatises* was written to intervene in the Exclusion Crisis, as a call for revolution rather than the rationalization of one that it became when it was published in 1690, and Knights maintains that "pamphlets debating the succession issue . . . showed a remarkable sophistication in their discussion of the origin of government and the extent of political obedience" (243–44).[16] The discussants themselves would no doubt agree, as Honest Hodge tells Ralph in a dialogue relating their "sober Discourse . . . Concerning Affairs in England": "[S]ince this *damnable Popish Plot* has been discovered, there have come out so many notable *good* and *bad Books* on all sides, that I vow to thee I am become sublime like a *Philosopher*."[17] A fair consideration of the "literature" of controversy may blur a sharp distinction between polemic and literature, as well as between politics and philosophy.

Another reason for concentrating on the Exclusion Crisis, besides the vigor of the debate then, is that it complicates a faith like Habermas's that the openness of argument in the public sphere will win out over those who want to keep it secret. The secret that the "Phanatick" Presbyterian in Richard Onslow's Whiggish *Dialogue between the Pope and a Phanatick, Concerning Affairs in England* (1680) ironically reveals is that he is in league with the pope to advance the Popish Plot even though in public they are archenemies, and in the dialogue the pope requests the Presbyterian to continue the deception of his public "Raillery" against him for in it "consists the strength of all our Stratagems."[18] But the Tories only returned the accusation of plotting against the Whigs. In Andrew Yarranton's *Coffee-House Dialogue* (1679?) a Whiggish captain accuses "all the Clergy of the Church of England" of neglecting "the Improvement of the Nation" and insinuates to his companion, a lawyer, that they "have another sort of Game to play;— no more of that—you understand me." The lawyer, however, questions not only the accusation but also the captain's manner of hinting at something even more sinister, presumably that the Anglican clergy have a "Game to play" with the Catholics: "Not I, I profess; I cannot be reconcil'd to half a Sentence join'd with a little push, a wink, a nod, a smile, or a Finger held up to the Nose; . . . Therefore Sir, if you would do any good upon me, you must speak, and not leave me to conjecture what you can say."[19] Both Whig and Tory accuse each other during the Exclusion Crisis of avoiding public argument for private insinuation, openness for secrecy and plotting. They accuse each other, as L'Estrange accuses the Whigs by putting these devious words into the mouth of his Whiggish character Citt, in his popular dialogue *Citt and Bumpkin* (1680), of "endeavour[ing] to compass that by *Stratagem* which we cannot gain by *Argument*."[20]

Habermas has been criticized for drawing a picture of a public sphere that is more open than closed, and based on the evidence of such dialogues I myself would criticize it for being too polite and disinterested.[21] But these qualifications aside, Habermas's account is indispensable because it gets the essential function of the public sphere exactly right: even with its passions and interests and its secrecy, it challenged the authority of arbitrary power.[22] Whereas before the advent of the public sphere what was meant by *publicity* was the physical, even bodily display of a monarch's power to the people, or what Habermas calls "representative publicness," now it designates the demand that "private people" issue to the authorities regulating the public realm to confront them "in a debate over the general rules governing relations in the . . . sphere of commodity exchange and social labor" (*Structural Transformation*, 7, 27). Or as the pupil in *A Dialogue at Oxford between a Tutor and a Gentleman* (1681) questions a bit more elegantly the ability of the state to govern without accountability either the institutions of the public sphere or the private individuals who make it up, "how [is it] possible for force alone, to create a better Title over publick Societies, than it would do in the case of each private man?"[23] The public sphere that these dialogues call into being may not be as polite or disinterested as Habermas sometimes pictures it to be, but it is no less oppositional for that.

In this study I examine the dialogues (and other works) of a group of philosophers engaged in a more speculative controversy about the nature of civil society. I am interested in how the demand for dialogue in the public sphere affects the content of a form that has been thought of as particularly philosophical. But I am also interested in the demand itself: how the form, or particular examples of the form, imagines what kind of dialogue is being demanded. Although my study is not limited to the prose dialogue but looks to other genres for what each writer has to say about dialogue as a principle of public discourse, I focus on the dialogue because one can best confirm what a writer means by the principle of dialogue from a text that is deliberately constructed as one.

The Tradition of the Dialogue

I do not intend my (re)placing the dialogue in the early English public sphere to obscure the long and varied tradition of the dialogue in philosophy, a tradition that dates from at least the time of Plato. Others, for whom that tradition is more relevant, have related it in detail, so I do not do so here.[24] For obvious reasons, however, I do not to commit to a definition of dialogue derived from the philosophical tradition like Richard McKeon's, which sees controversy as the opposite of dialogue, an "interruption" of opinion (or authoritative doctrine), dogmatically asserted, into the search for truth. This is to restrict the definition of dialogue to "dialectic," "a method of definition and argument, of division and collection," and even Plato's dialogues, as

McKeon himself points out, are not always dialectical.[25] There are many varieties of dialogue between the extremes of dogmatic assertion and unlimited speculation, so many, in fact, that for the purposes of this study it seems best to define the dialogue not as a method or quality of argument but simply as an exchange of opinion in a represented conversation between two or more speakers that gives the other fair hearing (although what counts as fairness is itself open for debate, and it changes with history).

What the Restoration period especially adds to the history of the dialogue form is the extent to which it, like other controversial literature of the period, is meant to influence *public* opinion, not, or not only, the opinion of a relatively small coterie. The Renaissance dialogue described by Virginia Cox, for example, is a manual for gentlemen and -women of how to conduct polite conversation. Even when a Renaissance dialogue addresses the subject of politics, as Thomas More's *Utopia* does, it usually does so in the decorous tradition of "counsel" for a prince and his ministers.[26] But beginning in the late seventeenth century the ruling elite in England found itself having to solicit the opinion of a much wider public to implement, if not yet to legitimate, its commands,[27] and the dialogue was one of the less decorous places where that opinion was formed. *A Conference Between a Bensalian Bishop and an English Doctor, Concerning Church-Government* (1681), for example, casts its narrator in a foreign utopia like More's with the same object of contrasting its "happy" practices with the corrupt ones of England and its church, but the narrator soon speculates not on such timeless questions as the character of a proper citizen but on such topical ones as the number of Charles II's children.[28]

I have disavowed for my purposes the definition of dialogue as a quality of argument, but the dialogue and other organs of the public sphere did assume an audience that could be reasoned with, an audience that could, as Habermas supposes, sift through the variety of arguments competing for its attention and recognize the better one. The dialogue does exhibit its connection to dialectic, that is, in the weight it gives to "pure" argument relative to narrative; the dialogue writer, to appropriate the words of Milton's *Areopagetica* (1644), "openly . . . publish[es] to the world what his opinion is, what his reasons, and wherefore that which is now thought cannot be sound."[29]

Because laying the commonwealth open to the reasonable consideration of the public was such an innovation, it had to be defended. The "sober Tory" who confronts the "moderate Whig" in *A Brief Discourse* (1680?), for example, calls him and his party "very honest well-meaning People, but that you are so thoughtful and uneasie in matters of Government: which in my opinion very ill becomes a good man, or a true Christian." To be "thoughtful" in matters of government here is not a virtue, and the Whig replies that he is only asking that dissenters be "a little more mildely dealt with."[30] To a Tory like L'Estrange, such thoughtfulness was really an intolerable "meddling" in things above one's station. In the opening issue of his periodical *The Intelligencer* he warns that "a public mercury . . . makes the multitude too familiar with the actions and counsels of their superiors, too pragmatical and censorious, and gives them not only a wish but a kind of colourable right and license to the meddling with the government." But *The Intelligencer* was itself such a "public mercury," and although L'Estrange claims that he is intervening in public affairs only because "the press" is not now "in order" and "the people" are not in their "right wits," what is obvious about his (and others') fear of meddling is that he himself has to meddle in order to express it.[31] Once the people have begun to reason in public, they can only be persuaded to leave politics alone (or not) by a more reasonable argument.

Oratory/Dialogue/Rhetoric

Obviously, then, when the principle of dialogue is not prejudged as a certain quality of argument, it cannot be opposed to controversy in the early English public sphere. Rather, I would define dialogue, more simply, by form rather than by content and return to the ancients to oppose it in this period to oratory. Not that public figures stopped making speeches or that audiences stopped listening to them; neither am I claiming that sermons and other oratorical tracts declined in popularity as literary commodities. The pulpit remained a necessary instrument for disseminating both orthodox and heterodox doctrine.[32] But in the public sphere that these dialogues construct, the speakers consistently contrast what they are doing to making speeches. This is certainly true of the dialogues that could be grouped under the broad rubric "Conformist," for there it is an article of faith that Nonconformist preaching had stirred the passions of faction and schism that caused the commonwealth to disintegrate in the first place. But even Nonconformists, although they defend the inspirational fire of their preachers, do not use the dialogue form to defend it.[33] For Conformists especially, dialogue was preferable (and opposed) to oratory as a form of public discourse because while it could be used to wage controversy, it also expressed a desire to settle it.

The capacity of dialogue to unite as it disputes may explain why the public criticism that it engenders is represented as *private* conversation, surely the most obvious question to ask of the function of dialogue in the early English public sphere. But this is equivalent to asking why Habermas locates the public sphere in the private realm— the realm of civil society—and he has another answer: "Reason, which . . . was to be realized in the rational communication of a public consisting of cultivated human beings, itself needed to be protected from becoming public because it was a threat to any and all relations of domination" (*Structural Transformation*, 35). If the public sphere originated in the kind of private conversation that these dialogues portray, it was because what was being said there was too dangerous, at least "originally," to be said in the open. Habermas's answer suffices to explain why oppositional discourse often took the form of private conversation, but not all dialogues are oppositional, and the dialogue also proposes, as the dialogue writer John Eachard put it, that human beings are "apt to sort, to herd; they love to enquire, to confer, and discourse."[34] Oratory may divide the commonwealth into factions, but discourse and dialogue unite it. Because it represents political discourse as a sociable activity, in this deepened sense the "hallmark" of the public sphere, in Terry Eagleton's paraphrase, "is its consensual character."[35]

ONE OF MY claims in this study is that although they would reconstitute the commonwealth differently, the relationship between oratory and dialogue is more complex than a simple opposition. What relates them, in fact, is their use of and attention to rhetoric, and introducing the theme of rhetoric is the best way to distinguish my work from the other, recent book dedicated to the eighteenth-century dialogue, Michael Prince's *Philosophical Dialogue in the British Enlightenment*. Beginning with Shaftesbury's Neoplatonic philosophy of dialogue and concluding with the transformation of a dialectical moral philosophy into the "mundane ethics" of the novel, Prince produces a history of genre that takes seriously the dialogue's claim to represent difference, primarily, for Prince, differences of religious belief and primarily between skepticism and a rational Christianity.[36] "From the beginning of the Christian era" (5), writes Prince, the dialogue was a natural ally of theists because, like the argument from design for the existence of God, it could demonstrate how the reality of unity (of the cosmos or of theological positions) existed beneath the appearance of difference. Ultimately, however, the skepticism that develops toward the design argument in the secular Enlightenment—particularly as it is expressed in Hume's *Dialogues*—erodes the certainty that the dialogue form had tenuously sustained. The new discourse of aesthetics contains whatever certainty remains, and the novel replaces the dialogue with a moral philosophy that deals in probabilities rather than certainties.

Because he is primarily interested in the dialogue's place in the history of philosophy, Prince does not consider what his authors—of those also considered here, Shaftesbury, Mandeville, and Berkeley—have in common with even the polemical practitioners of dialogue: a condemnation, not of vigorous argument, but of rhetoric, which they figure as oratory or exhortation. He conceives of rhetoric as the formal elements of a text, and in his capacity as a literary critic he is a perceptive reader of it.[37] But he is not interested in the ambivalent relationship between dialogue and rhetoric in this period as alternative means of persuasion. Indeed, by placing the dialogue in the context of "the British Enlightenment," Prince is almost bound to accept its self-definition—actually a definition imposed on it by Shaftesbury, with whom Prince begins his study—as opposed to rhetoric, to controversy, and, I submit, to politics.

By examining how late-seventeenth- and early-eighteenth-century dialogues prosecute the political controversies of the time, I propose instead to treat dialogue as a species of rhetoric, which much of the philosophy about dialogue, both during the Enlightenment and before, was explicitly designed *not* to do. In the long "territorial dispute," as Brian Vickers calls it, between philosophy and rhetoric, dialogue, because it professes to hear both sides of an issue equally and evenly —without the "sway" that rhetoric can bring—has traditionally been allied with philosophy.[38] Plato attacked rhetoric as an art that, like poetry, was more likely to deceive than to lead to truth, and Lucian, in his own satiric dialogues, praises dialogue as "the son of philosophy" and "the enemy of rhetoric."[39] This dispute was revived during the Enlightenment. The Royal Society not only favored a dialogical rather than a declamatory method in its scientific investigations but also aspired to a "plain style," devoid of rhetoric, in its scientific prose, and John Locke spoke for many reformers when he complained that rhetoric was invented "for nothing else but to insinuate wrong *Ideas,* move the Passions, and thereby mislead the Judgment."[40]

As John J. Richetti has reiterated, however, the opposition between philosophy and rhetoric cannot survive if philosophy is to be anything other than private speculation.[41] It is not as rhetoric that these dialogues ask to be judged. Even the most polemical of them want their solutions to strike the reader with all the transparency of common sense, and the philosophical dialogues that I discuss in chapters 1 through 5 disdain the designs of rhetoric for the light of pure reason. By reading them that way, however, I am able to ask not only *what* is being said in them but also *how* it is said and especially *who* is allowed to say it. The standards of freedom and openness by which these dialogues proclaim themselves philosophical may be determined in the rarefied atmosphere of a polite and speculative conversation,[42] but they must be measured in the prosaic public sphere, where they are intended to intervene.

The Argument

Defined very loosely, the controversy in which the philosophers I study are engaged is about the origins, present state, and future prospects of civil society. With varying degrees of concern, they all regard the diversity of opinions as a problem for the commonwealth, and although they conceive dialogue among diverse opinions differently, they all regard it as part of the solution to that problem.

The controversy begins with Hobbes, who both defines the problem of diversity and proposes absolute sovereignty as the only solution to it. When disagreeing individuals realize that their controversies may "come to blowes," they "submit their Right"—the right to their own reason or opinion—to the reason of the sovereign.[43] Dialogue figures in this process at the beginning, when those individuals agree among themselves to "set up" the sovereign's reason for right (*Leviathan,* 111), but not at all at the end. From *Leviathan* and his other works of civil philosophy, however, I glean Hobbes's concept of "Counsell" (302), a kind of dialogue by which he, as a farsighted but impotent teacher of right doctrine, attempts to persuade the sovereign to put it into effect. I extend this notion of counsel to the dialogue that Hobbes has with his "sovereign" reader and show how thinking of Hobbes's civil philosophy itself as counsel moderates his political absolutism. Hobbes's last two works of civil philosophy—*Behemoth* (1682) and *A Dialogue between a Philosopher and a Student of the Common Laws of England* (1681)—further that moderation by placing a new emphasis on the role of Parliament in representing public opinion. It is no coincidence that they are also written in the dialogue form. By giving voice for the first time in Hobbes's philosophy to his opponents, *Behemoth* and the *Common Laws* dialogue reveal the inadequacies of his absolutist theory of representation.

Counsel is a very controlled kind of dialogue, however, and despite the examples of these late works, the way to end controversy for Hobbes is plainly not by assembling people to discuss their differences, an approximate image of the public sphere. That notion of political dialogue was first advanced by seventeenth-century republicans, the two most prominent of whom—James Harrington and his disciple Henry Neville—I discuss in chapter 2. As republicans, Harrington and Neville argue against Hobbes that the true solution to "civil war and confusion" is not the concentration, but a balance, of power.[44] But the participants in Harrington's dialogue *Valerius and Publicola* (1659) and Neville's *Plato Redivivus: or, A Dialogue Concerning Government* (1681), both of which present Harrington's solution to that confusion, already agree that power needs to be shared. The participants in fact exemplify part of that solution: the commonwealth needs virtuous citizens who can debate what is best for it in a *disinterested* manner. It is a peculiar feature of Harrington's civil philosophy, however, that such disinterestedness is purchased at the cost of political effectiveness. Neither Harrington's nor Neville's dialogue had the desired effect: Harrington was unable to persuade the populace to establish a true republic on the ruins of the old one, just as Neville, some twenty years later, was unable to persuade Charles II to give up "a great deal" of his power to settle the Exclusion Crisis (172). More important, my analysis suggests that a lack of power is a necessary consequence of the disinterested function of philosophy (and debate, and dialogue) in Harrington's philosophy. Harrington's and Neville's polite debaters can agree that power needs to be shared because they lack an "interest" in the commonwealth: like the members of Harrington's senate whom they represent, they have the power to debate, but not to "resolve" (or enact), their proposals.

In chapter 3, Shaftesbury, a member of the same civic-humanist tradition as Harrington and Neville, makes deliberate the association of dialogue with disinterestedness that had been almost accidental in their civil philosophy. For Shaftesbury is so offended by what he sees as Hobbes's reduction of all human motivation to self-interest that he sets up a realm of idealized conversation that, because it is "purely" philosophical, can be nothing but disinterested. Such dialogue, and the disinterested "*Love of God or Virtue* for GOD or VIRTUE'S sake" (*Characteristicks*, 2:45) that it cultivates, can be practiced only after a deliberate retreat from the political realm: indeed, Shaftesbury is convinced that it is difficult for a philosopher, or any other citizen, to exercise virtue "in so remote a Sphere as that of the Body Politick at large" (1:62). Shaftesbury's retreat from politics involves a retreat not only from interestedness but also from the sort of rhetoric that, by appealing to interest, is needed to effect persuasion in the political realm. But although Shaftesbury (like every other figure in this study) disdains rhetoric as a one-sided use of speech, he too must resort to rhetoric to gain assent to his philosophy. In his model of philosophical dialogue, *The Moralists*, Shaftesbury uses the rhetoric of "enthusiasm" when the skepticism that he associates with the purely philosophical realm becomes intolerable: his spokesperson, Theocles, appeals to the skeptic Philocles' sense of pathos to convince him of the community that is greater than the sum of his individual opinions.

Just as Shaftesbury sets his ideal of disinterested dialogue against Hobbes's paradigm of self-interest, in *The Fable of the Bees* (1714–29) Bernard Mandeville sets his idea of conversation as "Dissimulation" against Shaftesbury's disinterested virtue. Dissimulation—the art of representing something to be what it is not—he argues, is both what brings society together and what makes it prosperous.[45] "Skilful Politicians" dissimulate when they represent virtue as more desirable than vice, deceiving people into pursuing the common interest at the expense of their more immediate self-interest (1:47). Merchants dissimulate when they misrepresent the actual value of their commodities, pushing up prices, encouraging production, and making everyone richer. Dissimulation is frankly self-interested and yet—as in Mandeville's famous paradox—good for the commonwealth, producing "publick benefits" out of "private vices." Dissimulation is also, as an art of words, frankly rhetorical. As it drives the engine of commerce, it is a kind of "commerce," practiced in close conversation between disagreeing parties. In chapter 4 I note the contradiction between commerce and Mandeville's own conversations, the dialogues that make up part 2 of the *Fable*. They are not exercises in dissimulation but philosophical exchanges that lead to disinterested enlightenment.

In my fifth, and final, chapter I examine George Berkeley's response to the "freethinking" of both Shaftesbury and Mandeville, the polemical dialogue *Alciphron* (1732). For Shaftesbury, freethinking, or skepticism, is a necessary ingredient of philosophical conversation, and for Mandeville it is an inevitable consequence of thinking about commerce. About the only thing the two have in common, then, is a desire to stand above the prejudices and potential misguidedness of ordinary believers, and both rest their claim to be above prejudice on the cultivation of polite conversation. For the clergyman Berkeley, however, freethinking has a corrosive effect on civil society, and to discredit it he uses his dialogue to practice conversation as catechism: sometimes a methodical process of question and answer that drives the respondent into a contradiction, sometimes a freer conference that inculcates religious truths. His enlightened opponents regard such truths as the prejudices they claim to be above, but Berkeley uses the dialogue both to *defend* prejudice and to *attack* enlightenment, at least too much of it. The antithesis of Shaftesbury's disinterested dialogist, he proves the worth of his religious doctrines by appealing to his hearers' interest in salvation.

However he may regard dialogue as catechism, or disregard the Enlightenment ideal of dialogue, neither has much to do with Berkeley's vision of the commonwealth. What holds a political community together for Berkeley is prejudice, not enlightened conversation. (For that matter, neither does the sort of disinterested, enlightened conversation that takes place in his dialogues bring society together for Mandeville; commerce, a very different sort of conversation, does.) He signifies, therefore, a logical end to this study. In the conclusion I trace a general decline of political speculation in dialogue from the philosophers who begin this study (Hobbes and Harrington) to those who end it. The kind of speculation about politics that late-seventeenth-century philosophers and polemicists indulged in emerged from a perfect union of political instability and philosophical confidence. With the growth of political stability in the middle of the eighteenth century, however, this union began to fall apart. Political debate offered only old answers to new questions, and the consolidation of the Whig oligarchy under Walpole blunted for the time being the sense that disagreement in politics could be productive, or even rational. In this study, the disunion between politics and philosophy starts with Shaftesbury, who looks elsewhere than politics for a *sensus communis,* and culminates with Mandeville and Berkeley, both of whom express a renewed interest in politics but who question—as Berkeley does by defending prejudice rather than enlightenment—whether philosophy can profitably speculate about it. The growth of political stability means the decline of the political dialogue.

By setting the controversy that begins with Hobbes and ends with Berkeley in the context of the polemical literature of the period, I mean to challenge a facile distinction between politics and philosophy. This controversy is unique in that it is conducted in a certain atmosphere of philosophical contemplation, even leisure. Yet the range of ideological positions represented by these figures, the profundity of their influences, and the number of replies that they provoked give the entire controversy a certain representativeness: it is representative in its comprehensiveness. From Hobbes's absolutism to Mandeville's "free" market, from Shaftesbury's deism to Berkeley's theism, from Harrington and Neville's civic humanism to Berkeley's passive obedience, it surveys the range of ways that the early eighteenth century could conceive of society's being organized. The controversy is representative, too, in that by the end of it the dialogues of Mandeville and Berkeley relate a decline in the philosophical *content* of the public sphere that the less numerous dialogues of the 1730s and 1740s similarly reveal.

A Theory of Interest and Disinterestedness

What is ultimately at stake in these dialogues, as well as in the public sphere that they call into being, is what counts as "reason" itself. When controversy remains intractable to reason, it can destroy a given community's understanding of what reason is. As Hobbes announced in his first book of civil philosophy, *The Elements of Law*, published in 1640, at the outset of the civil war:

> [The] common measure of all things that might fall in controversy . . . some say, is right reason: with whom I should consent, if there were any such thing to be found or known in rerum natura. . . . But . . . seeing right reason is not existent, the reason of some man, or men, must supply the place thereof; and that man, or men, is he, or they, that have the sovereign power.[46]

Because of its uselessness in preventing or arbitrating real conflict, right reason, for Hobbes, has departed from the philosophical scene. The same conflicts caused Harrington, at the opposite end of the political spectrum from Hobbes, to conclude, with him, that right reason does not exist in nature. In *Oceana,* the philosophical epic that he set against *Leviathan,* Harrington makes the deceivingly innocuous pronouncement that since "reason is nothing but interest, there be divers interests and so divers reasons."[47] In one stroke Harrington both acknowledges that diversity is a problem for the commonwealth and determines that appealing to diversity—as in the diversity of interests, or reasons—is the only rational way to solve it. It cannot be solved, that is, by an appeal to some absolute standard of reason that does not acknowledge its connection to human interest.

Late-seventeenth- and early-eighteenth-century dialogues, through their appeal to diversity, often pursue a new standard of reason, a new consensus. In a dialogue whose very title bespeaks the anxiety to produce that consensus, *A Modest Attempt for Healing the Present Animosities in England* (1690), the moderator, a sensible individual with the same name as the marquis of Halifax's Trimmer, asks his fellow participants in the dialogue, a "zealous Dissenter" named Testimony and a "cholerick Bigot" named Hot-head, to "consent to a Truce for an Hours time" so that they might "reason calmly" together.[48] Testimony and Hot-head agree to suspend their dispute for the "Discourse" that Trimmer proposes, although not, at first, with the expectation of reestablishing a more civil communication between them: as Testimony puts it, it is rather "in hopes to make *you* [Trimmer] a Convert, tho' he's [Hot-head's] desperate, and I've quite given him over" (8, emphasis added). In the course of that suspension, however, Trimmer points out to Testimony and Hot-head the extremity of their positions and gets each to "swear," at the end of the dialogue, that he does not intend the worst that the other suspects him of. The new consensus that they agree to (which it takes a sworn oath to enforce) is simply to extend more trust to the reasons of the other than they had been willing to entertain before, and the most that can be hoped for is, as stated in the introduction, that both parties "can but be put into so good a humour, as to unbend their Browes, and laugh at their own and others Extravagancies" (4). That, however, may be all the reason that Testimony and Hot-head need. They were ready to come to blows before; now, while they may not agree, they can at least communicate their differences to each other.

More important, however, Hobbes, Harrington, and the author of *Modest Attempt* all realize that the ability to enter into such a discourse depends on the interests and identities that the participants bring to the conversational table. The "Hour" of discourse that happens in dialogue may temporarily suspend those interests, and the practical imperatives that accompany them, but it is not disinterested in the manner of idealist philosophy, where (as in Plato's *Timaeus* or Shaftesbury's *Moralists*) the ability to reason disinterestedly depends on the serene contemplation of a natural order.[49] On the contrary, if, as Harrington insists, reason is "nothing but interest," there is no natural (or transcendent, or "right") reason to contemplate or appeal to. There is only a variety of reasons, and interests, and whatever conclusion the participants leave the dialogue with will be the one that acknowledges and appeals to that variety.[50] In other words, disinterestedness is acquired by pursuing for others the very conditions that make it possible for oneself, and it has itself to be argued for, not merely asserted or assumed. It is the product of a just outcome, not the prerequisite for one.

Among the writers in this study only Shaftesbury really idealizes disinterestedness, but since he largely defines the meaning of dialogue for the eighteenth century and deliberately looks back at the classical tradition, his version of the concept is an enormously influential one. Indeed, by rejecting a disinterestedness that is meant to transform the world of practical imperatives for one that transcends it, Shaftesbury both initiates the decline of political speculation in the dialogue and depoliticizes what his own dialogues represent as the public sphere.

For the intellectual historian Reinhart Koselleck, that is exactly what happened to the public sphere on the Continent when a group of philosophes, disillusioned by practical politics, established their own private sphere of speculation to criticize the absolutist state.[51] Koselleck does not find the same problem in England, where at least following the Restoration there was an established avenue—the public sphere —whereby critically thinking individuals could communicate their opinions to the government. But Shaftesbury, among English philosophers, is alienated enough from practical politics to want to retreat from it anyway, and he takes the philosophical realm of dialogue along with him. Like his predecessor Socrates in Plato's *Gorgias,* rather than living the life "of a 'real man,' speaking in the Assembly and practicing rhetoric and playing the politician," Shaftesbury would spend his life conversing, "in philosophy."[52]

In the context of the early English public sphere Shaftesbury's disinterestedness is anomalous. It is the moral equivalent of the skeptical method pioneered in science by the Royal Society, and the controversy between a devotee of that method, the natural philosopher Joseph Glanvill, and the Roman Catholic priest Thomas White illustrates what happens when one tries to apply that method toward truths that the other would still consider sacred. Like Shaftesbury but much earlier, Glanvill, in *The Vanity of Dogmatizing* (1661), warned against "confidence in opinions" and emphasized the fundamental ignorance of human beings in most matters of science and religion. But White, in a tract aptly entitled *An Exclusion of Scepticks from All Title to Dispute* (1665), replies that it was no fault "to inculcate Truth to those that live in ignorance and error." The chance to enlighten others, says White, is more important than deferring to their wrong opinions, and the skeptical method of seeing all options but committing to none (which White likens to "Duelling") cannot demonstrate the "Principles for governing our life."[53] Glanvill's reply "To the learned Thomas Albius," in his "defence" of the *Vanity, Scire/i tuum nihil est* (1665), percolates with the irony that is characteristic of the period's polemic:

> I thought it was not improper in a squabbling, and contentious Age, to indeavour to detect the vanity of *proud* and *confiding Ignorance;* and thereby to bring the less engaged and more manly tempers to a *peaceable unconcernment* and *indifferency* in the doubtful Quarrels of divided

Parties and Interests. So that I cannot with some regret behold the Cross and unlucky issue of my Designs; For by my dislike of *Disputes* I am engaged in one; And by the very method I meditated of *Peace* and *Reconcilement*, am my self forced into the number of *Contenders;* whom, I confest, I have ever less *admired*, than *pityed.*[54]

Glanvill protests that he recommended the skeptical method against the vanity of dogmatizing because he wanted, in his own way, to put a stop to controversy. Now, unhappily, he finds himself in a controversy. Controversy, Glanvill learned the hard way, cannot be avoided by advocating a "peaceable unconcernment"—Shaftesbury's disinterestedness—to the opinions that people hold passionately or that touch on their vested interests. One's own opinions can only be argued just as vigorously, and controversy perhaps resolved, not avoided.

Shaftesbury's disinterestedness is anomalous even in the more refined public sphere circumscribed by the dialogues of the other philosophers in this study. Hobbes—the first writer here—views the dialogue that is counsel not as an interest-free realm but as an opportunity to persuade the sovereign (and the "sovereign" reader) of his or her farsighted interest, and Berkeley—the last writer in this study—doubts that Shaftesbury's disinterested "Love of God or Virtue" is enough to make us good members of either church or state. For Koselleck, philosophy's separation from politics is one of the "pathological" legacies of the Enlightenment.[55] To the extent that Shaftesbury's ideal of disinterested dialogue, and the skeptical stance that goes along with it, aggravates that separation, I intend my title to call attention to it as a philosophical "luxury."

Besides, Shaftesbury's disinterestedness, which claims to be apolitical, is itself a political stance, or at least a culturally powerful one. "Whilst PHILOSOPHY is taken (as in its prime Sense it ought) for *Mastership in* LIFE and MANNERS," he concludes in the *Miscellaneous Reflections,* "'tis like to make no ill Figure in the World" (*Characteristicks,* 2:205). I would prefer that philosophy "make a figure in the world" by admitting its interests, not by claiming to be above them. This, in turn, requires that philosophical dialogue or discourse "hear" the interests that enable it to be disinterested, much as Dryden's dialogists "attentively listened" for the sound of the cannon that, by ensuring victory, enables them to discuss dramatic poetry (29). The conversation should recognize that philosophy can never be untainted by the world and its practical concerns. To call skepticism a luxury is to say that it often ignores those concerns, pretending that speculation can go on forever. When the world demands a decision, even polite conversation has to end.

1

HOBBES
Dialogue as Counsel

IN "On the Life and History of Thucydides," appended to his translation of the *History of the Peloponnesian War* (1629), Thomas Hobbes
defends the historian against the charge that his style is "obscure and
licentious." "So much was this work esteemed, even for the eloquence,"
Hobbes says, that the famous orator Demosthenes "wrote over the
history of Thucydides with his own hand eight times." Still and all,
Hobbes continues, Thucydides' eloquence was "not at all fit for the
bar; but proper for history, and rather to be read than heard. For
words that pass away (as in public orations they must) without pause,
ought to be understood with ease, and are lost else: though words
that remain in writing for the reader to meditate on, ought rather to
be pithy and full."[1]

In some way, Hobbes's entire career after his translation of Thucydides—his entire career, that is, as a civil philosopher—can be seen as
a gloss on the contrast that he draws here between writing and "eloquence," or speech. Just as Demosthenes practiced his style as an orator
by effacing a prior historian, Hobbes would practice his style—and
"style" his practice—as a historian and civil philosopher by effacing
prior orators. In *The Writing of History,* Michel de Certeau reminds us
of the "confidence" that Enlightenment philosophers had in writing:
it was "to refashion society in the same way that it had indicated the
power that the enlightened bourgeoisie was ascribing for itself." Society
would "construct its progress" through writing, and displace orality to
the uncivilized realm "of nature, of the woman, of childhood, of the
people."[2] Remarking in his "Life" that Thucydides was "sufficiently
qualified" in rhetoric "to have become a great demagogue, and of

great authority with the people," Hobbes draws a similar connection between orality and social disorder:

> But it seemeth he had no desire at all to meddle in the government: because in those days it was impossible for any man to give good and profitable counsel for the commonwealth, and not incur the displeasure of the people. For their opinion was such of their own power, and of the facility of achieving whatsoever action they undertook, that such men only swayed the assemblies, and were esteemed wise and good commonwealth's men, as did put them upon the most dangerous and desperate enterprizes. (571–72)

It is difficult not to see how strongly Hobbes identifies with Thucydides here. Like Thucydides, Hobbes was well qualified in the art of rhetoric. But also like Thucydides, Hobbes was disillusioned with political oratory, one of the traditional provinces of rhetoric, for it only swayed "assemblies" and urged "dangerous and desperate enterprizes." For Thucydides the citizen of ancient Athens, as well as for Hobbes the subject of pre–civil war England, the time for speechifying was at an end. The writer who wishes to do good for the commonwealth must devise some other means of "counsel."

Hobbes found that means, I believe, in dialogue: both in the written dialogues—*Behemoth* (1682) and *A Dialogue between a Philosopher and a Student of the Common Laws of England* (1681)—of his later career and in the process of dialogue between an authoritative but not necessarily knowing sovereign and a knowing but not necessarily authoritative teacher that he called "Counsell" (*Leviathan,* 302). Counsel, not oratory, is the proper use of speech in Hobbes's political science. Always limited to the one-on-one interaction between sovereign and teacher, dialogue as counsel never attains the semblance of a full-blown public sphere. Hobbes remains suspicious of the volatility of public opinion and no respecter of its legitimacy to authorize the commands of the sovereign. But the status of dialogue in these two late works suggests that Hobbes has moderated his political absolutism. The works themselves emphasize the sovereign's need to solicit the people's consent to the laws by which they are governed; and rather than presuming that the sovereign speaks for all, the "sovereigns" being advised in them—Hobbes's readers—are allowed to speak for, to represent, themselves.

Hobbes's Rhetorical Crux

Hobbes conceived of his political science, as he says in "A Review, and Conclusion" to his masterpiece *Leviathan,* as a response to "the disorders of the present time" (728). Those disorders were signified for him by the sheer diversity of opinions—about politics, religion, and how each influenced, or should influence, the other—that flourished in England with the rejection of royal authority at the time of the civil war. In *Leviathan* Hobbes censures "the tongues, and pens of unlearned Divines" for preaching the "Private Judgement of Good and Evill," a doctrine that leads to the "diversity" of "private opinions" and "tend[s] to the DISSOLUTION of a Common-wealth" (365–67, 363). Similarly, in *Behemoth,* his history of the civil war, he blames the translation of Scripture into vulgar languages for producing "diversity of opinion, and consequently (as man's nature is) disputation, breach of charity, disobedience, and at last rebellion."[3]

To solve this problem (as Hobbes defined it) of diversity, it was of no use to appeal to reason. Not only does Hobbes declare that "right" reason does not exist in nature—he cynically adds that "commonly they that call for right reason to decide any controversy do mean their own"[4]—but he knows that the diversity of opinions in the commonwealth prompts people to lose faith in the prospect of rationality itself. In the *Common Laws* dialogue, for example, Hobbes expresses his concern that "the variety and repugnancy of Judgments of Common-Law do oftentimes put Men to hope for Victory in causes, whereof in reason they had no ground at all."[5] What "encline[s] men to Peace" is not reason but a passion: the "Fear of Death" (*Leviathan,* 188). For fear of the violent conflict that may result, the parties in a controversy are persuaded not to press their sides of it. They are persuaded, in other words, to reconstitute "right reason":

> [W]hen there is a controversy in an account, the parties must by their own accord, set up for right Reason, the Reason of some Arbitrator, or Judge, to whose sentence they will both stand, or their controversie must either come to blowes, or be undecided, for want of a right Reason constituted by Nature; so is it in all debates of what kind soever. (*Leviathan,* 111)

Similarly in *Leviathan,* Hobbes makes the idea "That they that are at controversie, submit their Right to the judgement of an Arbitrator," one of the nineteen "Lawes of Nature" (213).[6] This arbitrator, or judge, is the sovereign authority or a representative; indeed, the act of submission *creates* the sovereign. Individually, the subjects of a commonwealth can appeal only to partial standards of reason; collectively, they can appeal to the impartial reason of the sovereign. The reason of the sovereign is not inherently more right (or impartial) than that of any subject; it has simply been "set up" for right reason.

For the parties in a controversy to agree in this way is for them to make a "Contract," which Hobbes elsewhere defines as "The mutuall transferring of Right" (*Leviathan*, 192). Unfortunately, that transferring is not always so mutual. It is true that philosophically minded subjects—as Hobbes fancies those who read, or have read, his works to be—readily see the consequences of living without some artificial standard of right reason. They possess what Hobbes calls "Prudence" or "Foresight" (*Leviathan*, 97), a quality much like Aristotle's "practical wisdom," which keeps the target of the good life steadily in view.[7] But most people are in fact shortsighted. When they are urged otherwise by "preachers and theologians-philosophers," they will often do what is directly contrary to their self-interest.[8] If it proved nothing else, the civil war proved this. Rather than holding out the fear of death and expecting them to fall in line, people must be shown not only that so submitting themselves will preserve their lives but also that preserving their lives and the safety of the commonwealth is the right thing to do. If his contract is to work, Hobbes has to *persuade* self-interested and naturally equal human beings that someone else's reason—the sovereign's—is better than their own. As Victoria Kahn perceives, Hobbes's contract "has not solved the problem of diversity. . . . He has simply transferred it from the realm of cognition to the realm of persuasion."[9]

The "realm of cognition" is the realm of science, but the "realm of persuasion" is the realm of rhetoric. The uneasy relation between the farsighted solution of a social contract and the shortsighted passions and opinions of most of the people expected to submit to it creates a crux in Hobbes's political science that is less than scientific:[10] it takes rhetoric to maintain the sovereign's reason as "right" or to provide the foresight that reason is "impotent" without.[11] Although he was the first to translate Aristotle's *Rhetoric* into English—published as *A Briefe of the Art of Rhetorique* in 1637—Hobbes's attitude toward rhetoric was mostly negative. He invariably denounced "the use of Metaphors, Tropes, and other Rhetoricall figures, in stead of words proper" in the "seeking of truth" (*Leviathan*, 114–15), and he warned of the dangerous effects of oratory as far back as his translation of Thucydides. The very definition of rhetoric that Hobbes supplies in the *Briefe* is suspicious in tone. To Aristotle's "ability, in each [particular] case, to see the available means of persuasion," Hobbes makes an addition: rhetoric, according to the *Briefe*, is "that Faculty, by which we understand what will *serve our turne*, concerning any subject, to winne beliefe in the hearer."[12] In this definition rhetoric is more than mere eloquence, but its end is not truth, nor even impartial persuasion to the more probable point of view, but simply victory.

A closer look at the distrust of rhetoric that Hobbes expresses throughout his works, however, reveals that it is consistently directed, not so much at persuasive discourse in general, but at persuasive speech. In *De Cive*, for example, Hobbes distinguishes between good and bad kinds of "eloquence":

> Now, *eloquence* is twofold. The one is an elegant, and cleare expression of the conceptions of the mind, and riseth partly from the contemplation of the things themselves, partly from an understanding of words taken in their own proper, and definite signification; the other is a commotion of the Passions of the minde (such as are *hope, fear, anger, pitty*) and derives from a metaphorical use of words fitted to the Passions: That forms a speech from true Principles, this from opinions already received. . . . The art of that is Logick, of this Rhetorick; the end of that is truth, of this victory.[13]

One could recast the distinction that Hobbes draws here as one between rhetoric considered in a broad sense, a sense that, as James P. Zappen says, preserves its "traditional association . . . with other intellectual disciplines—with logic, on the one hand, and with politics and ethics, on the other," and rhetoric in a narrow, negative sense, as mere eloquence, or fine speaking.[14] Or, again, because understanding words "in their own proper, and definite signification" requires, as Hobbes said of Thucydides' history, that they "remain in writing for the reader to meditate on," the distinction might also be recast as that between *writing* and speaking. Many of Hobbes's critics have made the point that for all of his distrust of rhetoric, he often resorts to it himself to make the truths of his political science more persuasive. But few have seen the difference between logic and rhetoric, or between rhetoric in its positive and negative senses, as a difference between writing and speech.[15] Again and again in his works, and especially in *Behemoth*, Hobbes maintains that fine speaking can never serve the commonwealth or serve in its reconstitution.[16] If he recognizes that eloquence in writing is necessary to make his political science efficacious,[17] Hobbes opposes the writing of that science to the speech of those who would disorder the commonwealth.

For example, just as demagoguery "swayed the assemblies" in Thucydides' Athens, in *Behemoth* Hobbes blames the speeches in Parliament for inciting civil war. When the less knowledgeable speaker in the dialogue, B, asks how the Long Parliament came to sentence Thomas Wentworth, the earl of Strafford, to death, the more knowledgeable A replies, "Impudence in democratical assemblies does almost all that's done; 'tis the goddess of rhetoric, and carries proof with it. For what ordinary man will not, from so great boldness of affirmation, conclude there is great probability in the thing affirmed?" (68–69). For Hobbes, there is something intrinsically unstable in the situation of a single speaker addressing a large group: if an orator is bold enough and the assembly large (or "democratical") enough, the group will believe anything that is said, no matter how "dangerous and desperate." Later in *Behemoth*, B declares that he understands now "how easily, by the help of seditious Presbyterian ministers, and of ambitious ignorant orators," the Long Parliament "reduced this government into anarchy." Significantly, B's understanding follows immediately after A distinguishes between that time of anarchy and before, when, over the issue of Parliament's mustering an army, king and Parliament "shot at one another nothing but paper" (108–9). Hobbes does not explicitly say that the transition from paper to shooting war was caused by the speeches of impudent (or "ambitious ignorant") orators, but the conjunction of the two is more than coincidental.

Oratory is the means by which the common people are encouraged to disobey the sovereign authority. Hobbes blames another kind of speech for encouraging disobedience among the elites of the commonwealth: disputation. Disputation was a formal academic exercise whose prominence in the primary and secondary curricula of Hobbes's day exhibited the humanist belief that training in rhetoric was needed to create a *bonus civis,* or good citizen. In a disputation, the first participant, called a "respondent," was posed a question "left doubtful by the best authorities," offered some kind of answer to it, and was responded to by an opponent supporting the contrary proposition. At the end, a moderator "summed up the arguments pro and con" and decided the question.[18] The participants in a disputation were pitted against each other, as opponents, and their aim was to defeat each other's arguments. Because of its polemical nature, and because the questions treated—for example, "Is there any certain knowledge of things?"—were, and probably remained, unresolvable, disputation was "much more a test of verbal facility in Latin and of skill in oral argument" than an investigation into the truth of things or training in how to reason independently.[19] This, Hobbes believed, tended to corrupt the students it was supposed to be cultivating. By demanding that one argue *in utramque partem,* on both sides of a question, disputation fostered the suspicion that there was *no* truth to be found in controversial questions. Deciding for one side or another of such questions was simply a matter of being swayed by rhetoric, not reason.[20]

Teaching versus Counsel

If Hobbes's criticisms of both oratory and disputation make it difficult to imagine a proper use of rhetoric in his political science, it is possible to find a proper use of speech. In his first work of civil philosophy, *The Elements of Law,* circulated in 1640, Hobbes distinguishes between two uses of language in general, which he names "teaching" and "persuasion":

> The first use of language, is the expression of our conceptions, that is, the begetting in another the same conceptions that we have in ourselves; and this is called TEACHING. . . . But if there be not such evidence [i.e., conceptions "from experience"], then such teaching is called PERSUASION, and begetteth no more in the hearer, than what is in the speaker, bare opinion. . . . There is therefore a great deal of difference between teaching and persuading; the signs of this being controversy; the sign of the former, no controversy (49–51).

Persuasion, by its very definition, is rhetorical: it must somehow convince the other that the "bare opinion" with which it starts is something more than that. Teaching, however, because it proceeds on the basis of "evidence" rather than opinion, seems to get by without using rhetoric and produces truth. When, in *Leviathan,* Hobbes equates teaching with science, the differences between it and persuasion are fully drawn. A "certain" sign of science, he says, is "when he that pretendeth the Science of any thing, can teach the same; that is to say, demonstrate the truth thereof perspicuously to another" (117). On the side of teaching are science, truth, logic (demonstration), and foresight (perspicuity). On the side of persuasion are belief, opinion, rhetoric, and shortsightedness.[21]

An even greater "advantage," or proper use, of speech than teaching, says Hobbes in *De Homine* (1658), is that speech can be used to "command."[22] By declaring command to be more advantageous than teaching, however, Hobbes is measuring not merit but magnitude. Command is greater because one who commands has more authority than one who teaches. Hobbes implies, both in *De Homine* and in chapter 25 of *Leviathan,* where he treats the subject at length, that the only person who can legitimately issue commands is the sovereign in speaking to his or her subjects. But the sovereign is not the only person who can teach. Unlike command, which requires the authority of the sovereign, teaching requires only knowledge—the "authority" of the truth—and the desire to impart that truth to a subject or student. A teacher will always possess more knowledge than a student, but their relationship may involve any mismeasure of authority.

When Hobbes's subjects "submit their Right"—the right to their own reason or opinion—to the reason of the sovereign, they give him or her the ultimate authority to determine what is true. As the person with the most truth (and the most authority) in the commonwealth, the sovereign is also its "primary" teacher. The sovereign, Hobbes says, judges "what Doctrines are fit to be taught" (*Leviathan,* 233). But what happens when the sovereign needs to be taught? Educating the sovereign was the traditional task of Renaissance advice books, like Machiavelli's *The Prince* and Thomas Elyot's *The Book Named the Governor,* and it is the "hope" that Hobbes expresses in the closing sentence of part 2 of *Leviathan:* "I recover some hope, that one time or other, this writing of mine, may fall into the hands of a Soveraign, who will consider it himselfe, . . . [and] convert this Truth of Speculation, into the Utility of Practice" (408). But, if Hobbes's doctrine is interpreted strictly, no subject can teach the teacher—that is, the sovereign—

without, as he puts it in the conclusion to *Leviathan*, "usurpation" of the sovereign's place. Indeed, Hobbes there says that he offers "such Doctrines as I *think* True" rather than doctrines that simply *are* true not because he lacks faith in his own philosophy but because according to that philosophy, a subject like Hobbes does not have the authority to determine what is true (*Leviathan*, 726, emphasis added). Hobbes risks offending the sovereign even by implying that his "Truth of Speculation" is being ignored in practice. Even if a subject knows what is best for the sovereign, he or she must lead the sovereign to that truth with discretion.

Taking into account the fact of sovereignty, Hobbes, in chapter 25 of *Leviathan*, modifies the difference between command and teaching to that between command and "Counsell." Like teaching, counsel requires only the authority of the truth, not, as does command, the authority of the sovereign. But while teachers do not have overly to concern themselves with how their students receive that truth, counselors do. The practice takes its name from the advice that a privy counselor gives to the sovereign, and so the one who is being counseled (hereafter, the "hearer") possesses more power, at least of the worldly, political kind, than the one who is doing the counseling. A counselor's authority derives solely from foresight, not from any advantage of power. As a result, a counselor is much more vulnerable to his or her "student" than a teacher.

A further difference between teaching and counsel becomes apparent when Hobbes properly defines the terms *command* and *counsel:*

> COMMAND is, where a man saith, *Doe this*, or *Doe not this*, without expecting other reason than the Will of him that sayes it. . . . COUN-SELL, is where a man saith, *Doe*, or *doe not this*, and deduceth his reasons from the benefit that arriveth by it to him to whom he saith it. . . . [A] man may be obliged to do what he is Commanded; . . . But he cannot be obliged to do as he is Counselled, because the hurt of not following it, is his own. (*Leviathan*, 303)

As Hobbes distinguishes them here, counsel, unlike command (but like the scholastic practice of disputation), admits of disagreement. But if counsel is unlike command, it is also unlike teaching. Counsel, like command, is an "Imperative" (302), but because the one who is being counseled requires reasons—in *Elements of Law* Hobbes says that a counselor must "furnish" a hearer "with arguments, whereupon to deliberate within himself" (52)—and may freely choose not to follow a counselor's advice, counsel has to be persuasive in a way that teaching, the mere indoctrination of authoritative opinion, does not. Yet counsel retains a didactic purpose: it is still, like teaching, devoted to telling the truth, albeit the truth to power. Thus, counsel may be defined provisionally as *persuasive* teaching.

Even though he defines it as "Counsell vehemently pressed," Hobbes takes care also to distinguish counsel, or at least good counsel, from oratory, which he calls "Exhortation" (304). First, counsel "deduce[s] the consequences" of a proposed action; exhortation encourages action without regard to consequences (304). Second, counsel is dispassionate; exhortation has "a regard to the common Passions" (304) and even aims to "enflame" them (309). Third,

> the use of Exhortation and Dehortation lyeth onely, where a man is to speak to a Multitude; because when the Speech is addressed to one, he may interrupt him, and examine his reasons more rigourously, than can be done in a Multitude; which are too many to enter into Dispute, and *Dialogue* with him that speaketh indifferently to them all at once. . . . [I]n hearing every man apart, one may examine (where there is need) the truth, or probability of his reasons, and of the grounds of the advise he gives, by frequent interruptions, and objections. (305–9, emphasis added)

Finally, exhortation uses "Similitudes, Metaphors, Examples, and other tooles of Oratory"; counsel, says Hobbes, is tied "to the rigour of true reasoning" (304). Hobbes makes these distinctions to exclude rhetoric from his description of counsel, but, as usual, rhetoric has a way of sneaking back in. Delivered to a single hearer, counsel is considerably more controlled than the rhetoric an orator uses to enflame the passions of a crowd. But the possibility that the hearer may interrupt and object to what a counselor says means both that he or she must be persuaded and that the persuasion occurs in the context of a genuine conversation. For Hobbes, counsel is more than persuasive teaching: it is persuasive *dialogue*.

As when he hopes that the sovereign who attempts to put the doctrine of *Leviathan* into practice will "[protect] the Publique teaching of it" (408), Hobbes prefers to describe his political science as a form of teaching. Teaching imparts truth, not opinion, and it does so without the need of rhetoric. Given the rhetorical crux of that political science, however—the fact that Hobbes has to persuade self-interested people that their greater interest lies in submitting themselves to the sovereign authority—it would be more accurate to describe it as a form of counsel, an advantage of speech that persuades of opinion. In recent years several critics have amply demonstrated how Hobbes, in Quentin Skinner's words, "uses rhetoric to support science."[23] Developing that insight, I would describe Hobbes's political science, because it uses rhetoric to support it, as a form of counsel.[24] To describe Hobbes's use of rhetoric as counsel helps us to see how vastly different Hobbes thinks the uses of rhetoric can be. An orator can use it to advance impudent designs, and a disputant can use it to talk for victory, but a counselor must use it to advise what is good for the sovereign and the commonwealth. Even more important, if Hobbes truly does intend his civil philosophy as "good and profitable counsel for the commonwealth," then he must regard the reader of it as a kind of sovereign.

The Reader as Sovereign

Obviously, to say that the reader is a kind of sovereign in Hobbes's civil philosophy is not to say that he or she has the power to arbitrate or judge the controversies that beset the commonwealth or any of the other powers that Hobbes reserves for the sovereign authority. Neither is it to say that Hobbes is any more sanguine that the bulk of the populace is not shortsighted: even sovereigns can be so, and often are. The ordinary readers of Hobbes's civil philosophy do tend to prefer the present good before the future one. Yet, as readers of his philosophy, they presumably have not yet made up their minds about it. They are not like the passive subjects who, in Hobbes's mind, compose the audience of an orator, ordinary hearers who cannot help having their passions enflamed. They are, rather, like the monarch who receives the advice of a privy counselor, who can choose to reject his advice and walk away (or put his book down). Like a monarch, that is, they cannot be obliged to do as they are counseled. If he is more didactic than persuasive—if, that is, his writing resembles teaching more than counsel—Hobbes risks offending his readers. He must counsel rather than teach them because they always have the capacity to disagree.

Simply because he delivers his advice via the printed page rather than the spoken word, then, Hobbes must respect his readers' "sovereignty." But there are other signs that Hobbes viewed what he was doing by writing to readers as being like counseling a sovereign. I have discussed the differences between the activities of teaching and command as Hobbes defines them: command requires the authority of the sovereign, but teaching requires only knowledge, the authority of the truth. Despite the "commanding" tone of voice in which he delivers his civil philosophy, Hobbes never pretends to command his audience into submitting themselves to the sovereign authority. As he originally defines the activity of teaching, he does not have to: it is supposed to impart "conceptions" in the student that are indisputable because they are founded in "evidence" or "experience" that both teacher and student share. In *Behemoth,* however, Hobbes further distinguishes between command and teaching in a way that qualifies the power of teaching, and he hints that "students," or subjects, are "taught" because they *cannot* be absolutely commanded. Discussing the claims of other authorities, namely, "the Popish and Presbyterian factions," "to govern us," B asks by what "right" the Catholic Church makes that claim. When A cites the verse from Matthew in which Christ commissions his disciples to "go therefore and teach all nations" because "All power is given unto me in heaven and in earth," B corrects his reading: "[F]or the text in St. Matthew, I know the words in the Gospel are not *go teach,* but *go, make disciples;* and that there is a great difference between a subject and a disciple, and between teaching and commanding" (5–6). Because it cannot extend the absolute authority required to command disciples to the temporal realm (the realm of subjects), that is, B asserts that the jurisdiction of the Catholic Church is limited to the spiritual realm (the realm of disciples). Unlike disciples, who can be commanded to obey the dictates of God, their sovereign power, subjects can only be taught to obey theirs. But if they can only be taught rather than commanded, then there is always the chance that the lesson will not take and they will disobey that power. Paradoxically, in promoting the absolute jurisdiction of the temporal power, Hobbes opens up a space wherein those subjects can disagree with that power. At least in this passage, teaching—the sort of teaching that Hobbes would be doing in his books of civil philosophy—sounds more like counsel than command.

That is, however, admittedly slim evidence for the proposition that Hobbes changes the conception of his reader from a mere recipient of indisputable doctrine to the subject of a dialogue. A supporting thesis that takes in the whole of Hobbes's career is provided by David Johnston, who surveys how Hobbes's conception of his audience evolved from his beginnings as a civil philosopher to the publication of *Leviathan*. In the beginning, Hobbes limited his audience to those who were already disposed to agree with him. He addressed his translation of Thucydides to "the few and better sort of readers" (xxiii), those like himself who were disillusioned with political discourse that "only swayed the assemblies." But Johnston describes how, as the reading public grew throughout the seventeenth century, Hobbes became interested in the phenomenon of public opinion and altered the style of his philosophical works to make them more accessible to a larger variety of readers. His first work of civil philosophy, the *Elements of Law*, was written for the powerful elite that could actually put his doctrines into effect (in fact, it was initially circulated only in manuscript) and "is essentially scientific as opposed to rhetorical in design." In contrast, *Leviathan* "was perhaps the first work in the history of political philosophy" that "was intended for a large, public audience and aimed to shape popular opinion directly." "*Leviathan*," Johnston concludes, "was designed less as a scientific treatise than as a work of rhetoric."[25]

I would extend Johnston's thesis about *Leviathan* to *Behemoth* and the *Common Laws* dialogue—Hobbes's last works of civil philosophy[26] —with the stipulation that the "large, popular audience" Hobbes intended them for was an audience of readers. Even though Hobbes's model for counsel is a spoken exchange between the sovereign and a counselor, the "sovereign" subjects whom Hobbes counsels are not hearers. Hobbes, in other words, may have expanded his audience from a "few" readers to many, but those readers remain the "better sort" because they *are* readers. How, B plaintively asks in *Behemoth*, can any teacher of civil philosophy—"the science of *just* and *unjust*"—"teach it safely," when "people always have been, and always will be, ignorant of their duty to the public"? A's reply deserves to be quoted at length:

> The rules of *just* and *unjust* sufficiently demonstrated, and from principles evident to the meanest capacity, have not been wanting; and notwithstanding the obscurity of their author, have shined, . . . to men

of good education. But they are few, in respect of the rest of men, whereof many cannot read: many, though they can, have no leisure; and of them that have leisure, the greatest part have their minds wholly employed and taken up by their private businesses or pleasures. So that it is impossible that the multitude should ever learn their duty, but from the pulpit and upon holidays; but then, and from thence, it is, that they learned their disobedience. (39–40)

Here Hobbes simultaneously appreciates and depreciates the intelligence of his potential audience—his "common" readers. He appreciates it because to many readers the truth of his civil philosophy is self-evident. He depreciates it because so many in that audience remain only potential readers of it, some because they do not take the time to consider it and others because they are illiterate. Hobbes, it seems, is himself unsure about just how large an audience he is writing to. What he is sure about is that hearers—that "multitude" who "learn their duty" only "from the pulpit"—are not a part of it. They do not have sovereignty and must simply be commanded to do their duty. Only readers have sovereignty and can—indeed, because they deserve respect, must—be counseled.[27]

Among Hobbes's works, *Behemoth* and the *Common Laws* dialogue grant the reader the greatest degree of sovereignty. This can be shown by contrasting the role of the reader in these works with the role of the hearers in Hobbes's earliest, though not original, attempt at dialogue, the "Melian dialogue" contained in his translation of Thucydides. Because of the unequal relationship that exists between the dominant Athenians and the intransigent colony of the Lacedaemonians that they have invaded, this dialogue is doomed from the start. The Athenians may say that they want to "confer" with the Melians "about the saving of your city"—to find some way, as they delicately phrase it, to "have dominion over you without oppressing you" (366)—but they also know "that in human disputation justice is . . . only agreed on when the necessity is equal; whereas they that have odds of power exact as much as they can, and the weak yield to such conditions as they can get" (365). Rather than "yield," the Melians reject the Athenians' terms of surrender and are overwhelmed. Precisely because they lack sovereignty, the Athenians' offer to counsel (rather than command) them lacks credibility.

In Hobbes's two later dialogues the situation is entirely different.

Although he must believe that the fate of the hearer who rejects his counsel will be the same as that of the Melians, Hobbes himself does not have the power to exact that fate. In other words, in both dialogues the hearer or "student" being counseled, unlike the Melians, does have a kind of sovereignty: he is not "obliged," as Hobbes might say, to do as he is advised to do. Yet there are also differences between the hearers—the subjects—of these dialogues. In *Behemoth*'s opening exchange B defers to A's knowledge of the time "between the years of 1640 and 1660," which puts him on a "Devil's Mountain," and he prays that A "set me (that could not then see so well) upon the same mountain, by the relation of the actions you then saw, and of their causes, pretensions, justice, order, artifice, and event" (1). B's tendency already to agree with A's interpretation of events means that A—and Hobbes —has to worry less about the interruptions and objections that B might pose in the course of the dialogue and that Hobbes and his spokesman can proceed simply to demonstrate (rather than dispute) the conclusion that he has drawn from the history of the civil war: that the sovereign must rule by force of persuasion as well as the (sometimes violent) force of his authority because people hold their opinions as passionately as, and sometimes more than, they passionately fear for their lives.[28] Of course, that conclusion, while it may not be subject to dispute in the dialogue, is itself a conclusion about disputability. It advises the sovereign to counsel rather than command his or her subjects, to respect *their* sovereignty.

The two discussants in the *Common Laws* are not, at least not initially, so agreeable. In fact, in the controversy about the common law that the dialogue treats, they begin as opponents: the philosopher speaks for Hobbes and absolute sovereignty, and the lawyer speaks for the independent jurisdiction of the common law and its courts. The lawyer thus represents a position—the "Private Judgment" of just and unjust—that, like the private judgment of good and evil preached by "unlearned Divines," contributes to the dissolution of the commonwealth, and Hobbes could have used the dialogue to reject his position absolutely. But the lawyer represents not only the common lawyers, whom Hobbes the disputant wants to defeat, but also the common readers who might be (or already are) misled by them, whom Hobbes wants to persuade. For that reason, and because the initial opposition of the lawyer gives him all the more sovereignty, the *Common Laws* dialogue resembles counsel, as Hobbes defines it in *Leviathan*, even more than does *Behemoth*.

What finally makes Hobbes's imitation of counsel in the dialogue form so remarkable is that in its open portrayal of disagreement it contradicts his famous claim that he had devised a civil philosophy that was as indisputable, and as scientific, as geometry. As he makes the comparison in one of his mathematical works, "Geometry, therefore is demonstrable, for the lines and figures from which we reason, are drawn and described by ourselves; and civil philosophy is demonstrable, because we make the commonwealth ourselves."[29] In *Leviathan* Hobbes anticipates that claim when he states that geometry is "indisputable" (because only geometers use his scientific method of beginning to reason from "Definitions" [114]) and implies that he intends to make civil philosophy indisputable—that is, absolutely certain—as well. According to Skinner, Hobbes's "drive towards demonstrative certainty" is a reaction to "the entire rhetorical culture of Renaissance humanism," particularly its practice of arguing *in utramque partem*.[30] It was the culture from which Hobbes learned the arts of rhetoric and disputation, but, by reacting to it, Hobbes expresses his hope that civil philosophy would not have to be persuaded of but could simply be taught.

Thus, in the opening exchange of the *Common Laws* dialogue the philosopher contrasts statute laws, which he says he reads "not to dispute, but to obey them" (54), with the common law, which, like the opaque religious doctrines debated by unlearned divines, *are* disputed, and endlessly, by common lawyers. By itself, this is nothing unusual: Hobbes always favors obedience and unanimity over the diversity of opinions that produces conflict. But in a later exchange the philosopher compares the common law to "Philosophy" itself as a "disputable Art" (69). Philosophy, that is—including and especially civil philosophy —is less like geometry than it is like the common law itself. We know what makes the law disputable: even though the "unwritten Law of Nature," which supposedly informs both the common (unwritten) and the statute (written) law, is "easy to such, as without partiality, and passion, make use of their naturall reason," Hobbes says in *Leviathan*, it has become "obscure" (and thus less "easy" or accessible) from years and years of misinterpretation (322). Philosophy may not be that obscure, but it is, Hobbes admits here, subject to disagreement.

When Hobbes demands authoritative interpretation, as he does of the law in this passage, he is not concluding that he has succeeded in making his philosophy indisputable but conceding that it never can be.

Despite his lifelong antipathy toward at least exhortative rhetoric, Hobbes comes to believe that his audience must not be taught or disputed with but persuaded and that civil philosophy is less a matter of science than of opinion, less a body of certain knowledge than a disputable art. In other words, Hobbes accepts that his political science is a form not of teaching but of counsel. Other works of Hobbes's may, as Johnston's thesis implies, resemble counsel more than command, but alone among them *Behemoth* and the *Common Laws* dialogue actually depict what counsel does. They do so not least because they *are* dialogues, a literary form that can portray not just the didactic questioning and answering of teaching or the combative thrust and counterthrust of disputation but also the persuasive give-and-take of counsel. To say that Hobbes comes to believe that philosophy is a disputable art rather than an indisputable science, however, is not to say that he abandons his attempt to make it reasonable. Hobbes proves this, in the *Common Laws* dialogue, by the contrast he draws between the reason of common lawyers and the reason of philosophers like himself, a reason that is right not because it is perfect (or absolute) but because it is prudent.

Right Reason and Prudence

In the *Common Laws* dialogue the readers whom Hobbes particularly wants to counsel are themselves "counselors": common lawyers. It was a fundamental tenet of Hobbes's political science that the law, like every other potentially independent entity in the commonwealth, is, or at least should be, subordinate to the sovereign authority. The law "subjects" everyone except the sovereign. Common lawyers held instead that the sovereign should be subject to the law, and despite the return of the sovereign himself at the Restoration, their view, not Hobbes's, was politically ascendent.[31] In *Leviathan* Hobbes explains that this is one of the opinions that tends to the dissolution of the commonwealth because it "setteth also a Judge above" the sovereign "and a Power to punish him; which is to make a new Soveraign; and again for the same reason a third, to punish the second; and so continually without end" (367). If, according to Hobbes, the only way to end controversy is to submit one's right to the judgment of an arbitrator, the error of common lawyers is obviously not that they fail to acknowledge any arbitrator or judge at all but that they fail to acknowledge the sovereign as "sole Supream Judge" (*Common Laws,* 68). For Hobbes, to set the law above the sovereign is to sentence the commonwealth to perpetual controversy.

What English tradition designates as the "common law" is that unwritten law or body of customs and usages that was administered in Hobbes's time by two courts, the Court of Common Pleas and the King's Bench. The principle that guided the administration of the common law, according to William Holdsworth in his monumental *History of English Law,* was "continuity,"[32] and it was a principle that tended to inspire awe among its advocates. The lawyer in the *Common Laws* dialogue, for example, describes the continuity of the common law in almost mystical terms: "[I]f all the Reason that is dispersed into so many several Heads were united into one, yet could he not make such a Law as the Law of *England* is, because by many Successions of Ages it hath been fined and refined, by an infinite number of Grave and Learned Men" (61–62). To the lawyer, the most grave and learned man of all was Edward Coke (1552–1634),[33] chief justice of both common-law courts—Common Pleas from 1606 and the King's Bench from 1613—who, according to Holdsworth, "has some claims to be considered the central figure in English legal history" (4:ix). The chief rival of the common-law courts in Hobbes's time was the Court of Chancery, which Francis Bacon considered to be "the Court of [the king's] absolute power."[34] In contrast to continuity, the principle that supposedly guided the Chancery was equity, "the idea that law should be administered fairly and that hard cases should so far as possible be avoided" (Holdsworth, 5:215). In practical terms, this meant that aggrieved parties could appeal to the Chancery judgments that were delivered in the common-law courts. To the philosopher in the *Common Laws* dialogue (and Hobbes), the other alternative besides the Chancery to the common law and the eminence of learned men like Coke is the sovereign's ability, as "sole Legislator" as well as sole supreme judge (68), to make *statute* law.

In the debate between Hobbes's philosopher and lawyer the philosopher tries to draw the lawyer away from his adherence to the common law and Coke toward absolute sovereignty and statute law. The lawyer, without claiming to be against equity, begins the dialogue by professing belief in something he calls "Artificial" or "Legal" reason (55). He understands equity to be "fined and refined" over time, not immediately (or naturally) apprehensible, and he draws support for his position from precedent, custom, and history, the traditional sources of reason in the common-law tradition.[35] In contrast to the lawyer, the philosopher professes belief in "Natural," not artificial, reason. As he replies to the lawyer's opening gambit,

> I understand well enough, that the knowledge of the Law is gotten by much study, as all other Sciences are, which when they are studied and obtained, it is still done by Natural, and not by Artificial Reason. I grant you that the knowledge of the Law is an Art, but not that any Art of one Man, or of many how wise soever they be, or the work of one and more Artificers, how perfect soever it be, is Law. It is not Wisdom, but Authority that makes a Law. (55)

The philosopher's reply collapses the lawyer's and Coke's distinction between "Natural" and "Artificial" reason: even the long study that Coke thinks is necessary to understand the law is "only natural."

If the lawyer's artificial reason distinguishes between cases of the common law, what does the philosopher's natural reason "distinguish"? Not surprisingly, it is the familiar Hobbesian doctrine that the good of the commonwealth depends on submitting that reason to the reason of the sovereign authority. As we know from *Leviathan*, and as the philosopher states here, "There is not amongst men an Universal Reason agreed upon in any Nation" (67). When coupled with Hobbes's assumption that all human beings are equally reasonable, the absence of a universal (or absolutely "right") standard of reason raises the familiar problem of diversity (and controversy), or, as the philosopher expresses it here, of disobedience to the law: "When I consider this, and find it to be true, and so evident as not to be denied by any Man of right sense, I find my own reason at a stand; for it frustrates all the Laws in the World: for upon this ground any Man, of any Law whatsoever may say it is against Reason, and thereupon make a pretence for his disobedience" (54–55). The blessing of natural reason is also its curse: available to everyone, it nevertheless produces different, sometimes seditious opinions. The philosopher's solution to this problem is also familiar: to "set up" the sovereign's reason "to supply the place of that

Universal Reason, which is expounded to us by our Saviour in the Gospel, and consequently our King is to us the Legislator both of Statute-Law, and of Common-Law" (67). Coke would have us believe that natural reason—or, rather, the natural reason of a few "Grave and Learned" men—could directly perceive a mode of living in conformity with abstract concepts like equity and justice. But Hobbes knows that the natural reason of most people, even common-law judges, is too limited, or too shortsighted, to do anything but conform to the sovereign's commands. What makes a law equitable or just is not its reasonableness: it is just (*and* reasonable) because the sovereign has commanded it. Conforming to the laws of the sovereign is what makes our natural reason, which commands that conformity, "right." The only "naturally" universal law in which the philosopher professes belief is the maxim "*Salus Populi* is *Suprema Lex;* that is to say, the safety of the People, is the highest Law" (102), and because the sovereign is the one who can best preserve that safety, the sovereign is also the one who determines just what the "safety of the People" is. The sovereign is the ultimate judge and legislator in the commonwealth.

Because the reason that Hobbes chooses to call right rests on a palpable perception of that which preserves our physical and mental well-being, the decision we make to obey the sovereign authority is an "interested" one. This is where Hobbes's previous analogy between geometry and civil philosophy breaks down: "pure" sciences like geometry, as Gary Shapiro affirms, are in Hobbes's view "subjects of disinterested curiosity," but civil philosophy is "bound up with questions of authority, right, and power."[36] It is also important to note, however, that this "interest" is not the narrow self-interest that might, as the philosopher previously said, make a "pretence" for disobedience. It is, rather, a farsighted interest, the sort that Hobbes elsewhere calls prudence.[37] In rhetorical terms, prudence is a product of pathos, one of the three kinds of proof or modes of persuasion in Aristotle's *Rhetoric*. We do what is prudent—that is, in our farsighted interests—because we fear for our lives, and fear is one of the emotions that Aristotle says a rhetor can arouse in order to effect persuasion.[38] In political terms, Hobbes's prudence is roughly equivalent to what later civil philosophers would term the "public interest."[39] Civil philosophy, then, is not a disinterested science for Hobbes, but neither can it, as A says in *Behemoth,* "appear propitious to ambition" or be exempt from the "obedience due to the sovereign power" (96). It is interested because it plays, as does the appeal of rhetorical pathos, on the passions—mainly the passion for self-preservation—but it is not shortsighted or self-interested.

Ironically, Hobbes's contractual approach to the law—to set up as law the commands of a sovereign to whom ordinary subjects have *agreed* to subject themselves—makes law, and the reason of the sovereign authority that legitimates it, just as "artificial" as the legal reason that, for Coke, distinguishes the common law. There is, however, an important difference between the artificiality of Coke's common law and the artificiality of Hobbes's sovereign law. When, in the concluding section of the *Common Laws* dialogue, the philosopher and the lawyer turn to talk "Of Punishments," the lawyer stubbornly adheres to his position that the common-law courts and their lawyers should be independent of the sovereign authority, and he is amazed to find the philosopher—because of the problem of diversity—denying even the *king* the right to determine "according to natural Reason" the just punishment for a given crime:

> LA. If the natural Reason neither of the King, nor of any else be able to prescribe a Punishment, how can there be any lawful Punishment at all?
>
> PH. Why not? For I think that in this very difference between the rational Faculties of particular Men, lyeth the true and perfect reason that maketh every Punishment certain. For, but give the authority of defining Punishments to any Man whatsoever, and let that Man define them, and right Reason has defin'd them suppose the Definition be both made, and made known before the Offence committed: For such authority is to trump in Card-playing, save that in matter of Government, when nothing else is turn'd up, Clubs are Trump. (140)

With the pun on "Clubs," the philosopher repeats that it is not the wisdom (or natural reason) of the sovereign but his or her authority (backed up here, presumably, by the threat of force) that makes the law. But he also adds an important caveat to his standard definition of law (and of reason) as anything that the sovereign—the "any Man" to whom the other subjects in the commonwealth have given the "authority of defining Punishments"—commands, or "defines." That caveat, that the definition "be both made, and made known before the Offence committed," makes *publicizing* a law and its punishments as essential to its reasonableness as whether it is prudent, or preserves the safety of the people. Although it guarantees only that the people will know (not agree with) the laws that they are compelled to obey, publicity is nevertheless imperative to Hobbes's new theory of representation in the dialogue. If before he envisioned only the sovereign representing the commonwealth, with wiser but weaker counselors advising him what was best for it, now he imagines a sovereign having to solicit the consent of a people allowed to represent themselves. And soliciting the consent of the people requires publicity.

From Representative Publicness to True Representation

To understand that change, and what dialogue has to do with it, however, we need first to understand the theory from which it changes. Hobbes conveys his original theory of representation most concisely in a passage from chapter 16 of *Leviathan*, "Of PERSONS, AUTHORS, and things Personated":

> A Multitude of men, are made *One* Person, when they are by one man, or one Person, Represented; so that it be done with the consent of every one of that Multitude in particular. For it is the *Unity* of the Representer, not the *Unity* of the Represented, that maketh the Person *One*. And it is the Representer that beareth the Person, and but one Person: And *Unity*, cannot otherwise be understood in Multitude. (220)

This "authorization" theory of representation parallels the contract-making process that, for Hobbes, brings human beings out of a state of nature into a state of society.[40] It recasts the arbitrator or judge whose sovereign reason solves controversy as a sovereign representative. The "consent of every one" being represented is necessary to authorize the representative, but only at the beginning of the process. Thereafter, those who disagree can only agree, or be unified, when the representative imposes his will on them. It is significant that Hobbes does not think that agreement among the subjects of a commonwealth can be achieved through discussion and argument, by people talking out their differences; it can only be imposed by a will that draws its strength from being singular.

Hobbes's single-minded view of representation is an instance of "representative publicness," the theory that Jürgen Habermas finds prevailing in Europe before the rise of the bourgeois public sphere at the end of the seventeenth century. In representative publicness, as in Hobbes's theory, the actual person of the representative "displayed himself, presented himself as the embodiment of some 'higher' power,"[41] and thus the only persons able to be representatives were the monarch and members of the nobility. Indeed, it could be said that representative publicness is not a theory of representation at all but a scheme to avoid it altogether. It is representation as conceived in an absolutist form of government.

It is hardly surprising that Hobbes would resist a more modern, possibly even a more "bourgeois" theory of representation. For him to extend the power of representation to persons other than the monarch would be a step toward a democracy, or at least a republic, and Hobbes had expressed his low opinion of democracy as early as his translation of Thucydides: democracy produces demagogues vying for "authority and sway" among the common people by exhorting them to "desperate actions" (572). Just as for Hobbes there is no "unity" outside the person of the representative (the Leviathan), in representative publicness there is no "public" outside the bodies of the person or persons who display that power. "What is it that can be called public," complains B in *Behemoth*, "in a civil war, without the King?" (113). The members of Parliament do not represent the public, for Parliament is simply a gathering of private individuals, each of whom presses his own interests. Neither can Hobbes conceive that a public comes into being when an assortment of other private individuals, independent of the government, assemble to discuss the interests that they may have in common, an approximate image of the public sphere that Habermas opposes to representative publicness at this time. In Hobbes's experience, assemblies only produce further discord, not Habermas's consensus.

To those more comfortable with democratic theories of representation the problems with representative publicness seem obvious. Because it asserts "that the interests of the sovereign and the people are identical," it raises the specter of tyranny, of a monarch who, acting to further only his or her own interests, governs arbitrarily and cruelly.[42] But tyranny—the most negative outcome of absolutist government— concerns Hobbes less than anarchy, or no government at all. A more pertinent objection to Hobbes's theory of representation is raised by Hanna Fenichel Pitkin, who calls it a "verbal game" that conceals the "real problem of the creation of political consensus."[43] It does not solve what I have been calling the problem of diversity. It simply assumes that all opinion in the commonwealth will be unified because the sovereign's opinion, being singular, is unified.

Pitkin herself slights the rhetorical consensus building that lies behind the original authorization of the representative. But her objection does expose the practical problem that a theory like representative publicness has with sustaining a collective will once the authorization process is over. In addition, as the population of the commonwealth grows, it becomes more and more difficult for the king actually to show the people that he represents them, as representative publicness requires him to do. Significantly, the party that understood this during the civil war was the Long Parliament, not the king. As B recalls in *Behemoth,* when the king might otherwise have made his "stoutness . . . known to the people" through a military victory or the promise of one, Parliament forced his party to make its response "couched in declarations and other writings." This "paper war" eventually exhausted both his will to respond and the people's willingness to follow him (116, 115). The spread of literacy in the seventeenth century and the plethora of controversial writings that arose to respond to it were surpassing the kind of publicity that required the king to show himself.

The civil war exposed another problem with representative publicness: by dividing king from Parliament, it forced the issue of precisely where sovereignty resides. B notes in *Behemoth* that when Parliament "first took up arms against the King," its members "[styled] themselves the King and Parliament, maintaining that the King was always virtually in his Parliament" (140). Similarly, when it leveled its grievances against the king, Parliament, in A's words, "accused . . . the bishops, counsellors, and courtiers, as being a more mannerly way of accusing the King himself" (82). In both cases, Parliament drew a distinction between the king's private person and his public person and assumed that someone other than the king—his private, physical person —could bear the sovereignty that had been his alone. Just as the threat of censorship often causes controversial writers to cloak their criticism of a government in irony, saying one thing and meaning another, so did the threat of punishment (for criticizing the king directly) cause Parliament to fall back on a theory of representation that separated the king's public person from his private one.[44]

In *Behemoth,* as the previous quotations imply, Hobbes resists the abandonment of representative publicness as a theory of representation. Although A, dismissing B's concern about an "inhuman" or tyrannical ruler, assures him that the king "commands the people in general . . . as a politic, not a natural person" (51), he later calls that same distinction, when Parliament draws it, an impudent and foolish one, only "an university quibble" (124). To draw that distinction, Hobbes knows, is to liberate the notion of representation. If what the monarch does as a "politic" (or public) person—that is, as the sovereign—is different from what he or she does as a "natural" (or private) person, then other persons can act for the monarch in the sovereign, public capacity. When B, referring to Parliament's attempt in 1642 to hold the republican town of Hull (and to bar Charles I from it) by right of its claim to "represent" all the people of England, asks who held it when Parliament was not in session, A replies, "I think it was the King's, . . . because the King himself did then and ever represent the person of the people of England. If he did not, who then did, the Parliament having no being?" (120). As usual, A's answer ties the notion of representation to the natural body of the representative: if that "body" is absent, as it is when Parliament is not in session, then the act of representation itself ceases to exist.

In the *Common Laws* dialogue, however, Hobbes seems to recognize that there *is* a difference between the monarch's natural, or private, capacity and his "politic," or public, capacity, and it is the lawyer who brings the philosopher to see the difference. When the lawyer asks the philosopher, "Do you think the distinction between natural and politick Capacity is significant?"[45] the philosopher replies in the negative, but when he elaborates on his answer, it becomes clear that the distinction, if not "significant," does in fact exist: "Whatsoever a Monarch does Command, or do by consent of the People of his Kingdom, may properly be said to be done in his politick Capacity; and whatsoever he Commands by word of Mouth only, or by Letters Signed with his hand, or Sealed with any of his private Seals is done in his natural Capacity" (162). As Joseph Cropsey points out, the way the philosopher draws the distinction in this passage has "made it appear" that what the king does "in his public or politic capacity" he does "*with consent*" (47, emphasis added). If Hobbes were still tied to the theory of representative publicness, there would be no need for the monarch to solicit the consent of the people to the laws by which they are governed. The monarch, acting in his or her politic capacity, would represent the people. But the people's own representatives are necessary to make their consent known to the monarch. Unlike representative publicness, the theory of representation that the philosopher advances here involves less "commanding" than consensus building.

Typically, the lawyer looks to history to establish the legitimacy of the monarch's soliciting the people's consent, reviewing "the Laws and Customs of our Ancestors" for other examples of the practice (162). What he finds there causes the philosopher finally to abandon the theory of representative publicness. Coke, the lawyer relates, inferred that as far back as the time of the Saxons "the Kings called together the Bishops, and a great part of the wisest and discreetest Men of the Realm, and made Laws by their advice" (166). Even considering that the philosopher had challenged him to find such precedents, the philosopher's response—with the lawyer calling once again on the authority of Coke and of history—is uncharacteristically agreeable, in content as well as tone:

> I think so; for there is no King in the World, being of ripe years and sound mind, that made any Law otherwise; for it concerns them in their own interest to make such Laws as the people can endure, and may keep them without impatience, and live in strength and courage to defend their King and Countrey, against their potent neighbors. . . . I confess, that the Parliaments of the old *Saxons*, and the Parliaments of *England* since are the same thing, and Sir *Edw. Coke* is in the right. (166)

"In other words," says Cropsey, the philosopher admits that "for the good of the people and also of the king it is necessary that legislation be with the advice and consent of the people, or, in this case, Parliament" (47). As if to encourage this new, conciliatory tone of the philosopher, the lawyer brings up another, equally old example of the king's soliciting the people's advice and consent. That custom, he reasons, must be "more ancient than the City of *Salisbury*" or Old Sarum because that borough, now totally decayed and deserted, still returns representatives to Parliament. Such "Cony" boroughs, which for nineteenth-century Parliamentarians meant that the system needed reform, are evidence for this seventeenth-century lawyer of the legitimacy of parliamentary representation: "[A] good Argument may be drawn from thence," he continues, "that the Townsmen of every Town were the Electors of their own Burgesses, and Judges of their discretion; and that the Law, whether they be discreet or not, will suppose them to be discreet till the contrary be apparent" (166). In reply, the philosopher makes an even more remarkable admission than before: "I think your reason is good: For I cannot conceive, how the King, or any other but the inhabitants of the Boroughs themselves, can take notice of the discretion, or sufficiency of those they were to send to the Parliament" (166–67). Thus, at this, the crucial end of the dialogue, the philosopher not only thinks for once that the *lawyer's* (and Coke's) "reason is good," but—by conceding that the subjects closest to a representative are the best judges of his or her abilities, that they can best "discern" or see who should represent them—actually limits the king's supply of right reason or foresight.

Those few critics who find a place for the *Common Laws* dialogue among Hobbes's works are divided about whether the philosopher's "confession" to the lawyer amounts to much of a change in his civil philosophy; that is, whether Hobbes has changed his attitude toward Parliament.[46] The *Common Laws* dialogue obviously does place a new emphasis on soliciting consent, however, and to my mind that is the more important change. Although Hobbes retains for the sovereign the ultimate authority to determine the law, soliciting consent requires that the sovereign obey the "imperative of publicity" that the philosopher outlined in reply to the lawyer's concern about lawfulness of punishments. The sovereign must make the law known to the people, and make it known before he or she can expect them to obey it. This may be only a practical imperative—the people's consent is required, not to authorize the law, but only to encourage their obedience—but it does ask the sovereign to speak rather than simply show, to persuade, and, nominally at least, to listen.

Hobbes's philosopher thus makes a crucial concession to the lawyer at the end of the *Common Laws* dialogue that Hobbes's A did not feel the need to make in *Behemoth,* but both dialogues make it a consistent theme that legitimate policy requires publicity, and in the *Common Laws* dialogue it is the philosopher, not the lawyer, who sounds that theme. Earlier in the dialogue, he makes it a part of the definition of law that it be "Publickly, and plainly" declared, adding that the members of Parliament "should be bound to furnish People with a sufficient Number of Copies (at the Peoples Charge)" of the statute laws they have just passed (71). The lawyer protests that to print and distribute so many copies would be "almost Impossible," but the philosopher persists: "[W]hat Reason can you give me why there should not be as many Copies abroad of the Statutes, as there be of the Bible?" (72). The idea that every subject, no matter how common, should have access to statute law is a radical one, comparable, as the philosopher alludes, to the Reformation demand that the Scriptures be made available to every believer. Although Hobbes the civil philosopher wants to promote obedience, and the religious reformer to save souls, the effect of their proposals is the same: to shift the responsibility for knowing the law, and the justification for obeying it, from private, learned men to the individual subject or believer.[47]

Besides, those who discount the difference between these dialogues and Hobbes's earlier works forget who has the "sovereignty" when the goal is cultivating public opinion. Whether Hobbes the civil philosopher is counseling his reader or the monarch—Hobbes's Leviathan —is soliciting the consent of the people, those subjects who had been only ordinary readers in Hobbes's earlier works are in command of the exchange. At the same time, soliciting the consent of the people is not the same as seeking their counsel.[48] If the people—rather than, in a sense and all along, Hobbes—were now counseling the sovereign, they would have to advise what is good for him or her. In *Behemoth* and the *Common Laws* dialogue, however, Hobbes depicts representatives of the people as advising the sovereign, or at least the sovereign reader, what is good for *them*. This is a change, not in the direction of counsel, but from representative publicness to true representation, and even if Hobbes ends up disagreeing with what those representatives would advise, at least he shows them advising it. It is a change that, like counsel, is symbolized by the dialogue form: Hobbes can now imagine persons other than himself, be they the people's representatives in Parliament, an innocuous student named B, or an argumentative common lawyer, representing the safety of the people to the sovereign. *Counsel,* the word I have used to describe the dialogue that Hobbes the civil philosopher has with his sovereign reader, may no longer be the appropriate term for this kind of public interaction, but it is still a kind of dialogue.

2

HARRINGTON
AND NEVILLE
Dialogue and Disinterestedness

THAT ONE can have a disinterested relationship to the pursuit of knowledge is an idea that both defies history and begs to be historicized. In eighteenth-century aesthetics, where historians of ideas have traditionally located the origin of the concept, to be disinterested was to contemplate a work of art "for its own sake," not from any desire to possess it, and to dismiss the moral, political, or otherwise practical concerns that might have gone into its making. In her book *The Author, Art, and the Market* Martha Woodmansee shows that the shift from an earlier, "instrumentalist" theory of art to this modern theory of art as "an autonomous object that is to be contemplated disinterestedly" —roughly, from the idea that art should work real effects in the world to the idea that it exists only to please—was born from the inability of certain serious artists to compete with the more popular sensational and sentimental ones. Instead of attempting to outdo the sensationalists, the advocates of disinterestedness turned their "loss of direct instrumentality"—their *lack* of effect—"into a supreme virtue."[1] What they gained for their disinterestedness was, in Pierre Bourdieu's terminology, a kind of "cultural capital."[2] Their disinterestedness was valuable not because it made them richer but because it distinguished them from the artists who produced more immediate gratifications and from the consumers who enjoyed them.

I mention Woodmansee's thesis because I want to draw an analogy between the cost of disinterestedness in aesthetics and its cost in political thought. Well before the rise of aesthetics in the eighteenth century, seventeenth-century civic humanists formulated the concept to counter the political science of Hobbes, who argued that because of their interest in self-preservation, human beings would subject themselves to the authority of an absolute sovereign. Civic humanists, in contrast, contended that human beings fulfill themselves only when they act as autonomous citizens (rather than subjects) in a republic and that to do so fully required a certain *dis*interestedness, to which they gave the classical name *virtue*.[3] Virtue designated "not merely a moral life but a life of service":[4] a virtuous citizen was one who subordinated private interest to the good of the community or polis. The polis could only be a republic, and not the absolute monarchy favored by Hobbes, because a republic left its citizens free to pursue their particular goods,[5] but citizens could only be virtuous if they exercised that freedom to choose the public good over their private ones.

In this chapter I examine the most prominent republican replies to the civil philosophy of Hobbes, by James Harrington (the theorist who imported civic humanism to England) and his disciple Henry Neville, in order to determine the costs and benefits of disinterestedness and to discover what dialogue has to do with it. In Harrington's dialogue *Valerius and Publicola* (1659) two virtuous citizens discuss why the republican solution to the crisis of the commonwealth has failed to capture the imagination of those charged with restoring it, and in Neville's *Plato Redivivus: or, A Dialogue Concerning Government* (1681), three other citizens adapt that solution to the new political reality of the Exclusion Crisis. Such dialogues take the debate about the commonwealth out of the king's private chambers (where Hobbes, by conceiving of dialogue as counsel, had sought, at least initially, to keep it) and place it in the public sphere. On the other hand, the solution they propose also restricts that debate to a "wiser few" citizens who, because they *are* disinterested, are disabled from actually doing anything about it. Harrington's civil philosophy bifurcates the commonwealth into a "debating few" and a "resolving many," and it has the effect of separating philosophical thinking from political action.

The Debating Few and the Resolving Many

What gave a civic humanist the power to act as a citizen was the possession of property. In *Plato Redivivus* Neville's spokesperson, the English Gentleman, announces that his "intent" in this discourse "is to prove, that in all states, of what kind soever, this aphorism takes place: Dominion is founded in property" (89).[6] But, plainly, in all states, and particularly in England without the benefit of Harrington's reforms, political power was not in balance with the power bestowed by property: not all those with the capacity to act as citizens, or with property, had a share in the "dominion" of their government. In his ideal commonwealth, *Oceana* (1656), Harrington attempts to ensure the proper balance of power to property through the famous Agrarian Law, which requires that property be distributed evenly among many citizens of the commonwealth rather than concentrated among a few.[7] The more balanced the distribution of property, the more stable the commonwealth and the more virtuous its citizens.

Just as he takes care to balance property in his ideal commonwealth, Harrington balances the unequal intellectual capacities of its citizens. In a random group of twenty persons, he says in *Oceana,* "about a third will be wiser, or at least less foolish, than all the rest." In a republican commonwealth a representative council of these wiser persons makes up the senate, whose function is "to debate the business whereupon they are to give advice, and afterward to give advice in the business whereupon they have debated." A council of the remainder of the twenty makes up the commons, whose function is to choose, or "resolve," among the alternatives that the senate has debated. As Harrington elucidates, it is the wisdom of the few that incapacitates them from choosing: "The wisdom of the few may be the light of mankind, but the interest of the few is not the profit of mankind, nor of a commonwealth. . . . As the wisdom of the commonwealth is in the aristocracy, so the interest of the commonwealth is in the whole body of the people" (172–73). The point of this passage is not that the few who debate are without interests but that, because they *are* "few," their interests cannot be representative of "the whole body of the people." Their private interests cannot be public. The interests of the many who choose, on the other hand, do represent the "interest of the commonwealth," or the public good. The debating few know what is best for the commonwealth but do not have the power to enact it; the resolving many do have that power but do not know how best to use it. In *Plato Redivivus,* Neville's Englishman agrees with Harrington that the peers "cannot have any interest or temptation to differ with the commons in anything wherein the public good is concerned" because the interests of the peers and of the commons are "exactly the same" (193). This is true not because the peers are less self-concerned than the common people but because their private interests remain private. In short, the commons in Harrington's ideal commonwealth not only has, as his character Valerius says, "a great deal of business" (790); it has the power of sovereignty itself.[8] The debating few are removed from governing, or at least from taking action on behalf of the public.[9]

It is significant that political wisdom, or civic virtue—which, according to his philosophy, only the senate can possess—is most saliently expressed for Harrington in counsel or debate, rather than in some other activity. Nearly a century after Harrington, David Hume, in an essay entitled "Of Eloquence" (1742), wondered why no "cultivated genius for oratory, as WALLER'S for poetry," had arisen in England "during the civil wars, when liberty began to be fully established" and when "popular assemblies," which "can be supposed to lie under the dominion of eloquence," began "to enter into all the most material points of government."[10] Twenty years after the civil war, Neville is still blaming the failure to implement Harrington's reforms on the lack of something like that "genius." In *Plato Redivivus* the Englishman supplies two other reasons besides the "politic debauch" of the English commonwealth, a consequence of the imbalance of property, for doubting that his reforms will be heeded:

> The first is; because most of the wise and grave men of this kingdom are very silent . . . and although they dislike the present condition we are in as much as any men, and see the precipice it leads us to, yet will never open their mouths to prescribe a cure. . . . For it is the nature of all popular councils . . . in turbulent times, to like discourses that heighten their passions and blow up their indignation; better than those that endeavour to rectify their judgments, and tend to provide for their safety. (196–98)

Both reasons have to do with the corruption of public discourse. Government has gone wrong because the "wise and grave men of this kingdom" do not speak and because the common people speak, or rather are spoken to, too much. If the wiser few had more virtue, they would be moved to "open their mouths to prescribe a cure"; if the ignorant many had less passion, they would not be moved by mouths that should remain closed.

In truth, both Harrington and Neville, although great believers in popular assemblies, would have disagreed with Hume's implication that the kind of discursive "genius" that the commonwealth needed at this time was oratorical. In the previous chapter I reviewed Hobbes's well-known distrust of oratory, a distrust that Harrington and Neville share. Neville, for example, achieved his first bit of notoriety during the civil war by publishing, in 1647, *The Parliament of Ladies,* a satire on the Long Parliament that mocks not only its Puritan propensity for making the private a matter of public concern—it is in this sense that Neville calls the male members of Parliament "ladies"—but also its oratorical excesses.[11] Harrington suggests that there is something in the enthusiasm for oratory that suppresses real debate. In *Valerius and Publicola* the contrary Valerius, denying the possibility that Parliament will ever agree to Publicola's (Harrington's) reforms, imagines that a senate debating them would conclude instead that the present form of the English government, with the balance among "king, lords and commons" tipped toward the king, is "the ancient, the only, the most happy government that this nation, nay, that the world ever knew." Amused by Valerius's scenario, Publicola insists that "ten to one" of the speakers in his senate "will be longer-winded than you have allowed" and, more important, that "they would have been debating upon that point at least a fortnight" (798–99). But this is to say that the senate did not "debate" on that point at all. Such long-winded speeches are displays of impassioned oratory, not reasoned debate. It is, again, because debate must be intelligent that Harrington separates the debating power from the resolving power in the commonwealth.

The strictness with which Harrington separates those powers has led even his most sympathetic critic, J. G. A. Pocock, to dismiss it as Harrington's "furthest departure from reality": "The prospect that any political gathering of seventeenth-century Englishmen could be persuaded to vote without debating, or *vice versa,* is . . . laughably remote."[12] But Harrington never says that the commons will *not* debate the issues that the senate puts in front of it to resolve; in fact, as in the example above, he says just the opposite. What is at issue is not the quantity of debate but the quality, and to keep it intelligent and reasonable—and on track toward a republic—Harrington restricts it to a wiser few. There is discussion and argument about the issues of the day all over Harrington's commonwealth, both in and out of government, and Harrington, much more than Hobbes, encourages this plethora of discursive activity:[13] it shapes, if it does not finally steer, the resolution of the commons. The debate that counts, however, the debate that does so steer that resolution, occurs in the rather small senatorial sphere of a representative government.

The Nature of Debate

If Harrington is quite specific about the kind, or at least the class, of person who can debate, about the debate itself he tells us little. In the conversation between Valerius and Publicola just recounted, the former does say that debate should be conducted in an "orderly" manner and "maturely," and that it should be reasonable: that a person, "much less an assembly, resolveth not upon anything without some considerations, motives or reasons thereunto conducing" (790). This would seem to align debate with the capacity for "judgment" that Harrington opposes to "invention" in *Aphorisms Political* (1659). Invention, the kind of reason that can pitch on "the formation or reformation of government," is best left, he explains there, to "one man" (a civil philosopher like Harrington himself), a single reasoner, whereas "Judgment is most perfect in an assembly," where one reasoner can bounce an idea off another.[14] Harrington's thoughts about judgment confirm that debate, which by its definition can only occur between two or more people, looks as different from pure ratiocination as from oratory. It is not a solitary thought or a speech but a rational dialogue between two or more persons.

Harrington may not tell us much about debate, but if it is equivalent to dialogue, we should be able to take *Valerius and Publicola* itself, and especially, because of its greater range, Neville's *Plato Redivivus* as examples of what Harrington means by it. From the evidence of Neville's dialogue, the first thing to say about such debate is that it is moderate in tone. The Englishman makes a plea for moderation in the dialogue when, lamenting the current state of public discourse, he calls for persons of "high and unquestionable a reputation" to "venture upon bold, that is (in this case) moderate counsels, for the saving of their country" (199). Some twenty years after speaking up for Harrington's proposals as a member of Parliament,[15] Neville, like Hobbes before him, believes that the commonwealth now needs not oratory but "moderate counsel." It is symptomatic of the disordered state of the commonwealth that it takes a paradox to describe the nature of such counsel: in order to be "bold," or efficacious, it must be moderate, or un-"rhetorical." In the passionate atmosphere of the Exclusion Crisis, moderation *is* bold.

Second, the debate that is *Plato Redivivus* is more instructive than persuasive. It does not have to be persuasive because, at least among its small, private group of debaters, it has nothing to prove. The Englishman, in fact, compares the "private conversation" that he is having with his friends to the "interlocutory" ones that the early Christians had among themselves when they "assembled together." Such conversation "served very much to the instructing and edifying those who had long believed in Christ, and possibly knew as much of him as their pastor himself," and it was in direct contrast to the "concionary" or oratorical preaching that "was used by the apostles and other missionaries, when they spoke to those who had never heard of the mysteries of Christian religion." The audience, that is, determined the speaker's manner, and the speaker determined how the audience could respond: unbelievers were obliged "to hear, and not reply, or any way interrupt the harangue" because the object of the preaching was their conversion; believers were encouraged "to interpose and desire to be heard" because they only needed to be confirmed in the faith (76). In Neville's dialogue the Englishman is "preaching" to the already converted; indeed, he acknowledges that his "congregation" —a Noble Venetian and an English Doctor, the other two characters in the dialogue—know as much as he does about what it takes to be a good citizen in the commonwealth. Among friends he can dialogue rather than "harangue."

Predictably, given that these friends already have much in common, the third characteristic of the debate exemplified by *Plato Redivivus* is that it is uncontroversial. The politics of the Englishman, as Neville's spokesperson, are already known; the Doctor introduces him to the Venetian as one who, like Neville himself, has "had a great share in the managing affairs of state here" and avouches that "really no man understands the government of England better than he" (75). The Venetian too, according to Neville's introductory "Argument," "had born office and magistracy in his own commonwealth" (71), a commonwealth that was "the most powerful contemporary embodiment of the discourse of civic humanism" in the seventeenth century, mythically renowned for its stability.[16] The third character, the "eminent physician" (71), falls in with the Englishman's proposals too. He also supplies the occasion for the dialogue, for he was called when the Venetian, visiting the Englishman and other friends in England, took sick.[17] While the Doctor attends and the Englishman visits the sick man in his chamber, the Englishman consents to divert the Venetian with "some account of our affairs here, and the turbulency of our present state" (75). That such a conversation is thought to be diverting to a man recovering from a near-fatal illness is a sure indication that the intelligent debate that this dialogue exemplifies will not be "disagreeable." For Neville, counsel is polite, not controversial, conversation.

Not only because of who they are, then, but also because of the instructive things they say and the moderate and polite way in which they say them, the characters in Neville's *Plato Redivivus* function like the debating few in Harrington's commonwealth. By "discoursing and arguing with one another," as Harrington says in *Oceana,* they "show the eminence of their parts" (172). Discoursing and arguing, perhaps, but not, in the end, disagreeing. Because "reason," as I quote Harrington in the introduction to this study, is "nothing but interest" (171), and because these virtuous debaters lack an "interest" in the commonwealth, there is no reason for them *to* disagree. That is the fundamental reason for the lack of controversy in this dialogue, but it can also be explained, more immediately, by the nature of the civic-humanist "cure" to the disease that ails the commonwealth, a cure that, as Neville never tires of saying, is "perfect" and "infallible" (e.g., 172 and 161). Just as Hobbes thought that he had made civil philosophy "indisputable," Neville thinks that the truth of Harrington's civil philosophy is self-evident, at least to better reasoners like these.

The Cure

Before the cure, however, the disease. What, according to Neville's debaters, is wrong with England's "body" politic? The Englishman, noting first that a considerable part "of the lands which were at the beginning in the hands of the peers, is not there now," diagnoses the disease thus:

> [T]he natural part of our government, which is power, is by means of property in the hands of the people; whilst the artificial part, or the parchment in which the form of government is written, remains the frame. Now art is a very good servant and help to nature, but very

weak and inconsiderable, when she opposes her, and fights with her;
it would be a very uneven contest between parchment and power.
This alone is the cause of all the disorder you heard of, and now see in
England. (133–34)

In short, as the Englishman summarizes a bit later, "for want of outward orders and provisions, the people are kept from the exercise of
that power, which is fallen to them by the law of nature" (145). The
problem with England, in other words, is not that property, or natural
power, is unbalanced—in this respect England already observes the
Agrarian Law—but that constitutional, or artificial, power, the political
power of representation, has not followed the historic redistribution
of property. No artificial "parchment" can long constitute a government that does not pay due service to property.

In the previous chapter I spoke of the "rhetorical crux" of Hobbes's
political science, that he has to persuade shortsighted and self-interested
human beings to submit to what should be self-evidently reasonable.
The coercive power of the sovereign authority will maintain a state
that has already been established, but because it *is* artificial, rhetoric
must establish (or authorize, through a contract-making process)
the state in the first place. This is emphatically not the case for Harrington and Neville. The individuals who are most "interested" in
Harrington's solution to political controversy—those freeholders
who now hold most of the lands—do not need to be persuaded to submit to his scheme because it recognizes and depends on their power.
The contrast between Hobbes's rhetorical task and their apparent
lack of one becomes even clearer when Neville's Englishman reveals
his "cure" for the English commonwealth:

> The cure will follow naturally, if you are satisfied in the disease and in
> the cause of the disease. For if you agree that our government is bro-
> ken; and that it is broken, because it was founded upon property, and
> that foundation is now shaken: it will be obvious, that you must either
> bring property back to your old government, and give the king and
> lords their lands again; or else you must bring the government to the
> property, as it now stands. (152)

Of course the Venetian and the Doctor already do agree that the foundation of the English government is shaken: even before the Englishman
has a chance to map out exactly how he would "bring the government
to the property," the Doctor assures him that "I am very well satisfied

in your grounds" (152). His reply reflects the customary, uncontroversial atmosphere of *Plato Redivivus,* as well as the apparent lack of a rhetorical task on Neville's part: as long as the Englishman is among friends and freeholding civic humanists, he does not have to persuade anyone of anything.

The problem is that outside of the sphere of polite debate that Neville's dialogue represents the Englishman and his fellow debaters are *not* among friends. The self-evidence of the republican solution strikes only other republicans. In the real world of public opinion, as the Doctor complains in reply to the Englishman's cure, "this fundamental truth is little understood," and "in all conversations men will be offering their opinions of what the parliament ought to do in their meeting" (152). In 1681 the balance of power remained in the hands of the king and his party.[18] It may be that Harrington and Neville, far more than Hobbes, ended up on the right side of history, with England finally, if more than a century later, taking on the characteristics of a republic, but in the meantime those who most need to hear their supposedly self-evident solution have not been listening.

The problem is also that neither Harrington nor Neville has the power to compel them to listen. They may know what is best for the commonwealth, but because they do not themselves have the power to enact their proposals, they can only talk (or write) about them. (In this sense, Harrington and Neville are exactly like the characters in their dialogues, with the "power" to debate or talk but not to resolve or act.) Since they are civil philosophers ("debaters" themselves), the only power they have is suasive. It turns out, then, that Harrington and Neville have a rhetorical task after all. If Hobbes had to persuade self-interested human beings that their greater interest lay in submitting their right to the sovereign, Harrington and Neville have to persuade individuals with vested interests in the status quo to enact Harrington's proposals for change. Because their dialogues were written some twenty years apart, however, the individuals whom Harrington had to persuade—his audience—differed sharply from that individual—Charles II himself—who was Neville's audience.

Harrington: Persuading the People

Besides the slight immediate effect that his proposals had, the most distinguishing fact of Harrington's career was how often, and in how many forms, he persisted in presenting them. His published works between 1656 and 1660 included, in addition to *Oceana, Pian Piano* (1657), a book of epistolary "intercourse" in which he replies to hostile questioning about *Oceana* from the clergyman Henry Ferne; pale fictions like *Politicaster* (1659), a play or "comical discourse" written in answer to the criticisms of Matthew Wren; *Aphorisms Political; A Letter unto Mr. Stubbe* (1660); and of course the dialogue *Valerius and Publicola*. It is as if Harrington, frustrated that his proposals were not being enacted, thought that all that was needed to get them enacted was the proper form and was casting about for what that form might be. The particular occasion of the publication of *Valerius and Publicola* was the southern march, from Scotland to London, of the army of General George Monck, which in late 1659 and early 1660 held the power either to reinstate the commonwealth—this time on true republican principles—or to restore the monarchy.[19] Harrington recognized that "New possibilities attended the southern march of Monck,"[20] either for the real beginning or the end of the republican cause. In "To the Reader," the prefatory note to *Valerius and Publicola,* he writes that "the work of the nation, being not understood, is in horrid danger of utter ruin" (782); and in the dialogue itself Valerius "confesses" that "our army hath it now in their power to introduce a commonwealth" (784). "Ruin" would obviously follow if it did not.

Given the "horrid danger" of this ruin, what is most striking about the opening of Harrington's dialogue is how utterly calm Valerius and Publicola seem in their discourse about it. Valerius comments on "the favorable silence of this long walk" that allows him to converse with his "Dearest Publicola" about the "extravagant changes" now taking place in English politics, and he contrasts the "tumult" of those changes to the "attention" that he managed to devote to the last discourse they had about them (782). The timing of this conversation parallels the place of the dialogue among Harrington's works: *Valerius and Publicola* restates, in the popular form of the dialogue, much of what Harrington had already written in *Oceana* and elsewhere, and Publicola describes it as building on the "foundation" of his commonwealth, about which, "by what hath already passed between you and me, . . . we are long since agreed." (That foundation, as he restates it, is that power is out of balance in England because most of the political power is in the "king and lords" and most of the property, or material power, is in the people [783].) The contrast between the dire state of the common-wealth and Valerius and Publicola's calm recounting of it is Har-rington's attempt, like that of Neville's after him, to make the repub-lican solution appear more moderate and ultimately more rational. Their tone turns Valerius and Publicola themselves into the wiser few capable of intelligent debate that the commonwealth needs at this dangerous time.

The timing of the dialogue, if not the tone, also turns Harrington's audience into the "many" that the wiser few need to advise. At this time, when Monck was on the move, the citizenry, even more than any pol-iticians, held the balance of power in the Commonwealth because Monck, although in command of the bulk of the army and invited south by the Rump Parliament (composed of those members who had voted to execute the king in 1649), responded most immediately and sensitively to "the middle ground of public opinion."[21] Harrington, then, addresses his dialogue not so much to his fellow republicans, who dominated (but did not control) the Rump, nor to the oligarchs, like Monck himself, who had dominated it during the Protectorate, but to the "people," that is, the gentry and taxpayers, who would decide, by supporting or withholding support from Monck, which way the govern-ment would turn. In *Valerius and Publicola* Harrington seems to vacil-late between denial that he has to persuade the people that a republic is in their best interests and frustration that they have yet to be so per-suaded. At one point in the dialogue Valerius, who often voices the popular concerns that Harrington's philosophical confidence other-wise discounts, demands to "see it more plainly and particularly dem-onstrated" how the people, who have never yet decided in favor of Harrington's republican reforms, even during the Commonwealth, should now be expected to: how they "must presently lose that incli-nation, which now plainly they have, to set up monarchy." Publicola's reply denies that he has to show anything of the kind: "You will put me then . . . to show by what reason it is that a pear tree must bear pears, or why men gather not grapes on thorns, or figs on thistles." A govern-ment "sufficiently founded or balanced upon" interest, he replies, is the only government that can long endure, because it is the only one that is fundamentally just and natural (796). At other times, however, even Publicola recognizes that what his philosophy must classify as "irrational" inclinations, such as the affection of the people for the institution of monarchy, often determine the course of human events. "[W]e are certain never to go right, while there remains a way to go wrong" (794), he admits to Valerius, and he sometimes reacts with exasperation, sometimes with good humor, when the latter reminds him of the continual failure of the republican cause (800).

When Publicola bemoans his latest failure—his neglect even after printing his proposals "over and over"—Valerius tells him that he "should have laid it, as they say, in their dish, by some direct address, as a petition or so." Not even the supposedly "wiser few" presently in Parliament, it seems, "take . . . great notice of books" (800–801). This may be why *Valerius and Publicola* itself is unlike any other book that Harrington ever wrote. As a represented conversation between a Harringtonian spokesperson and a sympathetic, albeit skeptical friend, it attempts to petition the people (and Parliament) "directly," beginning with Harrington's brief plea "To the Reader": "The way of dialogue, being not faithfully managed, is of all other the most fraudulent; but being faithfully managed, is the clearest and most effectual for the conveying a man's sense unto the understanding of his reader." Dialogue, as we have seen, can be the most fiercely polemical of literary forms, but if "faithfully managed," it can also be the fairest. It is also among the most accessible. He chose the form, Harrington concludes with uncharacteristic eloquence, because "There is nothing in this world, next the favour of God, I so much desire as to be familiarly understood" (782), and the word "familiarly" here has connotations both of "common," as in addressed (unlike the aforementioned parliamentary petitions) to a popular audience, and "intimate," as in treating that popular audience like friends and confidants (like, in short, Valerius).

Harrington's view of this popular audience—of the "many" that would send their representatives to the commons rather than to the senate in his commonwealth—is, to say the least, a complicated one. On the one hand, given that he is addressing the people directly and "familiarly" in his dialogue, he is reluctant to disparage their reasoning abilities or the depth of their knowledge of the kind of government that might be best for them. Thus, when it comes to the failure of the republican cause, Publicola is quick to assign blame elsewhere. "[T]he people," he says to Valerius, may have been "wholly unacquainted with the means" by which "a commonwealth should be introduced in

England," but "their leaders" were also "adverse to it" (783). Later, he utters the dangerous truth that the former "Commonwealth," the Rump and "Barebones" Parliaments that governed England from 1649 to 1653, was nothing but an oligarchy that ruled coercively. Indeed, this truth—and the unpopular government of the country that resulted from that rule of the few—accounts for some of the people's present inclination toward monarchy: "The people, having been governed by a king without an army, and being governed by a commonwealth with an army, will detest the government of a commonwealth and desire that of a king" (794). According to this interpretation of recent English history, the failure of the republican cause was due to the inept management of the few rather than to the ignorance of the many.

On the other hand, Harrington's philosophy can only conclude that the people have so far resisted the republican cause *because* they are ignorant. To do otherwise would be to conclude that "reason" is something more, or something other, than "interest," or that human beings can consciously act *against* their interests, either altruistically or irrationally. If the commonwealth is reordered along Harringtonian lines, with a debating senate and a resolving commons, both legislative bodies refreshed with new members (or "rotated") at regular intervals and standing perpetually, asserts Publicola, there is no way that it "can go one hair's beside the common and public interest of the whole diffusive body of the people" (787). True, assents Valerius, "except through ignorance" (788). Harrington neither singles out the people as the only ignorant members of the commonwealth—he includes the few along with the many in this "representative" body—nor sees them, as do so many others, as led astray by their passions. He blames ignorance, not passion, for their transgressing against interest.

Persuasion, then, should not be necessary because of the sheer reasonableness of Harrington's proposals. But persuasion *is* necessary because of the ignorance of the many (the people) who are, at least in this dialogue, Harrington's "familiar" audience. To skirt this dilemma, Harrington refers the ultimate vindication of his reforms to history, when, even if his audience remains ignorant of their wisdom, they will triumph anyway. Drawing a botanical analogy, Publicola insists that there is no difference "between the growing of a plant and of a commonwealth . . . seeing a commonwealth, knowing as little, doth no less." A commonwealth will "grow" in England "through mere necessity of nature" (783–84) whatever intelligent debaters say about it, or whether or not ignorant resolvers listen to what they say. But persuasion can make the transition easier. Just as the senate in Harrington's commonwealth advises a commons that has the power to reject that counsel and do as it pleases, Harrington advises his common readers of the wisdom of his reforms not because their assent, given the historical inevitability of those reforms, is necessary to enact them but because persuasion is a nonviolent, noncoercive way to effect historical change. The "mischief," says Publicola, is all in the "other things" that the people "will be trying" while a commonwealth grows, and his "desire . . . is to know how it [a commonwealth] should be *rationally* introduced, or by seeing; and that with more ease and better speed" (783–84, emphasis added). According to Harrington's way of thinking, power will inevitably follow property. All the best philosophers, and those talking with them, can do is to facilitate the process: to help history proceed rationally, not violently.

Harrington's view of the people, his popular audience, is complicated because he both needs and does not need them, because he wants them to be rational and knows that they have not been and may never be. Neville's view of the people is more generous. In his revision of Harringtonian doctrine he gives them, through their representatives in the commons, more credit for their reasoning abilities than does his mentor, for "if there be any dissenting upon bills between the two houses, when each of them shall think their own expedient conduces most to the advantage of the public," then (says the Englishman) "this difference will ever be decided by right reason at conferences; and the lords may as well convince the commons, as be convinced by them" (193–94). Given that concession to the commons, and although Neville's dialogue is only a little less "familiar" than Harrington's (it is much longer and more elaborate), it is perhaps surprising that the ultimate audience of *Plato Redivivus* is not the people but the king, Charles II.

Neville: Persuading the King

As a member of Parliament from 1656 to 1660, Neville was able to speak for what Harrington, who was never a politician, could only propose in writing.[22] It was Neville alone who, having survived his mentor, adapted Harrington's proposals to the Exclusion Crisis, a controversy that had its beginnings in the fears surrounding the probable succession of a Catholic—Charles II's brother, James, duke of York—to the throne of England. Suspecting that the Catholic Church, in league with France, was scheming to assassinate the king and destroy the Protestant religion in England,[23] the Commons passed, during 1679–81, three bills that "excluded" James from succeeding to the throne. In response to each bill Charles dissolved Parliament: his actions, while ensuring that James did succeed, in 1685, also gave rise to the first organized opposition to such "arbitrary" monarchical rule, and to a party that supported such uses of royal power. The royalists, who became known as the Tories, found ideological support in the publication of Robert Filmer's *Patriarcha,* an absolutist tract written before the Restoration but published at the height of the Exclusion Crisis, in 1680. The parliamentarians, known as the Whigs, looked to Harrington and Neville. Published in 1681, Neville's *Plato Redivivus,* says Pocock, "may be taken as the first attempt to restate Harringtonian doctrine in a form appropriate to the realities of the Restoration."[24]

Neville's spokesperson in the dialogue, the Englishman, denies that the exclusion of James would be any "cure" for England's present difficulties, but he asserts that *because* of the crisis Parliament "may be encouraged to propose, in the first place, the true cure" (161). Like Hobbes (and Harrington), Neville is confident that a "true" cure—one "determined by the 'immutable laws of nature'"[25]—will "absolutely lay" the causes of this crisis "asleep forever" (172). But Hobbes's (and Filmer's) authoritarian solutions are no cures at all. When the Venetian compares his plan to ask the king to "voluntarily [part] with power" to a poor monk's hapless propitiation of God, the Englishman flatly rejects the analogy. The difference between "the Friar's case and mine," he says, is that "omnipotency is wanting" (175–77). Because the people no longer believe that the king has absolute power, either by earthly agreement or divine right, authoritarianism is outmoded. The Englishman and his fellow debaters must find some other solution to "civil war and confusion" (177).

Neville's debaters propound that solution in an atmosphere devoid of polemics, if not of politics. "Plato redivivus" is Plato "renewed" or "renovated," but the method imitated is the expositive one of Plato's later dialogues, not the adversarial one of the earlier. Setting the tone, the Englishman claims, "I hate nothing more than to hear disputes amongst gentlemen and men of sense, wherein the speakers seem (like sophisters in a college) to dispute rather for victory, than to dis-cover and find out the truth" (77). But just as the timing of *Valerius and Publicola* made the English people (rather than, more specifically, Parliament) the audience of Harrington's dialogue, the timing of *Plato Redivivus* during the Exclusion Crisis does give Neville a specific audience to "discover" the truth to, and a rhetorical task to perform. When his debaters turn from their analysis of the problem with the English commonwealth to their solution, Neville's rhetoric, his "preach-ing" not to the already converted but to the unbelievers, becomes increasingly evident. Paradoxically, the first sign of this is the English-man's reluctance to continue the discussion. He has not hesitated before; now, he proclaims himself "afraid to speak" and wonders, "How can any man, without hesitation, presume to be so confident as to deliver his private opinion in a point, upon which for almost two hundred year (for so long our government has been crazy) no man has ventured?" The Englishman's lack of confidence here does not last long—when the Venetian assures him that "it will not be so much presumption in you, as charity, to declare yourself fully in this matter" (152), he proceeds to do so—but he has dissociated himself from a too obvious investment in his own solution. Like a member of the senate in Harrington's ideal commonwealth, he seems interested in solving the problem but does not seem especially interested in having his way with it.

To persuade unbelievers further of his good intentions, the English-man agrees "to examine some of those expedients," or other solutions to controversy, that they have proposed (152). As the Doctor "reduce[s] them," those other expedients amount to two: "the hindering the growth of popery" and "declaring the duke of Monmouth's right to the crown" (153). The Englishman regards restrictions on Catholics as necessary but no solution: popery, he says, is not "the cause of our present distemper, but the effect of it" (159). Installing James, duke of Monmouth—Charles's illegitimate son, a Protestant, and a popu-lar favorite—as heir apparent, too, will "miss our cure" and keep the English commonwealth "in the confusion we now suffer under" (171). But, again, the Englishman's reaction to the "expedient" that is Monmouth, the pressing of which has precipitated the present crisis, is notable for what he does not, or refuses to, say. When the Doctor

first raises the subject of Monmouth's claim to the crown, the Englishman replies that Parliament cannot "ever suffer such a thing to be so
much as debated amongst them" (164). The Doctor stays with the
issue, however, and when he adds that "there are others, who . . . do
yet pretend that there is great reason to keep up the peoples' affections" to Monmouth, in order to secure "their government and religion," the Englishman rejoins:

> What you have started is not a thing that can safely be discoursed of,
> nor is it much material to our design; which is intended to speculate
> upon our government, and to show how it is decayed. I have industri-
> ously avoided the argument of rebellion, as I find it couched in mod-
> ern politicians; because . . . a politician (as well as an orator) ought to
> be an upright man; so ought to discourse nothing, how rational soever,
> in these points under a peaceable monarchy which gives him protec-
> tion, but what he would speak of his prince if all his counsel were
> present. (167)

Even among friends, apparently, one topic, the "argument of rebellion," can not be spoken of. That Neville so precipitously drops the
possibility of rebellion is understandable, given that republicans were
the first to be accused of sedition and Harrington was arrested for
treason in 1661.[26] By refusing even to speculate what the people
might do if James succeeded to the crown, however, Neville ignores
his natural constituency, those readers who already agree with him
about the dangers of absolute sovereignty.

He does so, and rationalizes his reticence by appealing to his loyalty
to the king, because the king is his ultimate audience. According to
his diagnosis, England is in crisis because constitutional power has
not followed the property that has shifted to the people: in such an
unnatural situation, the Englishman says, the king must "have a great
deal more power, or a great deal less" (172). But giving the king more
power, as Hobbes and Filmer would do, would only make the situation even more unnatural, and prone to violent change. The only real
solution is to persuade the king to give up "a great deal" of power. The
difference between Neville's rhetorical task and Hobbes's could not be
clearer: Hobbes argues for absolute sovereignty but directs his argument
at an audience of common readers, while Neville argues for a mixed
government or a "balance of power" but directs his argument, ulti-

mately, at the sovereign. In Hobbes's political science it is the ordinary subject who must submit his or her right to the sovereign. In Neville's dialogue it is the sovereign himself who must submit his right to Parliament, the elected representatives of his ordinary subjects.

In fact, Neville the republican is much more like the privy counselor whom Hobbes identifies with in chapter 25 of *Leviathan* than Hobbes the authoritarian ever was. Hobbes's common readers, while they were deserving of some respect, were "sovereign" only in their capacity to disagree. But Neville's audience—the real sovereign—does have much "right," or power, left, and persuading him to give it up is, to say the least, a delicate matter. Approaching the king like a privy counselor, Neville's Englishman is circumspect, wary, a "better [conjurer] than any we have yet at court" (177).

When the Venetian asks the Englishman how his civil war began, for example, he dissembles:

> [T]his gracious prince [Charles I] never pretended, (as some divines have done for him,) that his power came from God, and that his subjects could not dispute it. . . . So that our war did not begin upon a point of right; but upon a matter of fact. For without going to lawyers or casuists to be resolved, those of the people who believed that the king did intend to destroy our liberties, joined with the parliament; and those who were of opinion that the prevailing party in parliament did intend to destroy the king or dethrone him, assisted vigorously his majesty with their lives and fortunes. . . . [B]oth parties pretended and believed they were in the right; and that they did fight for, and defend the government. (150)

In *Oceana* Harrington analyzed the cause of the civil war much as Neville analyzes England's present troubles, as "the natural consequence of the fact that the balance in lands and hence in power had passed into the hands of the people,"[27] and concluded that "the dissolution of the late monarchy was as natural as the death of a man" (203). Essentially, Harrington held Charles I and his party responsible for not recognizing that their private interests no longer represented the public interest. But Neville, much as did Hobbes, makes the civil war more a conflict of interpretations (over a "matter of fact") than a conflict of interests (a "point of right"). Neither Parliamentarians nor Cavaliers any longer believed that the king had a divine right to rule; both parties were guilty only of mistaking each other's motives (or "opinions"), not of too forcefully asserting their interests or claims to power. Neville, although obviously sympathetic to the side of the Parliamentarians, dissembles here because he does not want to offend the present-day king, the son of Charles I, and his party.

When he does address the consequences of reform head on, Neville employs a two-pronged strategy of flattery and threat. Immediately after the Englishman asserts that it is in the king's "own interest" to consent to his reforms, for example, he offers two reasons "why the king will please to grant this after the thorough discussing of it." The first, "because all great princes have ever made up matters with their subjects upon such contests, without coming to extremities," plays on Charles's desire for "true greatness." The second, that the king "cannot mend himself, or his condition, if he do not" (178), recalls a warning, made earlier, that princes like Richard II, "who have abused their power to the prejudice of the subjects," have gotten themselves killed. Although he adds that such acts "are no way justifiable," the Englishman raises them to "serve for an instruction to princes" (126). This curious buttressing of flattery with threat, a moral appeal with a practical one, most characterizes Neville's rhetoric of counsel in *Plato Redivivus*. His prince is led to think that he is submitting to Neville's reforms because he is good, but he really does so because he has no choice.

Although Neville seemed to have possessed the better political sense, at times his solution seems just as utopian as Harrington's. Before the Englishman details his reforms, he describes the benefits that would accrue to England on their enactment:

> When this is done, we shall be as if some great hero had performed the adventure of dissolving the enchantment, we have been under so many years; and all our statutes from the highest to the lowest, from Magna Charta to that for burying in woollen, will be current: and we shall neither fear the bringing in popery, nor arbitrary power in the intervals of parliament; neither will there be any dissensions in them; all causes of factions between the country and court party being entirely abolished; so that the people shall have no reason to distrust their prince, nor he them.

The utopian republic that the Englishman envisions here is not so different from Hobbes's or even Filmer's patriarchal commonwealth:

both are, as Hobbes put it, "more than Consent, or Concord"; they are "a reall Unitie of them all" (*Leviathan*, 227). As the Doctor, whose infrequent skepticism is the only trace of disagreeableness in this polite dialogue, comments of the Englishman's vision, "You make us a fine golden age" (185). In reality, however, Neville's reforms are not nearly as utopian as Harrington's were, at least in *Oceana*. Many of them were in fact realized seven years after *Plato Redivivus*, in the revolution of 1688.[28]

Philosophy and Powerlessness

It is of course impossible to determine definitively what historical cause or causes effected those reforms. It necessarily follows from Harringtonian doctrine, however, that the cause cannot be the arguments of Harrington's debating few, whether those debaters are represented by Valerius and Publicola, the characters in *Plato Redivivus*, or Harrington and Neville themselves. Harrington's singular contribution to political theory, after all, was to place the impetus for historical change—ultimately, to place the source of power itself—in the material force of property rather than in some more traditional source like the authority of great men. Power *will* follow property, Harrington and Neville say over and over, no matter what politicians or philosophers say about it. The arguments of civil philosophers and intelligent debaters may facilitate the progress of history, but they cannot finally impede it.

Harrington's and Neville's critics understood that Harrington's placing power in property undermined the more traditional sources of power. Platophilus, the character who parodies Neville in W.W.'s reply to *Plato Redivivus*, *Antidotum Britannicum* (1682), for example, is so besotted with Harringtonian doctrine—in particular, "as *Plato Redivivus* saith, . . . *That Empire is founded in Property*"—that he fears "this goodly Fabrick of the *British* Monarchy" because power *has* shifted from it to the people, "hath had no sure Foundation for many years to support it." His friend Britanicus, however, assures him that neither the monarchy nor the nation at large is in danger of collapse because the "Authority or Legal power" in England is still in the hands of the king. "[H]ow the shifting and change of the Property or possessions of Lands, from the King and Peers to the Commons, should work a change in the Government of *England*, I must protest I am to learn," scoffs Britanicus about Harrington's central doctrine, and then he declares "Commoner[s]," even those with "great Estates," to be "but as Cyphers, and insignificant," without such authority. Britanicus seems to be making a case for the immateriality of power—as Hobbes might originally have conceived it, singular, mystical, and mute—but he immediately backs up the force of that authority with the very material, coercive power of the army: even if the people are "disgusted" with the present government, he tells Platophilus, they "can act nothing to the prejudice of the Government, so long as the King keeps the Militia in his hands and at his dispose."[29] Hobbes too depended on the threat of force, but his appeal to it was hardly so blatant, so crassly dismissive of the sentiments of the populace: he tried to persuade his readers of the authority of absolute sovereignty, not bludgeon them into it. That W.W. so quickly resorts to coercion as the final "reason" for monarchical power suggests that by 1682 Harrington and Neville may have been on the right side of history after all.

The problem with such old-style, absolute authority for Harrington was that it was not—could no longer be—representative. When Publicola, trying to be fair to the arguments of royalist opponents like W.W., attests that there are some who "hold the king to be nothing else but the representor of the people and their power," Valerius interrupts him by comparing such a king to the tyrannical Turk and asserts that "The people's power at that rate comes to the people's slavery" (785). Because what is represented in government for Harrington is interest, and because the interests of the commonwealth are many and diverse, no one person can accurately represent or even approximate the interests of the whole body of the people. Yet, despite his pronouncements against absolute authority, Harrington recognizes the power of a certain kind of immaterial authority: the wisdom of the few, which leads the people differently than the force of property leads them, that is, noncoercively. In the "Preliminaries" to *Oceana*, Harrington describes the difference between the force of property and the force of wisdom thus:

> The principles of government then are in the goods of the mind, or in the goods of fortune. To the goods of the mind answers authority; to the goods of fortune, power or empire. . . . [T]he learning or prudence of a man is no more power than the learning or prudence of a book

or author, which is properly authority. A learned writer may have authority, though he have no power; and a foolish magistrate may have power, though he have otherwise no esteem or authority. (163)

The characters in Harrington's and Neville's dialogues are meant to embody this kind of authority. They may not represent the *whole* body of the people any more than does Hobbes's Leviathan—Harrington has the commons for that—but they do represent their class, and differently from the way the single "representor" of royalist theory could represent anyone (except him- or herself). Furthermore, one gains admittance to the "class" of the wiser few, in Harrington's words, "not by hereditary right, nor in regard of the greatness of their estates only," but by "their virtue or authority that leads the people" (173).[30] Neville confirms this in *Plato Redivivus* by presenting meritorious debaters who are not necessarily aristocratic: the Venetian certainly is, but the Englishman comes from the minor gentry, and the Doctor is a professional man. They constitute more a meritocracy of judgment than an aristocracy of birth.

Harrington, then, sets up an "enlightened" distinction between power and authority, force and reason, and places himself in the latter camp. Indeed, he makes that distinction the centerpiece of his perfect commonwealth. It is the separation of power and authority that ensures, according to Harrington, that there will be no conflict between the commons and the senate, or—with the power (and interest) in the commonwealth in the commons and not the senate—that the interests of the parties will be, in Neville's words, "exactly the same" (193). In the commons itself, where the private interests of individual members may *not* be "exactly the same," the potential for conflict is tempered by the senate's advising which result is best to take; and in the senate, where the private interests of individual members have been disabled from ever coming into play, the only conflict that can result is the relatively harmless clash of opinions, not the potentially harmful clash of interests. The "double point" of Harrington's separation of power and authority, writes Pocock, is thus "to assure an uncorrupt assembly by placing decision in the hands of those not committed to a particular outcome," that is, the debating few, and to ensure "that the senate and assembly cannot possible come into conflict."[31] It may take force to constitute such a perfect commonwealth in the beginning—Publicola says that "if there be no other way, except that only of invasion, whereby the present balance can receive a change sudden enough to admit of any other form, the reason why we must have a commonwealth is coercive" (783)—but once it is constituted, only the force of authority, the "unforced force" of the better argument, is needed to keep it going.

Yet, as much as Harrington tries to assure us of the perfect reasonableness of his proposals, the sticking point remains the "ignorance" of the many, who, if they are not exactly expected to "see" the wisdom of a republican form of government, are at least expected to "feel" the prudence of being led by a wiser few.[32] In one of those moments that seems to occur in every dialogue, when (despite the writer's best intentions) the respondent raises an objection that seems more sensible than anything the writer's spokesperson could answer to it, Valerius expresses "little doubt" to Publicola that "there is in your form a full security unto the people of their liberty" but wonders whether "there is in it any full security that the people shall not cast off this form." He wonders, in other words, how Publicola can know that his reforms will really mean the end of conflict in the commonwealth: why the people may not, at some future date, decide to change their government away from Harrington's "perfect" commonwealth. Publicola answers bluntly, "They cannot, without going against their own interest"; and Valerius's retort is just as blunt: "But they *can* go against their own interest" (795, emphasis added). Publicola insists on the reasonableness of interest, but Valerius raises the possibility that the people will not always be reasonable. In their "ignorance," Valerius realizes, the people may elect to ignore authority.

Thus, Valerius interrupts Harrington's dialogue where the philosopher himself began *Oceana* and the whole of his civil philosophy: with the uncomfortable realization that authority is *not* power. Publicola cannot know that his reforms will mean the end of conflict or that they will even be heeded, and Harrington and Neville, as I have said, cannot compel the populace to listen to their better arguments. No writer can, of course, but my point is that Harrington's civil philosophy sets up an opposition between power and authority that reproduces the relationship that Harrington and Neville, as writers and civil philosophers, have with their respective audiences, which culminates in the atmosphere of polite but ineffectual debate that permeates their dialogues. If they themselves represent the wiser, debating few, their proposals put them at the margins rather than at the center of power. Just as the disinterested artists in Woodmansee's history of aesthetics found themselves alienated, or at least distanced, from popular "critical" opinion, so do the disinterested citizens in Harrington's ideal commonwealth, for all of their material property, find themselves alienated from popular political opinion. The cost of political disinterestedness—which, like aesthetic disinterestedness, is a kind of cultural capital—is political influence.

The political powerlessness of Harrington and Neville, as well as the discursive atmosphere of their dialogues, might be compared to that of Harrington's famous Rota Club, a group of disciples and "Virtuosi" (John Aubrey's term) who met to discuss politics at Miles's coffeehouse in the autumn and winter of 1659–60. The butt of many town wits and mocked by Milton in *The Readie and Easie Way to Establish a Free Commonwealth* (1660), the Rota nevertheless generated interest in Harrington's innovations, especially in the "rotation" of officers by ballot that gave the club its name. "Round the oddly shaped table," writes Caroline Robbins, "Harrington, Neville—by now his recognized lieutenant—and their friends, articulate and gifted, staged the best debates of the century." Aubrey, a member of the club, reports, "The Discourses in this Kind were the most ingeniose, and smart, that ever I heard, or expect to heare, and bandied with great eagernesse: the Arguments in the Parliament howse were but flatt to it." But as Robbins concludes, the members of the Rota "talked in a vacuum." They had no real power, and their discourses attracted only intellectual interest, not popular support.[33] As in the Rota, the conversation in *Valerius and Publicola* and *Plato Redivivus* is "articulate and gifted," as well as always polite, the paradigm of public discourse for a civic humanist. But one wonders whether Harrington's and Neville's dialogues are, like the Rota, paradigmatic because ultimately there is not much at stake.

I have said that the distinction between power and authority is an "enlightened" one, but the tension between political power and philosophical wisdom is at least as old as Plato's *Republic*. What seems unique about that relationship in this period is that civil philosophers were trying to influence public opinion to an extent that was unprecedented in its directness, while public opinion itself, by no means yet the "voice of God," was becoming a force that politicians (and philosophers) had to reckon with. To the extent that philosophers assert their disinterestedness from political affairs, they are proclaiming either that public opinion does not matter to them or that politics is not the appropriate means to shape it. According to Reinhart Koselleck, the latter is exactly what some philosophers of the Enlightenment period did: they used the separation that Hobbes had opened up between the demands of public order and the dictates of private morality—a separation Hobbes had intended to *protect* the state—to rationalize their lack of "interest" in politics, an activity that, in its interestedness, could not but violate their private consciences.

But the accuracy of Koselleck's thesis is more thoroughly born out in the dialogue and other writings of the subject of my next chapter, the third earl of Shaftesbury. Although they exacerbate the split between power and authority, Harrington and Neville intended no separation between politics and philosophy. They did not, that is, disavow politics as a means to shape public opinion or to effect social change. Far from it: they were philosophers who insisted that politics was the means by which the contrariety of interests (and opinions) in the commonwealth must be reconciled and that philosophy could profitably speculate (debate) about what the appropriate form for that "common-wealth" might be. Unlike Hobbes, Harrington and Neville did not deal with controversy by subsuming it in the single will and person of a supreme arbitrator or judge. Rather, Harrington's civil philosophy fully recognized that the solution to controversy in post–civil war politics could only be the product of some negotiation among various interests. But the dialogues that Harrington and Neville wrote in support of that civil philosophy do not as much demonstrate that solution as work around it. *Valerius and Publicola, Plato Redivivus,* and the senatorial sphere of polite debate that they represent are not the places where differing interests can actually be brought together. They are, rather, places where certain like-minded individuals can simply discuss what is best for the commonwealth without their interests getting in the way.

3

SHAFTESBURY
Dialogue and Distinction

SOON AFTER the third earl of Shaftesbury entered Parliament in
1695, "he had," according to his son, the fourth earl, "an opportunity
given him of expressing that spirit of liberty which he maintained to
the end of his life, and by which he always directed his public conduct."[1] The occasion was the debate in the House of Commons over
the Treason Act, which guaranteed a person indicted for the crime the
benefit of counsel. Shaftesbury, notes his son, felt the need of such an
act the more acutely for the troubles of his infamous grandfather, the
first earl, who had been accused of treason and worse for his machinations during the Exclusion Crisis. To the end of securing "the life of
the subject, which might be taken away almost at the pleasure of the
crown," continues the fourth earl,

> my father prepared a speech, which those, to whom he showed it,
> thought a very proper one upon the occasion. But when he stood up to
> speak it in the House of Commons the great audience so intimidated
> him that he lost all memory, and could not utter a syllable of what he
> intended. . . . The House, after giving him a little time to recover,
> called loudly for him to go on, when he proceeded to this effect:—"If
> I, sir, who rise only to speak my opinion on the Bill now depending,
> am so confounded that I am unable to express the least of what I pro-
> posed to say, what must the condition of that man be who is pleading
> for his life without any assistance and under apprehensions of being
> deprived of it?" The sudden turn of thought (which by some was
> imagined to have been premeditated, though it really was as I men-
> tion it) pleased the house extremely; and it is generally believed, car-
> ried a greater weight with it than any of the arguments which were

offered in favour of the bill which was sent to the Lords and passed accordingly.[2]

Whether Shaftesbury was feigning passion in his speech about the bill is unimportant. The incident illustrates his keen appreciation for the power of rhetoric and his awareness that the manner or ethos of a speaker means as much, if not more, to the success of an argument than its content or style. Perhaps more important, it exemplifies his ability to gain a political advantage from an apparent disdain for the political realm and the sort of machinations that made his grandfather infamous. It suggests that he knew how to emulate one of his philosophical heroes, Cicero, who, as Shaftesbury comments about his letters, "endeavour'd to throw off the Mein of *the Philosopher* and *Orator,* whilst in effect he imploy'd both his Rhetorick and Philosophy with the greatest Force" (2:139).

Shaftesbury's life and writings are full of such dichotomies. He was an aristocrat who extolled something called "common sense," a strict defender of "good breeding" and politeness who advocated the "freedom" of an often satiric "wit and humour," a country Whig who spoke of how "We polish one another, and rub off our Corners and rough Sides" through the "amicable Collision" of commerce (*Characteristicks,* 1:39), a civic humanist who retreated from active participation in government, an unconvinced religious conformist, a freethinking moralist, and a skeptical Neoplatonist. He often embodied the controversies that the writers who precede him in this study considered it the business of dialogue to resolve, and he was the foremost philosopher of dialogue in the eighteenth century. Michael Prince, in *Philosophical Dialogue in the British Enlightenment,* argues that Shaftesbury's philosophical and political interests remained "divided" and that he was drawn to the dialogue form because it expresses without resolving that division; his own dialogue *The Moralists,* for example, speaks as strongly for the skeptical position as for the Neoplatonic one.[3] My own view is that Shaftesbury is not as skeptical as he may appear and that his philosophy of dialogue actually suppresses difference for the superior perception of a like-minded few. For all of Shaftesbury's Whiggish tolerance for a diversity of opinions, he seeks a consensus of manners. He turns the problem of diversity into a virtue, the virtue that I call *distinction.*

Common Sense and Consensus

What Shaftesbury usually means by *skepticism* is less a radical doubt about the truth of religion or reality than an awareness that existing opinions about these and other matters are so diverse as to be irreconcilable. He describes this awareness as skepticism in the scene that concludes the *Miscellaneous Reflections,* his commentary on the preceding treatises, including *The Moralists,* that together compose his *Characteristicks of Men, Manners, Opinions, and Times* (1711). In this scene Shaftesbury "represent[s] a Conversation of the same free nature" as the philosophical speculations of Philocles and Theocles, the main characters in *The Moralists.* There, Shaftesbury admits, he gave free, if temporary, reign to Philocles, "the suppos'd SKEPTICK or *Free-thinker*"; here, a "Gentleman of some Rank" is "provok'd by an impertinent Attack of a certain violent bigotted Party," a group of religious zealots, "into an open and *free* Vindication not only of Free-*Thinking,* but Free-*Professing,* and *Discoursing,* in Matters relating to Religion and Faith." The zealots want to find "some way to reconcile Differences in Opinion; since so long as this Variety shou'd be thought on, *RELIGION,* they thought, cou'd never be successfully advanc'd." To the zealots, freethinking, which entails not only doubt about such doctrinal matters as revelation but also toleration of religious views other than the one officially sanctioned by the state, leads to civil unrest, and they want to suppress it. To the gentleman, however, "Variety of Opinion was not to be cur'd": it is simply "impossible" that "*All* shou'd be of *one* Mind" about religion, or, he implies, any other public issue (2:281). Half a century after *Leviathan,* Shaftesbury has apparently given up on the feasibility of bringing Hobbes's "Consent, or Concord" out of religious and political diversity. To Shaftesbury, an ideological consensus is not even necessary. What so worries the zealots is of no concern to him or to his gentleman: diversity, at least the diversity of opinions, is not a problem for the commonwealth.[4]

It is not a problem because the commonwealth is in fact governed by a force internal to the gentleman and those like him, a force that is all the more effective for being internal. Shaftesbury calls this bulwark against skepticism "common sense," and in the second treatise of the *Characteristicks, Sensus Communis; an Essay on the Freedom of Wit and Humour* (1709), he defends the satirist Juvenal, from whom he draws the term, for denying such a quality to the Roman court. A court can have no notion of a "public," or any "other *Sense* than that of *private Good*," and common sense, elaborates Shaftesbury, rightly signifies "*Sense* of *Publick Weal*, and of the *Common Interest*; Love of the *Community* or *Society*, Natural Affection, Humanity, Obligingness, or that sort of *Civility* which rises from a just *Sense* of the *common Rights* of Mankind, and the *natural Equality* there is among those of the same Species" (1:59). It is this innate and common sense, looking out for the good of the whole rather than the parts and pleasantly assured of just what that good is, that ensures for Shaftesbury that diversity will not be a problem for the commonwealth. "Common" by virtue of sensing what unites an individual with a greater community and a "sense" by virtue of being a feeling (or manner) rather than a thought (or opinion), it is impervious to skepticism. Shaftesbury, to apply David Fate Norton's useful distinction, may thus be classified as an "epistemological," but not an "ethical," skeptic. Like the skeptic Pierre Bayle, he "question[s] everything, every proposition, every method alleged to discover truth," but unlike Hobbes and Locke (Shaftesbury's tutor), he does not "deny the existence of any 'real good.'"[5] "For let us carry *Scepticism* ever so far," he pronounces at the conclusion of *An Inquiry Concerning Virtue, or Merit* (1699); "let us doubt, if we can, of every thing about us; we cannot doubt of what passes *within our-selves*. Our Passions and Affections are known to us. *They* are certain" (1:272). Epistemological skepticism is ultimately harmless because common sense—our "Passions" and "Affections"—is so secure.

As phrases like "Public Weal" and "Common Interest" signify, Shaftesbury's common sense is not limited to fellow feeling or one's immediate society. Through natural affection or sociability, he explains in *Sensus Communis*, "*a Clan* or *Tribe* is gradually form'd; *a Publick* is recogniz'd" (1:62). Indeed, it is only through the free expression of fellow feeling (rather than the suppression of it) that a public is recognized. "A Multitude held together by Force, tho under one and the same Head," Shaftesbury declares in the *Miscellaneous Reflections*, "is not properly united. . . . 'Tis the social Ligue, Confederacy, and mutual Consent, founded in some common Good or Interest, which joins the Members of a Community, and makes a People ONE. Absolute power annuls *the Publick*" (2:197). This is, of course, the "common sense" of civic humanism, inherited by Shaftesbury from such republican ancestors as the first earl and Harrington and Neville[6] and now the reigning ideology in England among royalists and republicans, Tories and Whigs, alike. The revolution settlement had validated the early republican vision of shared sovereignty and a balance of powers, and the hegemonic status it attained in England since the same ideas had gotten his grandfather exiled accounts for Shaftesbury's relative indifference to what an earlier generation had thought of as the problem of diversity.

What Shaftesbury adds to such principles is fellow *feeling*, the natural affection that is the "Foundation," as he says, of common sense (1:61). In his view, one must not only "reflect" on "what is *worthy* or *honest*"; one must also make that "Notice or Conception of *Worth* and *Honesty* to be an Object of his Affection" (1:204). His common sense must be felt as well as thought. As Lawrence E. Klein observes, when Shaftesbury talks about the "worthy" civic-humanist principle of "liberty," he is likely referring to the freedoms conversational partners take with one another rather than to the freedoms a state gives (or does not give) its citizens, which marks a "significant shift in emphasis" in the civic-humanist paradigm he inherited, "one that distanced liberty from its specifically cultural [and political] setting."[7] It would, however, be a bit more accurate to say that when he is enthusing about common sense, there is little difference for Shaftesbury between the feeling that brings two people together for fellowship and the sentiment that unites the members of the commonwealth: the personal is the political. As Terry Eagleton puts it, Shaftesbury's "affections are no mere subjective whims, but the key to a well-ordered state."[8]

The Retreat from Politics

The personal may be the political for Shaftesbury, but the personal always comes first. Common sense begins at home, with our natural affection for those human beings who are closest to us, and only then extends outward to found the well-ordered state. In fact, despite his civic humanism, which regarded participation in government as a positive good, Shaftesbury himself retreated from direct political activity. He did have a brief parliamentary career, including stints in both the House of Commons (1695–98) and the House of Lords (1700), and William III even offered him the post of secretary of state when the Whigs achieved a parliamentary majority in 1701. He was forced to resign both offices, as well as to decline William's offer, however, because of ill health, and both bouts of political activity were followed by periods of philosophical contemplation and writing. Robert Voitle, Shaftesbury's biographer, states that he was a political "idealist" who had trouble with "practical politics"; Klein concludes that political "engagement" presented him with an "existential [conflict]" between publicizing his philosophical project and preserving his personal integrity (16).[9] In the *Philosophical Regimen,* the posthumous collection of Shaftesbury's personal meditations that shows the private as opposed to the public person, Shaftesbury, perhaps reflecting on William's offer, poses the conflict between politics and the self thus:

> Thou wouldst serve thy country. Right. But consider withal and ask thyself wouldst thou willingly be perjured, wouldst thou be false, wouldst thou lie, flatter, be debauched and dissolute to serve it? Certainly I would not. But if I think to serve it as I am now bid, all this will necessarily follow. . . . I must grow corrupt, interested, false, and what then will be the service I shall render to my country?[10]

Despite his civic humanism, there is something about politics that Shaftesbury finds, in a word, distasteful. Elsewhere in the *Philosophical Regimen* he says that the critical question for him is not "How do I govern" the "world" but the question "how do I govern MYSELF?" and he vows to "Stop therefore in this [political] career" (102).

If he did participate in government, Shaftesbury says, he would grow corrupt and "interested." Politics, especially the party politics of post-Restoration England, had turned the civic-humanist ideal on its head: it was no longer (if it ever had been) a venue for disinterested gentlemen to serve the public interest but had become one for corrupt, false, and interested individuals—politicians of party—to satisfy their private interests. But Shaftesbury has more than material ambition in mind when he condemns the interestedness of party politics. Because "Partys are no good Registers of the Actions of the adverse side," his freethinking gentleman in the *Miscellaneous Reflections* says, it is "unlikely, that After-Ages shou'd know any other Truth than such as serves the ends of the Representers" (2:282–83). For one as committed to the Platonic ideal of a timeless truth as Shaftesbury was, this is a remarkable, almost Nietzschean admission that what we can know of truth in history is almost inevitably biased, a "story" told by the party in power. The party that triumphs, that is, lays claim not only to the material spoils but also to the power to "represent" truth itself. If Shaftesbury continues to believe that there is a truth that is not interested, it seems that one must retreat from politics in order to find it.

But again, Shaftesbury's primary concern is not political, or party, corruption. His real concern, as expressed in the private meditation above, is that politics will somehow corrupt *him*. Shaftesbury reveals the depth of that concern by the language he uses to describe his psychological conflict in *Soliloquy, or Advice to an Author* (1710), language that is itself tainted by party politics: his own "party of REASON and *good Sense*" does battle with the "party" of "APPETITE," which includes those "Imaginations or Fancys" that "conceal half their meaning, and like modern Politicians pass for deeply wise" (1:102, 101). Shaftesbury may retreat from politics, but politics—and the worst kind of factional politics—has apparently followed, and found, him.

There is, however, a considerable difference between the parties that confound the state and the parties that confound Shaftesbury. Political parties represent differing interests, interests, Harrington would have said, that—when conflict is resolved by appealing to them —look like reason itself. But Shaftesbury's reason is not an interest, and it cannot be appealed to as one would appeal to an interest or at all reconciled with his interested party of appetite; for Shaftesbury to resolve his personal conflict, reason must simply win out. The exercise of reason, that is, and the "party" of philosophy that commands it, are purely "disinterested."[11] Shaftesbury defines disinterestedness— an absolutely central concept in his philosophy—in *The Moralists* as "the *Love of God or Virtue* for GOD or VIRTUE'S sake," and he opposes it to Hobbes's "mere political" motive for behaving morally or religiously, "*a future Reward and Punishment*" (2:45).[12] In Shaftesbury's Neoplatonic philosophy the virtuous person must feel "Affection towards what is morally good . . . *for its own sake*" (1:221).

The Dialogue as a Purely Philosophical Realm

Shaftesbury combines his retreat from politics with a now familiar distrust of political oratory, although that distrust is tempered by his contrasting respect for the rhetorical tradition. As a humanist, Shaftesbury began to repair the breach between philosophy and rhetoric that had opened up when Hobbes and other rhetorical reformers, more committed to the new science than to humanism, rejected rhetoric as deceptive and manipulative. As Klein elucidates, Shaftesbury seems to regard the orators of classical Greece and Rome as exemplary public figures, and he attributes the rise in those classical republics of "politeness"—an "ideal of virtuous sociability" that, according to Klein, Shaftesbury devotes his entire philosophical project to promoting— to public figures' need to solicit the opinion of audiences that were not obliged to hear them (Klein, 186–87, 201–5). It is obviously more polite to persuade a populace, through the "art" of rhetoric, than to coerce or command it.

But like the other figures in this study, Shaftesbury denounces the one-sided rhetoric of mere exhortation, not only because it is commonly associated with politics and politicians but also because it appeals to interest (or appetite) rather than to reason and disinterested virtue. In *Soliloquy* he tells of a "certain Nation" that was

> remarkably fluent in Expression, much pester'd with Orators and Preachers, and mightily subject to that Disease which has been since call'd *the Leprosy of Eloquence;* till some sage Legislator arose amongst 'em, who when he cou'd not oppose the Torrent of Words, and stop the Flux of Speech, by any immediate Application, found means to give a vent to the loquacious Humour, and broke the force of the Distemper by eluding it. (1:88)

Shaftesbury uses the same medical imagery here as Harrington and Neville to warn of the dangers of eloquence. Oratory, or exhortative rhetoric, is a "Leprosy" that must be removed from the commonwealth if it is to be wisely governed. The trick to sage legislating (if only, for Shaftesbury, the legislating, or governing, of the self), is to find a more appropriate way to express the "loquacious Humour" that now finds "vent" in oratory.

That more appropriate way is through dialogue. In *Sensus Communis* Shaftesbury distinguishes between the methods of oratory and those of dialogue: "In matter of Reason, more is done in a minute or two, by way of Question and Reply, than by a continu'd Discourse of whole Hours. *Orations* are fit only to move the passions: And the power of *Declamation* is to terrify, exalt, ravish, or delight, rather than satisfy or instruct" (1:42). The method of "Question and Reply"—dialogue and conversation—serves the party of reason and good sense better than declaiming. But serving reason is not quite the same purpose for Shaftesbury as it was for the previous advocates of dialogue in this study; it is rather—and in a way that again distinguishes dialogue from oratory—a *lack* of purpose. When Shaftesbury imagines the scene of dialogue, that is, he does not imagine it, as Hobbes does, as a teacher counseling a recalcitrant student to a prudential end. Nor does he require, as Harrington and Neville do, that the speculations of a wiser few be directed to the good of the many. Shaftesbury's better reasoners indulge what he calls their "Habit" of reasoning in dialogue simply because it "teach[es]" them to reason better (1:42), and reasoning well is its own reward. Like the love of God or virtue—like the exercise of philosophy—dialogue is a "satisfying," even pleasurable activity in itself.

In other words, dialogue is disinterested. Like the polite sphere of debate that Neville represents in *Plato Redivivus,* dialogue for Shaftesbury is a realm in which reasoners can speculate "without offence" (1:42). Conversely, "The only *Poison* to Reason"—the only thing that makes speculative conversations disagreeable—he says, "is *Passion,*" and "if the very hearing certain Propositions of Philosophy be sufficient to move our Passion; 'tis plain, the *Poison* has already gain'd on us" (1:52). Of course the ability to be dispassionate or disinterested depends in part on what is being discussed. "Certain Propositions of Philosophy," like the proposition of the unity of all things that the characters discuss in Shaftesbury's dialogue *The Moralists,* do not stir the passions, or engage the interests, the way propositions of politics might. They do not, at least, for better reasoners. *The Moralists* does contain one character, "a formal sort of Gentleman, somewhat advanc'd in Years," who cannot reason disinterestedly, cannot help being passionately stirred by certain propositions of philosophy that he hears. A dogmatic believer, perhaps even a Dissenter, he interprets Philocles' skepticism as a serious attack on revealed religion. When Philocles, for the sake of argument, paints "an authentick picture" of virtue "triumph'd over, degraded, spoil'd of all her Honours, and defac'd," he is "violently decry'd" by the gentleman, who infers, wrongly, that Philocles' "Principle of Liberty" in conversation extends "to a Liberty from all Principles" (2:37). In essence, the old gentleman cannot separate his politics (his interests) from his philosophy (his own "propositions" and opinions). If one is to reason disinterestedly in dialogue, as

Shaftesbury implies with his negative example of the old gentleman, one must detach oneself from the world and one's investment in it.

One must also, Shaftesbury adds, have "a Liberty in decent Language to question every thing" in dialogue (1:42), the freedom to practice the brand of skepticism that so offends the old gentleman. As I have said, Shaftesbury questions not only whether the variety of opinions in the commonwealth can be cured but also whether it *should* be. His skepticism, that is, is both an epistemological point about the lack of certainty in human belief and a call for toleration in the face of this fact. At the beginning of *The Moralists,* in a letter to his friend Palemon about his conversation with Theocles, Philocles asserts that in the "*Academick* Philosophy" he is about to recount "there is a certain way of Questioning and Doubting, which no-way sutes the Genius of our Age. Men love to take Party instantly." The kind of philosophy that he prefers—the kind that this "dogmatical" age finds "most disagreeable"—is that

> which goes upon no establish'd Hypothesis, nor presents us with any flattering Scheme, talks only of Probabilitys, Suspence of Judgment, Inquiry, Search, and Caution not to be impos'd on, or deceiv'd. . . . Hence that way of DIALOGUE, and Patience of Debate and Reasoning, of which we have scarce Resemblance left in any of our Conversations, at this season of the World. (2:7–8)

Dogmatism is "superficial," "lazy and effeminate," and "cowardly"; in contrast, the philosophical reasoner or dialogist must have the courage "to dare *doubt*" (2:7). Philocles practices what he preaches to Palemon here, for in the dialogue itself Theocles compliments him for his "becoming manner of . . . SCEPTICISM," for not being "one of those timeorous Arguers who tremble at every Objection rais'd against their Opinion or Belief" (2:61). In the *Miscellaneous Reflections* Shaftesbury extends his critique of such dogmatists by making them, not skeptics, the enemies of the state. Skepticism, he affirms, is "no more than barely, 'That State or Frame of Mind in which every one remains, on every Subject of which he is *not certain*'"; thus, properly defined, dogmatism is "the most dangerous State of Opinion" and skepticism is "the safest" (2:163, 165). Contrary to the "Genius" of the age, Shaftesbury gives the skeptic the moral (and political) high ground.

But just as Shaftesbury counters the skepticism that he expresses most forcefully at the end of the *Miscellaneous Reflections* with common sense in the rest of the *Characteristicks,* he counters the skepticism on which Theocles compliments Philocles in *The Moralists* with dialogue —with *their* dialogue—itself. Dialogue, that is, is the formal equivalent of common sense: it reconstitutes the social body that skepticism would leave divided. Shaftesbury's "skeptical" dialogists are free to express whatever opinions they like, even if those opinions conflict because— since they are *disinterested* dialogists—their interests are not engaged. That they are able to talk about their differences is more important than the differences themselves: a difference of opinion does not cause a difference in manners (such as the old gentleman's) that would end the conversation before it even began. In a way their differences are like the "*Contrarietys*" that, according to Philocles after his full conversion to Theocles' deistic point of view, the "World's Beauty" is "founded . . . on." Just as "from such various and disagreeing Principles, *a Universal Concord* is establish'd" (2:18), from different opinions, and the need and desire to talk about them, the natural sociability of the discussants is manifested. Opinions may conflict, but dialogue reestablishes the natural order of things.

The Factions of Dialogue

To recall, this natural order of things is implicitly a political order. The problem that most concerned Shaftesbury's civic-humanist ancestors, the political problem of corruption, or pursuing one's private interest at the expense of the public interest, is not really a problem for the virtuous citizens who inhabit the philosophical realm. According to Shaftesbury at the conclusion of the *Inquiry Concerning Virtue,* being virtuous includes the understanding that it is "according to the *private Interest* and *Good* of every-one, to work towards the *general Good*" (1:273). As long as they are in the philosophical realm, retreated from the state, and talking about their differences—as long, that is, as they are in a world like that of *The Moralists*—Shaftesbury's disinterested dialogists seem to have no need for "government" at all.

But if Shaftesbury cannot imagine citizens who understand what it means to be virtuous deliberately choosing to be corrupt, or too "private," he *can* imagine them misconceiving just how large their "public" really is, or should be. In *Sensus Communis* he grants that "UNIVERSAL Good, or the Interest of *the World in general,* is a kind of remote Philosophical Object. That *greater Community* falls not easily under the Eye. Nor is a National Interest, or that of a whole People, or Body Politick, so readily apprehended." What is readily apprehended is the interest of smaller, more intimate groups: "In less Partys, men may be intimately conversant and acquainted with one another. They can there better taste Society, and enjoy the *common* Good and Interest of a more contracted Publick" (1:62). If common sense is the bond that holds society together (and makes government unnecessary), then it seems that citizens must actually "converse" with the "greater Community" in order for common sense to work.

Shaftesbury suggests that if citizens do not feel that intimate, conversable contact with the greater community, the human need for it can turn natural sociability into a real problem for the state. "Nothing is so delightful as to incorporate," and yet, "when the Society grows vast, and bulky," the only way to feel the delight of company is to find smaller and smaller companies to incorporate with. "Hence, in the way of Peace and Civil Government, that *Love of Party,* and Sub-division by *Cabal*" (1:63). This is, in a word, factionalism, and it is the corruption of common sense: it causes citizens to stop thinking philosophically, or disinterestedly, and to start thinking politically, or interestedly.[13] But if factionalism is corruption, it is only because it is natural sociability taken to its extreme. Paradoxically, Shaftesbury's common sense gives rise to the very factions that it was supposed to prevent. The "associating Genius" that causes societies to form also causes them to fall apart (1:63).

There is, then, an inherent instability in the philosophical realm of dialogue, an instability that is as much a crux in Shaftesbury's philosophy as the social contract was in Hobbes's. Hobbes presumed that human beings were naturally aggressive and had to persuade them to associate; Shaftesbury presumes that human beings are naturally sociable and has to prevent them from associating too much (or factionalizing). This instability is also the crux of *The Moralists:* the problem that Philocles expresses at the outset of the dialogue, and that he seeks out Theocles in order to solve, is his own propensity toward factionalism. "I cou'd love the Individual, but not the Species," he tells the philosopher when Theocles first informs him of his own love for that "remote Philosophical Object" that is the "UNIVERSAL Good" or "greater Community." "This was too Mysterious; too Metaphysical an Object for me" (2:32). Philocles' inability to grasp the greater good is his particular kind of *ethical* "skepticism," the only kind of skepticism that Shaftesbury finds of real concern. Philocles not only doubts not only the certainty of his own opinions; he also doubts the certainty of manners, common sense itself.

Like Hobbes, Shaftesbury is prone to talk as if reason itself can re-solve this instability. In *Sensus Communis,* for example, he says that unless the "*combining* Principle," or natural sociability, is "happily directed by right Reason, it can never find Exercise for it-self in so remote a Sphere as that of the Body Politick at large." But, again like Hobbes, as Shaftesbury goes on to describe what actually makes up this "right Reason" that is to "direct" natural sociability or common sense into a love of the greater community, it sounds less like reason and more like rhetoric. The difficulty with loving the "general View or Notion of a *State* or *Commonwealth,*" he continues, is that in it "No visible Band is form'd; no strict Alliance: but the Conjunction is made with different Persons, Orders, and Ranks of Men; not sensibly, but *in Idea*" (1:62). This is why Shaftesbury makes natural affection the foundation of com-mon sense: the only way that a citizen can love the greater community, or any community, is to feel as much as think it. Thus, Philocles con-tends to Theocles that he "cou'd love nothing of which I had not some *sensible material* Image. . . . [W]ere it possible for me to stamp upon my Mind such a Figure as you speak of, whether it stood for *Mankind* or *Nature,* it might probably have its effect, and I might become perhaps *a Lover* after your way" (2:32–33, first emphasis added). In strikingly rhetorical terms, Philocles describes here the crux of Shaftesbury's philosophy. The social spirit that both rightly creates community and wrongly causes a neglect of the greater community is more sensible than intellectual, and if common sense (the right social spirit) is to prevail over factionalism (the wrong social spirit), it must appeal more to our senses than to our reason. Philocles, who lacks common sense, needs an *image* of the greater community in order to believe in, or "love," it, and reason alone can neither create this image nor "stamp" it on the mind. The only thing that can do so is rhetoric.

The Rhetoric of Enthusiasm

Because he wanted to contrast it most sharply with Hobbes's cold, calculating rhetoric of self-interest, Shaftesbury named the rhetoric that creates a love for the greater community "enthusiasm." He did so

deliberately, knowing that enthusiasm was also associated with the worst
—that is, the most *irrational*—aspects of rhetoric in certain eighteenth-
century minds.[14] The religiously orthodox criticized enthusiastic (mostly
Nonconformist) believers and their preachers—such as the so-called
French prophets, a millenarian group that appeared in London during
1706 and 1707—for letting their passions "[get] *astride* on" their reason.[15] In *A Letter Concerning Enthusiasm* (1708), however, Shaftesbury
uses the prophets' appearance as an occasion for rehabilitating enthusiasm as the affective element in a natural religion, and in *The Moralists* he turns the rhetorical excesses of enthusiastic preaching into a
positive description of the greater community or unity of all things.
Indeed, because that unity is sensible and material, such enthusiastic
rhetoric is the *only* way to describe it. "All things in this world are *united*," enthuses Theocles at one point in *The Moralists*. "For as the *Branch*
is united with the *Tree*, so is the Tree as immediately with the *Earth, Air,*
and *Water,* which feed it. . . . See there the mutual Dependency of
Things!" (2:52). Such verbally florid rhetoric, which Theocles delivers
with a fervent emotionalism, eventually satisfies Philocles' desire to
perceive the greater community. In retrospect, he writes to Palemon,
he was "perfectly cur'd" of his skepticism by Theocles' enthusiasm
(2:20), and near the conclusion of the dialogue he himself exclaims,
"all sound *Love* and *Admiration* is ENTHUSIASM: 'The Transports of
Poets, the Sublime of *Orators,* the Rapture of *Musicians,* the high Strains
of the *Virtuosi;* all mere ENTHUSIASM!" (2:104).[16]

However satisfying it is to Philocles and other skeptics, it is ironic
that Shaftesbury's enthusiastic rhetoric has nothing to do with dialogue.
After attempting to convince Philocles logically of the unity of all
things, Theocles concedes that "I can never think of satisfying you
in any ordinary way of Conversation" (2:49), and after an extended
enthusiastic "rhapsody"[17] he gently scolds his friend for "suffer[ing]
me thus to run on, without the least Interruption" (2:92). Because the
"ordinary way of Conversation" does not satisfy, whenever Theocles
needs finally to convince his hearers of some truth he stops talking
with them and starts talking *to,* or *at,* them. To be sure, the suspension
of dialogue is not without the consent of those same hearers. Before
another of Theocles' rhapsodies, the old gentleman (never much of
a dialogist anyway) asks that "the *Law* of SERMON . . . be strictly
observ'd, and 'That there be no *answering* to whatever is *argu'd* or

advanc'd'" (2:50); and later Philocles, asking Theocles to give voice again to his "Divine Thoughts," assures him, "You may be still as much *alone* as you are us'd, and take no more notice of me than if I were absent" (2:78). Jack Prostko claims that Shaftesbury suspends dialogue at such moments because it "appears to threaten the 'will'" that he "fights so hard to substantiate in his private meditations; and oratory, at least, provides a degree of control,"[18] but this is to make Shaftesbury's choice of oratory, or enthusiastic rhetoric, more conscious than it is or can be. Shaftesbury constructed the dialogue as a realm in which virtuous individuals could discuss their differing opinions and yet remain united by a fundamental common sense; it turns out, however, that when those individuals differ on that fundamental level—when, that is, they are skeptical not only about opinions (or epistemology) but also about manners (or ethics)—*"Dialogue,"* as Shaftesbury says in a different context, "is at an end" (1:110). In wanting to inoculate his philosophical realm from all practical, prudential, and "interested" appeals, Shaftesbury inoculates it from the principle of dialogue itself. Ethical skeptics can neither be logically dissuaded from their skepticism (because common sense is sensible) nor be "counseled," as Hobbes would have it, away from it (because common sense cannot contain an appeal to self-interest); they must simply be converted. All sound love may be enthusiasm, but the one who is hearing such rhapsodic sentiments must take the enthusiast's word for it.

That enthusiastic rhetoric has nothing to do with dialogue in Shaftesbury's philosophy is proven by its painful consequence. Theocles launches into an enthusiastic "Fit" (2:80) to cure Philocles of his ethical skepticism, to bring him back into the greater community of humankind, but as Philocles suggested when he said that he would let Theocles "alone" to rhapsodize about that greater community, to be able to rhapsodize about it is necessarily to be lonely. Enthusiasm works to enlarge one's perception only in isolation: the wrong social spirit is still a sociable spirit, but one can only get the right social spirit without being sociable. At the end of his last rhapsody Theocles counsels that "we had better leave these unsociable Places, whither our Fancy has transported us, and return to our-selves again, in our more conversable Woods, and temperate Climates" (2:391), and Philocles agrees that he and other enthusiasts have always to be "recall[ed] . . . from these *solitary* Places" (2:394). For Shaftesbury, a view of the greater community—what we might call Shaftesbury's version of Hobbes's "foresight"—is possible only after solitary retreat.

Distinction

After the skeptic has been converted, however, dialogue (and a local community) can return to the philosophical realm. And after *his* conversion, and for the rest of *The Moralists*, Philocles talks with Theocles about how common sense can become something better, or more reliable, than the natural sociability with which every human being is born. Theocles' advice, however, is perhaps more than Philocles wants to hear: to be "*confirm'd* and *strength'd*" (2:112) in Theocles' way of viewing the world, he must take care to distinguish on just what, or whom, he chooses to bestow his greater perception. Our "Notions and Principles of *Fair, Just,* and *Honest*"—what Theocles has been calling common sense—may be "*innate*" (2:109),[19] but in the *Miscellaneous Reflections* Shaftesbury states that

> a TASTE or *Judgment*, . . . can hardly come ready form'd with us into the World. . . . Use, Practice and Culture must precede the *Understanding* and *Wit* of such an advanc'd Size and Growth as this. A legitimate and just TASTE can neither be begotten, made, conceiv'd, or produc'd, without the antecedent *Labour* and *Pains* of CRITICISM. (2:207–8)

A "TASTE or *Judgment*," it seems, is *not* innate, although it builds on the notions of fair, just, and honest—the natural affections—which are. Taste takes "*Labour* and *Pains*" to acquire. Thus, in *The Moralists* Theocles explains that as in "other Subjects of Art or Science," it is difficult and time-consuming to gain a "true *Taste*" for natural beauty, and Philocles agrees that beauty "lies very absconded and deep." Before, "Like the rest of the unthinking World," he continues, "I never troubled my-self with examining what *the Subjects* [of his "Enjoyment"] were, nor ever hesitated about their *Choice*" (2:104–5). Now, with Theocles' help, he will be more discriminating.

Theocles' invocation of a term of discrimination like taste raises a familiar problem in Shaftesbury's philosophy, the problem of diversity. When Theocles asks Philocles how he can doubt that "*Distinctions*" about what is "*fit* or *decent*" in the world, like the affections that give rise to them, "have their Foundation *in Nature*," Philocles answers that if they did, no one would ever disagree about such notions. But Theocles has a ready answer to Philocles' objection:

Even by this, . . . it appears there is Fitness and Decency in Actions;
since *the Fit* and *Decent* is in this Controversy ever pre-suppos'd. . . . *All*
own the *Standard, Rule,* and *Measure:* But in applying it to Things, Disorder arises, Ignorance prevails, Interest and Passion breed Distur-
bance. Nor can it otherwise happen in the Affairs of Life, whilst that
which interesses and engages men as *Good,* is thought different from
that which they admire and praise as *Honest.* (2:111–12)

To resolve controversy, individuals must make *beauty*—here "that which
interesses and engages" them—their *good*—"that which they admire
and praise."[20] It is here that Theocles advances Shaftesbury's famous
equation between aesthetics and morality, or as Theocles expresses it
here, "That *Beauty* and *Good* are still the same" (2:112).[21] To Shaftesbury, the morally good is aesthetically pleasing not only because the
qualities of order and unity themselves are inherently beautiful but
also because, again, goodness, like beauty, requires the discipline of
criticism. If most individuals err by applying a common standard of
goodness to the wrong things, the error can only be corrected by applying the standard to the right, or beautiful, things.

Yet being able to recognize the right or beautiful in things requires
a sense of taste to begin with—a sense or standard that is not at all
common—which raises the problem of diversity all over again. Just as
Hobbes merely shifted the problem from the realm of cognition to
the realm of persuasion, Shaftesbury shifts it to the realm of taste.
When he asserted that our passions and affections are "certain," he
appeared to have solved the problem: if common sense is merely natural sociability, all *do* "own the *Standard.*" Even if diversity, or controversy, is merely a problem for the self and not for the commonwealth
(as Shaftesbury seems to present it in his private meditations), the
conflicted individual, *any* conflicted individual, can appeal to his or her
own passion for goodness—a personal "party of reason"—to resolve
it. But if it takes taste to resolve controversy, either political or personal,
only the cultivated can do so. Shaftesbury has not solved the problem
of diversity either: he has merely recast difference—moral, political,
and otherwise—as aesthetic "distinction."[22]

Whereas in *Sensus Communis* and the *Miscellaneous Reflections* Shaftesbury impressed on his hearers that "Variety of Opinion was not to
be cur'd," Theocles now rails, in fact almost enthuses or rhapsodizes,
against the variety of opinions, convinced that he—that his opinion—

is in the right. "What shall we say to such-a-one" who alleges that "There can be no such thing as real *Valuableness* or *Worth*"? he asks. "Or shall we ask, *what Shame*, of one who acknowledges no *Shameful?*" (2:112–13). Such skepticism is of the dangerously ethical, rather than the therapeutically epistemological, kind—the kind that Theocles has just cured Philocles of—and Theocles no longer tolerates it. Indeed, he resolves to combat it, in part by noting that even skeptics, when pressed, resort to certain moral standards like shame and ridiculousness, standards that they simply know are true.

The more important point, however, is not that the skeptic has standards but that Theocles, faced with the problem of diversity, must assert his "distinctive" opinion against the skeptic's. It may not be possible to cure the variety of opinions, but at the same time one opinion, at least when it comes to beauty and the good, is *not* as good as another. One cannot be truly philosophical by negotiating or seeking consensus with every opinion that comes up for examination. Rather, one must simply, or not so simply, choose one opinion over another. The critical question for the philosopher who views the world distinctively is what kind of choices a person should make: "[E]verything in this World goes *by Exchange*. Nothing is had for Nothing. . . . A *good* MIND must be paid for, as other things" (2:123). When one is thinking philosophically (and distinctively), *every* choice that one makes is critical in at least two senses of the word. It is evaluative because every choice is a test of one's distinctive faculties, or taste, and it is crucial because one cannot have a "*good* MIND" except by approaching every choice as that sort of test. By being critical, by choosing the correct opinion over the incorrect one, one increases one's capacity for making the proper choices in the future.

One increases, in other words, one's virtue. By arguing that there are proper choices to be made, Shaftesbury makes a virtue out of what had been a problem, the problem of diversity. He elevates common sense to taste and in the process makes it all the more inaccessible. Theocles concludes *The Moralists* by asking for a critical "Measure" and "Rule" with which to make such choices and then lists a series of questions that an aspiring critic should ask to apply that standard: "'Where, then, is the Difference? Which Manner is *the best?*' . . . Everyone, of necessity, must reason concerning his own Happiness; 'What his *Good* is, and what his *Ill.*' The Question is only, 'Who reasons best?'"

(2:123–24). As Raymond Williams perceives, critical terms like *taste* and *cultivation* "make little sense unless we are able to contrast their presence with their absence,"[23] and the questions with which Theocles ends *The Moralists* necessarily exclude those things and persons who are judged not to be the "best." Everyone—because of the problem of diversity—will reason differently, but only Shaftesbury and other critical reasoners will reason distinctively. The liberal defender of toleration in the political realm turns out to be as intolerant of difference in the philosophical realm as the most ardent dogmatist.[24]

The Consequences of Distinction

As I have mentioned, the virtue of distinction limits the "freedom" that Shaftesbury boasted of in the philosophical realm. As long as Shaftesbury's virtuous dialogists are examining their philosophical opinions, all actually *is* free, or speculative. It makes little difference, for example, whether Philocles is or is not a skeptic about orthodox religion because one can be such a skeptic, at least according to Shaftesbury, without denying the moral fabric of the universe. Philocles' (and Shaftesbury's own) religious skepticism, in other words, questions merely such doctrinal matters as the reality of miracles, not the actual existence of God (whom Shaftesbury, as a theist, still upholds as the supreme source of the universe's meaning). But Shaftesbury will not permit a skeptic to question—or worse, laugh at—the reality of virtue. Thus Philocles, who in his prefatory letter warned Palemon of his "Inclination to SCEPTICISM," can simultaneously fear that he has given his friend "occasion to suspect me of the worst sort of *Scepticism,* such as spar'd nothing; but overthrew all Principles *Moral,* and *Divine*" (2:15–16). Similarly, in complimenting Philocles' "becoming manner" of skepticism, Theocles opposes it "to a kind of Bigot-*Scepticks;* who forfeit their Right to *the Philosophick Character,* and retain hardly so much as that of *the Gentleman* or *Good-Companion*" (2:61). One of the choices that critical reasoners must make, it seems, is just what kind of skepticism—"becoming" or "bigoted"—they are to assume, and what distinguishes bad skepticism from good is a matter of "manner."

Just as freedom has its limits in Shaftesbury's philosophical realm, the sense of taste—even, in fact, common sense itself—is not all that "common," or popular.[25] One does not, he concludes in *Sensus Communis,* know truth by "*counting Noses*" or by "poll[ing] an indifferent

Number out of a *Mob*" (1:80). That truth is determined not democratically but distinctively proves to be of powerful rhetorical force in *The Moralists*. Philocles is attracted to Theocles' view of the world in part because the philosopher appeals to his own desire for distinction, for setting himself apart from the mass of ordinary human beings. When, during a walk in the woods before his conversion, Philocles convinces Theocles that he is "conscious of a better Order" in creation, Theocles compliments him for being—as Theocles himself is— "Master of a nobler Mind" (2:51). Later, expounding on the virtue of disinterestedness, Theocles mocks those "inferiour Creatures" who find happiness in the actual "*Possession*" of the objects that give them pleasure, or in the "Joys of *Sense.*" "'[T]was not here," he explains to Philocles, "that we had agreed to place our *Good;* nor consequently our *Enjoyment.* We who were rational, and had Minds, methought, shou'd place it rather in those MINDS" themselves, or in disinterested contemplation (2:103). Those with taste or nobler minds both perceive the natural order of things and are able to contemplate it disinterestedly; those without taste are defective in both mind and manner. Just as Shaftesbury's morals take precedence over his politics, the primary appeal of taste is a personal one: not the good it provides to the commonwealth but the satisfaction it gives to its distinctive possessor.

It is true that Shaftesbury is aware of the presumption involved in asserting one's distinctiveness too forcefully, and he devotes an entire essay in the *Characteristicks* to mitigating that presumption. Through the practice described in *Soliloquy,* he makes himself the first target of his criticism. Whenever he feels himself in danger of giving offense to others by asserting his opinions dogmatically rather than agreeably, Shaftesbury "multipli[es] himself into *two Persons*" and becomes "*his own Subject*" of dialogue (1:87). Soliloquy, like a kind of conversational partner, addresses the vain imaginings, driven by the party of appetite, that one always knows best, that one's opinion is always superior, and it drives them out of one's mind in order to give way to the party of reason and good sense. Soliloquy thus displays the same skeptical "wit and humour," the same familiarity, as dialogue, except that now the liberty to question everything is directed at oneself.

Yet Shaftesbury's insistence that one must soliloquize with oneself before one can dialogue with others makes one wonder why dialogue has to be so mediated. If criticism, the practice of exposing oneself to alternative opinions, is morally improving, why is the first "alternative" opinion that occurs to Shaftesbury one of his own? Why, when he seeks to cure a "super-speculative Philosophy with a more practical sort," does he effect that cure by applying "chiefly to *my-self*"—or "to our Acquaintance, Friendship, and good Correspondence with *our-selves*" —and not to others (1:152)? Why, in short, does he not envision conversation with the world, or with other individuals, as a method of moral improvement?[26] The answer, of course, is that he does, but only *after* he—and, one assumes, those with whom he would converse—has improved himself through soliloquy. Soliloquy may be commendable as a method of self-examination, but it restricts the privilege of dialogue to those who are already distinctive, and Shaftesbury's virtue of distinction as it is pursued in his philosophical realm of dialogue actually aspires to "a monologic, single-voiced language."[27] Real dialogue —the conversation, possibly leading to mutual understanding, that occurs between individuals of differing interests—is impossible in Shaftesbury's philosophical realm.

That judgment, the most important consequence of distinction, may seem severe. But consider that Shaftesbury comprehends soliloquy as morally improving not because it constantly exposes one to alternative opinions but because it "pretend[s] to that *Uniformity of Opinion* which is necessary to hold us to *one Will*, and preserve us in the same mind, from one day to another" (1:100, first emphasis added). Consider also that the uniformity of opinion that soliloquy is meant to preserve is, like the philosophical realm itself, distinctive—Shaftesbury doubts that soliloquy will "be of any use towards making us either wiser, or happier," but he is "confident, it must help to make us *wittier* and *politer*" (1:169)—and necessarily excludes wrong opinions (and those who hold them) in favor of right ones. In fact, as Shaftesbury goes on to describe it, soliloquy seems less like a method for engaging the world (and others) and more like a method for detaching, or distinguishing, oneself from it. "Tho his Intention be to please the World," he says, the soliloquizer must "nevertheless be, in a manner, *above it;* and fix his Eye upon that consummate *Grace,* that Beauty of *Nature,* and that *Perfection* of Numbers, which the rest of Mankind, feeling only by the Effect, whilst ignorant of the Cause, term the *Je-ne-sçay-quoy*" (1:171). Shaftesbury suggests that everyone who soliloquizes will eventually come to value the same distinctive things; in effect, that everyone will have the same opinions. Thus, the possibility that a soliloquizer may eventually exchange opinions with others is finally insignificant. When opinion is uniform, and uniformly distinctive, one is likely to hear only the same opinions in return.

Distinction as Power

More committed to self-improvement than to social progress, Shaftesbury denies that soliloquy can benefit the commonwealth at large. "Our present Manners," he owns, "are not so well calculated for this Method of SOLILOQUY, as to suffer it to become a national Practice" (1:88). Toward the end of the essay, when he imagines an *"uncourteous"* reader asking why he bothers to publish if he writes only "for *SelfEntertainment"* (or improvement), he answers that "'tis of no concern to me, what regard *the Publick* bestows on my Amusements; or after what manner it comes acquainted with what I write for my private Entertainment, or by way of *Advice* to such of my Acquaintance as are thus desperately embark'd." Shaftesbury, it seems, has given up on reforming the commonwealth. All but conceding that he intends to engage in dialogue only with other like-minded soliloquizers, he maintains that he writes to give advice to "Friends," not to change the world (1:157–58).

Like the pathos that won over his audience in the House of Commons, however, Shaftesbury's disdain for publicity in *Soliloquy* is disingenuous. The essay purports to be about how authors can best give advice to others, and it is doubtful that an audience consisting only of friends could provoke the anxiety that he expresses at the outset of it, about how "to make ADVICE *a free Gift.*" Shaftesbury realizes here that the very act of giving advice assumes a certain "Mastery" over the other (1:86)—that it is, in other words, an act of domination—and he worries how to make that mastery seem not commanded but consented to.[28] His whole discussion of soliloquy, in fact, is framed as a response to this problem: the public will be more receptive to being criticized if authors can convince it that they have thoroughly criticized themselves. Shaftesbury soliloquizes not, like some eighteenth-century Hamlet, in order to question the reality of moral truth but to learn how better to enforce it, on others as well as on himself. Soliloquy is not a way to avoid the public: it is a better means of persuading it.

In *The Moralists* Shaftesbury similarly gives the soliloquizer politi-

cal, as well as moral, authority. In the beginning, Philocles "bemoan[s]"
the decline of philosophy as a public force: "She is no longer *active* in
the World; nor can hardly, with any advantage, be brought upon the
publick *Stage*. We have immur'd her (poor Lady!) in Colleges and
Cells." Critics have seized on this quotation as evidence of Shaftesbury's ambition to popularize philosophy[29]—to bring it, through such
accessible forms as literary dialogue, out of those same "Colleges and
Cells" and make it "active" once again—and I have already indicated
that the disdain for publicity that he expresses elsewhere is inconsistent with the larger aims of his philosophical project. But Philocles
follows his lament with a less frequently cited affirmation of how powerful philosophy already *is:* "But as low as PHILOSOPHY is reduc'd;
if *Morals* be allow'd belonging to her, *Politicks* must undeniably be
hers. For to understand the Manners and Constitutions of Men *in
common,* 'tis necessary to study MAN *in particular,* and know the Creature as he is in himself" (2:4–5). "Whilst PHILOSOPHY is taken (as
in its prime Sense it ought) for *Mastership in* LIFE and MANNERS,"
adds Shaftesbury in the *Miscellaneous Reflections,* "'tis like to make no
ill Figure in the World" (2:205).[30] As always in Shaftesbury's philosophy, to assume "Mastership" in life and manners is to assume mastery
in all walks of life, including politics.

At the beginning of *Soliloquy* Shaftesbury forswore such mastery: it
was precisely what he *did not* want the act of giving advice to look like.
By the end of the essay, however, he is less reticent about assuming the
mastery due to a soliloquizer. "The Question" to ask of the practice,
he says there,

> is the same . . . , as in *a Family,* or *Houshold,* when 'tis ask'd, "*Who rules?*
> or *Who is Master?*"
> Learn by the Voices. Observe who speaks aloud, in a commanding
> Tone: Who talks, who questions; or who is talk'd with, and who
> question'd. For if the Servants take the former part; they are the Mas-
> ters, and the Government of the House will be found such as naturally
> may be expected in these Circumstances. (1:167)

The "Servants" in this passage are, of course, the party of appetite;
the "Master," the party of reason and good sense, the party of philosophy. The practice of soliloquy, that is, enacts Shaftesbury's internal
controversy, which concerns him more than the external, political

controversies taking place in the state. But surely the dialogue taking place inside the self mirrors the many dialogues, or conversations, taking place outside it, and surely the same rules apply: the "commanding Tone" that allows a soliloquizer like Shaftesbury to master his own passions also allows him to assume mastery over others. Speaking in a commanding tone may not involve actual participation in government (or making effective speeches), but it will display the distinction that the practice of soliloquy has achieved. And distinction gives the soliloquizer mastery or "Government of the House" of state.

It may be objected that what I have said about Shaftesbury's interest in publicity invalidates my previous point that his dialogue is really a kind of monologue. The public, that is, includes more than Shaftesbury's friends or other like-minded soliloquizers. But the point stands: the mastery that distinction brings may call for one to speak to others, but that speech, if made less presumptuous through the practice of soliloquy, is still delivered in a commanding tone. It is more rhetoric than dialogue, and there is still no room for consensus, or even for conversation, between individuals of differing interests.[31] The closest thing to a representation of public engagement in the *Characteristicks*, for example, occurs when the freethinking gentleman defends his position against the religious zealots at the end of the *Miscellaneous Reflections*, and although the gentleman apologizes for acting "contrary to the Rule and Measure of Conversation" by "draw[ing] the Company's Attention towards me thus long," he "quit[s] the Place and Company" when his opponents become unmannerly (3:289, 293).[32] In his retreat from a public that he nevertheless intends to master, Shaftesbury is even more of an elitist than his fellow civic humanists Harrington and Neville, who similarly reserve the principle of dialogue for a wiser few. Harrington and Neville know that their elite few do not represent the diversity of interests beyond their company. Indeed, their unrepresentativeness is what gives them the ability—the disinterestedness—to debate the affairs of the commonwealth, if it leaves them powerless actually to resolve on those affairs. But Shaftesbury, because he sees no disparity between the public interest and a properly distinctive, private interest, believes that his elite few actually *do* represent the commonwealth. Their distinctiveness makes them both representative and powerful.

Force for the "Vulgar"

Distinction may entail the power to speak in a commanding tone to the undifferentiated, undistinctive public, but Shaftesbury often talks as if that particular power were best left to someone else. Looking back fondly on some indefinite golden age in *Sensus Communis,* for example, he contrasts the time when the "Opinions" of persons were "left to themselves"—a "time when Men were accountable only for their Actions and Behaviour"—to the present age, in which the "Magistrate" accounts for opinions (1:49). This negative image of the magistrate reappears in *The Moralists:* because "there is no Enforcement of Reason but by Reason," Theocles declares that "the Language of the Magistrate . . . has little in common with that of Philosophy" (2:40). The magistrate and his very real political powers do violence to the disinterested philosophical realm.

Although the magistrate may not be admitted to the philosophical realm, however, he is needed to police those who are allowed to enter it. There may have been a time when individuals were not accountable for their opinions, but they are now, and always were, accountable for their actions and behavior. Shaftesbury, as I have noted, excludes a number of unmannerly individuals from the philosophical realm. The bigoted and dogmatic older gentleman who disappears from *The Moralists* is one example; another is provided by the distinction that Shaftesbury, despite his reputation as a freethinker, carefully makes between two kinds of "atheists," the one "who *absolutely denies*" and the one "who *only doubts*" (the sort of unbeliever whom we would call an agnostic). "Now he who *doubts,*" says Theocles in *The Moralists,* "may bear a due respect to the Magistrate and the Laws," but "He who *denies*" is "obnoxious to them," "daringly presumptuous," and "therefore punishable" (2:40). The opinions of the atheist may be "obnoxious," but it is his ill manners—the difference between politely doubting (like the well-mannered Philocles) and "presumptively" denying—that justifies his exclusion from the philosophical realm. It also justifies the force by which the magistrate punishes, as well as excludes, him. "If Men are vicious, petulant or abusive," asserts Shaftesbury in *A Letter Concerning Enthusiasm,* "the Magistrate may correct them" (1:11); and in the *Inquiry Concerning Virtue* he urges "a virtuous Administration" to serve the public "by restraining the Vicious, and forcing them to act usefully to Society" (1:219). He may tolerate a diversity of opinions, but he does not tolerate a diversity of manners.

The vicious, or corrupt, are not the only ones to be restrained by Shaftesbury's "virtuous Administration," or at least excluded from the philosophical realm. In *Sensus Communis* he concedes that only "the Fear of *a Gibbet* or *a Jail*" may give the corrupt "a Reason for being *honest*"; "the mere Vulgar of Mankind often stand in need of such a rectifying Object as *the Gallows* before their Eyes" (1:69, 70, 127). The magistrate apparently excludes not only those who are unmannerly and should know better (the corrupt) but also those who are ignorant of what good behavior is in the first place (the "Vulgar"). The freethinking gentleman who closes the *Miscellaneous Reflections* verifies this exclusion when he apologizes for the "study'd Discourse and Decalmation [*sic*]" of his opening remarks by explaining that he was addressing "the *Ignorant* and *Vulgar*" (2:284). Dialogue may be Shaftesbury's preferred mode of discourse for himself and his philosophical few, but the rest of humankind still receives only oratory.

It remains only to ask whether moving from ignorance to knowledge, and thus acquiring the virtue of distinction, is possible for those who are not among that elite few. For no matter how difficult it may be to subject oneself to the "*Labour* and *Pains* of CRITICISM," anyone who takes those pains should be able to become distinctive. This, indeed, is one of the principles that inform the model of the public sphere that Habermas draws from the eighteenth century: judgments based on taste are not "cognitive" but result from reflection on one's "own feelings of pleasure or displeasure," and those feelings "by virtue of their very form can be present in every individual."[33] Of course, being able to practice the "art" of criticism and learning it in the first place require an education and a freedom from necessity that Habermas's model has been criticized for not taking into account fully, and this is true enough. But it is at least theoretically possible that those left outside its definition of a critical public can use the public sphere's own principles against it because they agitate *against* exclusion.

This is not true of Shaftesbury's "public" sphere. Because he makes a virtue of distinction and, more important, because he makes a certain preliminary distinctiveness a prerequisite for joining in the polite conversation that fully develops that virtue, his sphere of critical dialogue will always be more private than public. Shaftesbury, to recall, describes the kind of criticism that his distinctive reasoners conduct in dialogue as a "Habit," and he contends that the habit can be mastered only by practice, not by referring to "written" or "set" (and accessible) rules. Moreover, to practice the habit of reasoning requires that one be "invited" to it (1:42), an invitation presumably issued by one whom one knows, and who knows one, already. The capacity to master the habit of criticism (and to acquire the virtue of distinction), that is, demands a certain intimacy that cannot be extended to the general public: gentlemen have to know one another, know the extent of one another's capacities to take liberties and be critical with one another, if they are to reason together at all. Shaftesbury's sphere of critical dialogue thus displays the "remarkable irony" that Nancy Fraser finds in Habermas's public sphere: "A discourse of publicity touting accessibility, rationality, and the suspension of status hierarchies is itself deployed as a strategy of distinction."[34] Shaftesbury, that is, touts the freedom, the skeptical reasoning, and the disinterestedness of the philosophical realm of dialogue, attributes that seem to open it to everyone willing to abide by its *"Standard, Rule,* and *Measure,"* but it turns out that actually applying those standards or rules requires a sense of what is good and proper to begin with and that applying them further gains for one a sense of distinction that quickly separates those who have it from those who do not.

What, then, would a "public" sphere based on Shaftesbury's virtue of distinction look like? On the one hand, it would be vigorously discursive. There is perhaps no more eloquent expression of the promise of a once and future public sphere than Shaftesbury's description of the causal connection between a vigorous discursivity—the unrestrained exchange of opinions in dialogue—and the kind of enlightenment to which he gives his honorific name of politeness: "All Politeness is owing to Liberty. We polish one another, and rub off our Corners and rough Sides by a sort of *amicable Collision.* To restrain this, is inevitably to bring a Rust upon Mens Understandings" (1:39–40). At his best, Shaftesbury realizes the Enlightenment dream of a discourse *unre*strained by the traditional powers of church and state, a discourse that dispenses the knowledge most worth having in a fashion—conversation with one's fellow human beings—that is as delightful as it is instructive. On the other hand, when Shaftesbury further defines such discursive liberty, reminding the "friend" to whom he writes *Sensus Communis* that he is defending only "the Liberty of *the Club*, and of that sort of Freedom which is taken amongst *Gentlemen* and *Friends*, who know one another perfectly well" (1:45), he restrains it just as surely as did church and state. In short, Shaftesbury closes off the "public" sphere before he opens it again to the "freedom of wit and humour." The obvious point to be made about such a discursive realm is that it would actually be private, homogenous, and "clubbable." The less obvious point is that because of its homogeneity, it would have little interest in seeing that the conditions that make its freedom possible are extended to other spheres and to other publics.

In her essay "The Social Preconditions of Radical Scepticism," the sociologist Mary Douglas says that the sort of radical questioning of reality that Pascal, for one, attacked as Pyrrhonian tends to arise from "a social position that combines considerable privilege with lack of influence in an arbitrarily powerful political system." Shaftesbury's lack of political influence was self-, not arbitrarily, imposed, and his "skepticism" was hardly radical: opinions can be treated with the freedom of wit and humor, but only among a "better sort" (1:186) who know one another perfectly well (and who share a fundamental ethic or ethos that the universe has an ultimate structure and a meaning). Like the skepticism of the religious mystics whom Douglas discusses, however, even Shaftesbury's limited skepticism depends on a distinctive dissociation from the larger community of ordinary believers. It is in this sense that I would call it a "luxury." Shaftesbury's skepticism, and the kind of dialogue that it encourages (and that encourages it), is "contingent," as Douglas says, on his philosophical sense of the "futility or immorality of exercising power and authority," and this "contingency rests in turn on [his] place in a social structure," a privileged place from which one can criticize but need not engage.[35] However much the "Privilege of *Scepticism*" (2:83) that Shaftesbury takes in dialogue resembles the freedom and openness of an ideal public sphere, then, in its dissociation (and in its "disinterestedness") from more diverse publics it is finally antithetical to it.

4

MANDEVILLE
Dialogue as Commerce

THAT BERNARD MANDEVILLE, author of *The Fable of the Bees* (1714–29), provides one of the first apologies for the emerging capitalist order in early modern England is one of the commonplaces of Mandevillian criticism. For Mandeville, commerce brings human beings together in society: one of the "publick benefits" that the relentless pursuit of our "private vices" produces is the cooperation among otherwise disagreeable individuals to gratify those vices. "The reciprocal Services which all Men pay to one another, are the Foundation of the Society," he proclaims in the *Fable* (1:221), and then illustrates what he means by listing the "Multiplicity of Trades and Artificers" that "must be employed" to produce "a fine Scarlet or crimson Cloth" (1:356). Not only "Wool-combers, Spinners, the Weaver, the Clothworker, the Scourer, the Dyer, the Setter, the Drawer and the Packer; but others that are more remote and might seem foreign to it; as the Millwright, the Pewterer and the Chymist" must cooperate to produce the cloth, and they all cooperate "voluntar[ily]," aware that "every one Works for himself, how much soever he may seem to Labour for others" (1:356–58). Society according to Mandeville is not, as it was for social-contract theorists like Hobbes and Locke, "a constellation of independent moral agents" but a conglomeration of "contradictory but interlocking needs."[1]

What has received less emphasis in the criticism is the discursive nature of this social bond. It is discursive because it depends, in at least two ways, on the art of words that Mandeville terms "Dissimulation" (1:349). Because we should, rationally, pursue nothing but our private interests, "skilful Politicians" (1:47) dissimulate when they represent virtue as more desirable than vice. The ruse fools those who do not know better—the poor and ignorant public—and makes them more governable. But among those who do know better than to be privately virtuous, dissimulation also drives the engine of commerce, which makes a society materially prosperous. Merchants dissimulate when they misrepresent the actual value of their commodities, pushing up prices, encouraging production, and making everyone richer.[2] Dissimulation, the art of representing something to be what it is not, is necessary both to keep the poor on the straight and narrow path of virtue and to help the rich maintain their duplicitous advantage.

Commerce—and society itself—then, depends on conversation. It might even be said that commerce *is* a kind of conversation. Conversation is the circulation of opinions, and commerce is the circulation, or exchange, of goods and services. For Mandeville, indeed, *commerce* signifies both the exchanges that keep society going and the conversations in which those exchanges take place; and, unlike Shaftesbury's distinctive brand of dialogue, it is wholly indiscriminate: everyone, from the noblest aristocrat to the most humble tradesman, engages in it. But if commerce is conversation, it is a dissimulative, deceitful kind, not the free and open communication that Habermas says the bourgeois champions of civil society translate into political power. Mandeville would thus seem to have turned dialogue, as well as the discursive nature of the social bond, upside down from where Shaftesbury had left it: dialogue may bring human beings together in society, but it does so by betraying truth and beauty, not by revealing them.

And yet, in an implicit contradiction in his philosophy, Mandeville's own conversations—the six dialogues that "illustrate and explain" (2:7) his system in part 2 of the *Fable*—are not dissimulative but transparently truthful. He perceives of dialogue as commerce, but he practices dialogue as enlightenment. Mandeville may not intend his writing to spread his dangerous truth about dissimulation and the social order to the public at large, but there is nothing to prevent it from spreading anyway. Under the insidious logic of commercial capitalism, ideas, like goods, tend to traffic all too freely, a fact borne out by the nefarious popular reputation of a writer who maintained that he was addressing only "the few that can think abstractly, and have their Minds elevated above the Vulgar" (1:231). Mandeville's reputation was made for him, and his readers will be enlightened about the truth that he wants concealed from all but the wisest. Yet to enlighten them, according to his philosophy, can only be to ruin the commonwealth.

Emulation and the Origin of Society

From "The Grumbling Hive," a poem in Hudibrastic verse published without supporting documentation in 1705, *The Fable of the Bees* grew by accumulation. In 1714 Mandeville published the first part of the *Fable* itself, comprising the poem annotated by several prose "Remarks" and "An Enquiry into the Origin of Moral Virtue," an essay in which he recasts the paradox contained in the *Fable*'s infamous subtitle, "Private Vices, Publick Benefits." "[N]o Species of Animals is, without the Curb of Government, less capable of agreeing long together in Multitudes than that of Man," elaborates Mandeville; "yet such are his Qualities, whether good or bad, I shall not determine, that no Creature besides himself can ever be made sociable" (1:41). Humankind is paradoxical, according to Mandeville, because it is both naturally disagreeable and yet sociable, or at least "can be made" sociable by artificial means. In this version of his paradox, the "private vice" is humankind's innate disagreeableness; the "publick benefit," humankind's potential sociability.

As the *Fable* shows, however, Mandeville is not dissatisfied with the sociableness that the world *already* exhibits, along with the "grumbling." He is the first figure in this study simply to accept diversity rather than attempt to suppress it (as does Hobbes), compromise with it (Harrington and Neville), or deny that on some level it really exists (Shaftesbury). If different people desire different things, society nevertheless shows a certain capacity to satisfy those desires, and diversity is not really a problem.[3] Mandeville's lack of anxiety about social differences is certainly due, at least in part, to the increased sense of stability in English politics, as well as to his own political inclinations: by the 1714 publication date of the first part of the *Fable*, the Whigs—the party of "toleration" and the party for which Mandeville had propagandized—had begun to settle in for their long ministerial run.[4] Explaining how humankind can be made sociable amounts for Mandeville to explaining how society as it now exists came to be.

Society came to be, according to Mandeville in the "Enquiry into the Origin of Moral Virtue," when certain "Lawgivers, . . . Moralists and Philosophers," the aforementioned "skilful Politicians," took the fact of diversity and, rather than attempt to suppress or deny it, played it up. Observing the natural differences among human beings, "they divided the whole species into two Classes," an upper and a lower,

> vastly differing from one another: The one consisted of abject, low-minded People, that always hunting after immediate Enjoyment, were wholly incapable of Self-denial, and without regard to the good of others, had no higher Aim than their private Advantage. . . . [T]he other Class was made up of lofty high-spirited Creatures, that free from sordid Selfishness, esteem'd the Improvements of the Mind to be their fairest Possessions . . . and making a continual War with themselves to promote the Peace of others, aim'd at no less than the Public Welfare and the Conquest of their own Passion. (1:42–44)

The lower class was passionate and selfish, the upper class dispassionate (or disinterested) and selfless. Or so said the skillful politicians. Mandeville's own description of the difference between the two classes is so comically exaggerated that he appears to be imitating what the politicians say about that difference, not saying it himself. The difference is less real than rhetorical: diversity is a fact of life, but part of what makes politicians "skilful" is their ability to heighten it through the power of eloquence. What seems real or "natural" in Mandeville's description is not that difference but the passion that causes it to be proclaimed so vehemently.

Generated from the difference between the upper and lower classes is "Emulation" (1:43), a dynamic that is central to Mandeville's account of the origin of society. Individuals began to emulate one another, he explains, when the skillful politicians made "the People they were to govern, believe, that it was more beneficial for every Body to conquer than indulge his Appetites, and much better to mind the Publick than what seem'd his private Interest" (1:42). What makes the upper class upper is its ostensible devotion to this actually civic-humanist ethic; what makes the lower class lower is its ostensible neglect of it. Actually, neither class is devoted to it: human beings are ruled by their passions, and their passions dictate that they will behave self-interestedly. What the politicians realized, however, was that chief among these passions is the desire of human beings to think well of themselves and to have others think well of them; for Mandeville, pride is the most fundamental "passion" of all. They therefore gave the name of "VIRTUE" to that behavior "by which Man, contrary to the impulse of Nature, should endeavour the Benefit of others, or the Conquest of his own Passions out of a Rational Ambition of being Good" (1:48–49), praised virtue as the quality that distinguishes one class from another, and flattered individuals into thinking either that they already possessed the quality (if of the upper class) or that they could attain it (if of the lower). The upper class emulated the quality that supposedly distinguishes them from the lower, the lower class emulated the upper, and humankind was made sociable. In Mandeville's formulation, "the Moral Virtues" are not natural, primary, or even real, but "the Political Offspring which Flattery begot upon Pride" (1:51).[5]

That society originates in humankind's pride or desire for distinction clarifies the meaning of Mandeville's paradox. If their susceptibility to flattery causes otherwise disagreeable individuals to come together in society, that susceptibility is still, like the other passions, a "vice." If coming together in society is not exactly a "virtue" as a civic humanist might understand it, it is still a social good (perhaps *the* social good), or "benefit." Mandeville (acting as a skillful political writer) has managed to turn the private vice of human disagreeableness or desirousness into the public benefit of human sociability. As he affirms in "A Search into the Nature of Society," the essay that concludes the 1723 edition of the *Fable*, "not the Good and Amiable, but the Bad and Hateful Qualities of Man, his Imperfections and the want of Excellencies which other Creatures are endued with, are the first Causes that made Man sociable" (1:344). Paradoxically, human beings will come together in society because they desire to be something better—at least superficially, in the eyes of others—than the selfish, acquisitive creatures that they truly are.

Strictly speaking, however, the mere (immaterial) emulation of virtue by the upper class and the emulation of the upper by the lower class are enough to bring society together. What makes a society—like Mandeville's original, bustling beehive—"Great" (1:36) is commerce, which is the emulation of one's social betters by material rather than immaterial means. The more familiar interpretation of Mandeville's paradox assigns the "private vices" to the whole variety of human passions, not just to human disagreeableness, and the "publick benefits" not just to human sociability but to the vast array of material goods that come from associating to gratify them. Even if Shaftesbury's natural affection were a reality, Mandeville says, it would provide "no Reason or Probability . . . why Mankind ever should have rais'd themselves into such large Societies as there have been in the World" (1:346). Only material needs—not immaterial ones like the passions for self-preservation, affection, or even emulation—can make a society great.

Commerce as Conversation

Mandeville's commerce may not involve the sharing of opinions as Shaftesbury's polite dialogue does, but it does involve conversation. Society flourishes because the desires of human beings are in a constant state of flux, and those desires force people to meet, and to *talk*, with one another in the course of satisfying them. In part 2 of the *Fable*, Mandeville's spokesperson, Cleomenes, while conceding that virtue might be a more peaceable way to bring individuals together in society, remarks on the "conversable" nature of commerce: "[T]he whole Superstructure [of civil society] is made up of the reciprocal Services, which Men do to each other. . . . To expect, that others would serve us for nothing, is unreasonable; therefore all *Commerce*, that Men can have together, must be a continual bartering of one thing for another" (2:349, emphasis added). Not virtue but commerce—serving others for *something*, with the expectation of return—is conversable. Indeed, given that one of the eighteenth-century definitions of *commerce* was, according to the *Oxford English Dictionary*, the "interchange (esp. of letters, ideas, etc.)," a definition that is still current, if less common, the relationship between commerce and conversation is less analogy than literal correspondence. One can converse with material objects as well as people, and "bartering" can involve the exchange of opinions as well as goods.

If commerce corresponds to conversation in Mandeville's system, human beings themselves—the agents of conversation—correspond to commodities. Like commodities, humans are changed, or "processed," in the course of satisfying one another's desires. "Nature," Cleomenes states, "had design'd Man for Society, as she has made Grapes for Wine" (2:185). When his friend Horatio explores his analogy, saying that "if you would compare the Sociableness of Man to the Vinosity of Wine, you must shew me, that in Society there is an Equivalent for Fermentation," that is, some quality that "is palpably adven-

titious" to the "Multitudes . . . joyn'd together" in society, Cleomenes
has a ready answer:

> Such an Equivalent is demonstrable in mutual Commerce: for if we
> examine every Faculty and Qualification, from and for which we judge
> and pronounce Man to be a sociable Creature beyond other Animals,
> we shall find, that a very considerable, if not the greatest Part of the
> Attribute is acquired, and comes upon Multitudes, from their convers-
> ing with one another. *Fabricando fabri fimus.* Men become sociable, by
> living together in Society. (2:189)

The value that is added to individuals processed from a state of nature
to one of civilization is precisely their sociability, and they acquire that
quality simply by conversing with one another, acting "in mutual
Commerce." If getting them to interact in the first place may take
some artfulness, getting them socialized does not; it is as natural as
fermentation. It begins to happen as soon as individuals are thrown
together with, or rather against, one another.

Somehow, the changing that takes place when human beings satisfy
one another's desires in commerce, a satisfaction that must involve a
certain degree of conformity, does *not* eliminate their natural differences. Instead, they retain their distinctiveness, their "flavor," in the
process of becoming sociable. Mandeville emphasizes the diversity
rather than the conformity in commerce when, shifting his analogy
from society as wine, he compares

> the Body Politick (I confess the Simile is very low) to a Bowl of Punch.
> . . . The Water I would call the Ignorance, Folly and Credulity of the
> floating insipid Multitude; while Wisdom, Honour, Fortitude and the
> rest of the sublime Qualities of Men . . . should be an equivalent to
> Brandy. I don't doubt but a *Westphalian, Laplander,* or any other dull
> Stranger that is unacquainted with the wholesom Composition, if he
> was to taste the several Ingredients apart, would think it impossible
> they should make any tolerable Liquor. . . . Yet Experience teaches us,
> that the Ingredients I named judiciously mixt, will make an excellent
> Liquor, lik'd of and admir'd by Men of exquisite Palates. (1:105–6)

Although Mandeville uncharacteristically confirms class distinctions
here—the multitude is "insipid," while the elite is both tasty and "ex-
quisitely" tasteful—the metaphor of commonwealth as punch also

maintains a degree of diversity in unity. Together, the different ingre-
dients blend, or more accurately, complement, one another. When
Mandeville elsewhere asserts that the "Contraries" in the body politic
"are best cured by Contraries" (1:321), he is only repeating what by
the early eighteenth century had become a political truism. But to
"cure" contraries for Mandeville is not—as it is for others (like Shaftesbury) who would profess that principle—to eliminate them. A bowl
of punch, after all, is not a bowl of cherries.

Just what kind of conversation is commerce, the sort of talking that
makes society work? That Mandeville frequently contrasts his philosophy to Shaftesbury's—"[T]wo systems," he states, "cannot be more
opposite than his Lordship's and mine" (1:324)—implies that it is
not conversation as a civic humanist might understand it: it is not a
consummately polite good in itself.[6] In this, Mandeville is closer, if not
exactly close, to eighteenth-century periodical essayists like Joseph
Addison and Richard Steele, who, while they recognized that commerce
had its civilizing effects, nevertheless represented polite conversation, says Stephen Copley, "as being outside and apart from trade and
commodity exchange." Commerce may have given a newly monied
middle class the material resources to emulate, in consumption, the
distinctive virtues of the upper class, but commerce itself was too ardent,
too evidently self-interested, to stand in for the dispassionate "morality, manners, taste and discriminatory skill" that were "the defining
concerns of the polite."[7] When those essayists actually try to conflate
commerce and polite conversation, as Steele does in a backhand way
in number 219 of the *Tatler* when he calls it "a very great Error, that we
should not profess Honesty in Conversation as much as in Commerce,"[8] their very language betrays the feebleness of the attempt.
That Steele has to resort to a double negative—it is an "Error" that we
"should not" profess honesty, rather than an advantage that we
should—to describe the supposed veracity of commercial exchanges
suggests that he is hedging even as he pleads for truthfulness, and the
ambiguity of the verb "profess," which could signify the pretense of
"Honesty" as easily as it could the real presence of it, is an example of
just how deceiving Steele's own "conversation" can be. Depending on
whether one believes or disbelieves in the authenticity of polite conversation, Steele's sentiment betrays either the incompatibility of it
with commerce or the scandal of their actual similarity.

Indeed, most of what passes as polite conversation resembles commerce—the sort of conversation that makes society work—in its inauthenticity. If there are no (or few) individuals who can consistently
place the public interest before their own, there are those who *appear*
to be doing so, who appear, that is, to be virtuous. This "laudable quality" of "mak[ing] others believe, that the Esteem we have for them
exceeds the Value we have for our selves," explains Mandeville, "is
commonly known by the name of Manners and Good-breeding, and
consists in a Fashionable Habit, acquir'd by Precept and Example, of
flattering the Pride and Selfishness of others, and concealing our own
with Judgment and Dexterity" (1:76–77). Like virtue itself, Shaftesbury's cherished qualities of politeness and good breeding are nothing more (and nothing less) than what flattery begot upon pride. The
"true" sort of conversation in Mandeville's paradoxical system, the
conversation that brings society together and makes it great, is false to
its core. It is what Mandeville terms *dissimulation.*

Dissimulation

Because human beings are all fundamentally the same passionate,
self-interested creatures, dissimulation is necessary to create the illusion of difference, and thus the dynamic of emulation, in the first
place.[9] But that is the work of skillful politicians, who bring a society
together. Merchants, as I have said, also dissimulate to make a society
great. Taking note of "the innumerable Artifices, by which Buyers and
Sellers out-wit one another," Mandeville asks, "Where is the Merchant
that has never against his conscience extoll'd his Wares beyond their
Worth, to make them go off the better?" and then relates a story of
two merchants who barter over a parcel of sugar, each raising or lowering the price according to information that he conceals from the
other concerning its supply. "[A]ll of this is called fair dealing," observes Mandeville; "but I am sure neither of them would have desired
to be done by, as they did to each other" (1:61–63). Elsewhere he adds
that "Tradesmen are generally forc'd to tell Lies in their own Defence,
and invent a thousand improbable Stories, rather than discover what
they really get by their Commodities" (1:81). Just as society would be
impossible without the lies of politicians, commerce would be impossible without the lies of tradesmen. To simulate, or truly represent,
one's own "Pride and Selfishness" would both offend one's social

companions and scare off one's commercial partners; we dissimulate, or misrepresent those qualities, says Mandeville, both to keep society going and to drive its commercial exchanges.

If dissimulation is a kind of rhetoric, albeit a rhetoric as entirely deceptive as Hobbes, Locke, and other seventeenth-century reformers feared it was, then another way of putting Mandeville's point is that societies progress materially—they become "great"—as they progress rhetorically. Shaftesbury, it should be noted, said much the same thing: societies progress as they become more "polite,"[10] and politicians who persuade their populaces via the rhetorical arts are politer than those who simply command. For Mandeville, however, civilized discourse is a "rhetoric of dominion":[11] rhetorically sophisticated societies are more advanced, *and* more polite, but only because they have more ways—more words—to make immaterial qualities like virtue seem greater than they really are. Eloquence is not the gloss on a predominantly logical argument (as it is in Hobbes) nor the politically tainted "leprosy" that appeals to the "party of appetite" and interest rather than to reason and disinterested virtue (as it is in Shaftesbury), but just the opposite: a tool to appeal to the better angels of our nature. As making people believe that it is better to mind the public interest than it is to mind their private interest "has always been a very difficult Task," Mandeville says, "so no *Wit* or *Eloquence* has been left untried to compass it" (1:42, emphasis added). There is simply no society without "Hypocrisy," because "if by *Art* and *prudent Dissimulation* we had not learn'd to hide and stifle" the "Ideas that are continually arising within us," "all Civil Commerce would be lost" (1:349, emphasis added).

Human beings certainly do not "speak, in order that their Thoughts may be known, and their Sentiments laid open and seen through by others." This becomes evident when Cleomenes disagrees with Horatio's confident assertion to that effect in part 2 of the *Fable:*

> The first Sign or Sound that ever Man made, born of a Woman, was made in Behalf, and intended for the use of him who made it; and I am of Opinion, that the first Design of Speech was to persuade others, either to give Credit to what the speaking Person would have them believe; or else to act or suffer such Things, as he would compel them to act or suffer, if they were entirely in his Power. (2:289)

The first speech already had "designs" on us, concealing the fact that it was "intended for the use of" the speaker while it seemed to make that person's "Thoughts" and "Sentiments" known. But that we speak for our own good, to get others to think or act as we want them to, is only one "idea" or interest that we conceal through dissimulation, and speech is only one means of doing it: elsewhere Mandeville calls "Fine Cloaths" and other material signs of status "warrantable ways" of gratifying pride because they "stifle" it too (2:126–27). "Virtue," Mandeville tells us, "bids us subdue, but good Breeding only requires we should hide our Appetites" (1:72), and pride is the first "Appetite" or interest that we need to dissimulate if we are to behave sociably.

Dialogue as Commerce?

Given his analysis of the self-interested motives behind commercial conversation, one might expect that Mandeville's own conversations, the dialogues that make up part 2 of the *Fable*,[12] would be exercises in dissimulation. If commerce is a kind of conversation, that is, then when Mandeville attempts to represent real conversation, it should resemble commerce, the many dissimulative conversations that keep society going. What would such conversation look like? Mandeville has already given us a picture of it in the story of the two traders: if Cleomenes and Horatio were acting in kind, each would talk to deceive the other, driving up the value, if not of any goods he is trying to sell, at least of the opinions he holds (including the "virtues" that are attributed to him). Such dialogues might resemble the calculating transactions of Restoration comedy, where beneath the surface of civility we see the machinations of wits striving only to bed the innocent or fleece the foolish.

Outside of part 2 of the *Fable,* Mandeville doubts that conversation, whether polite or no, can be truly disinterested. At one moment, in the essay "A Search into the Nature of Society," he can sound as sure as Shaftesbury that the pleasures of "what I call good Company" are genuine: "There is nothing said in it that is not either instructive or diverting to a Man of Sense. It is possible they may not always be of the same Opinion, but there can be no contest between any but who shall yield first to the other he differs from. . . . The greatest Pleasure aimed at by every one of them is to have the Satisfaction of Pleasing others." Mandeville does not, however, luxuriate in this conversational idyll but counters that if such persons "could employ themselves in something from which they expected either a more solid or a more lasting Satisfaction, they would deny themselves this Pleasure, and follow what was of greater consequence to 'em" (1:339–40). Furthermore, the pleasure that one takes from good company, the "Satisfaction of Pleasing others," is itself suspect. "Even the most polite People in the World," he goes on to say, "give no Pleasure to others that is not repaid to their Self-Love," and he looks to polite, and pleasurable, conversation for proof:

> [T]he plainest Demonstration that in all Clubs and Societies of Conversable People every body has the greatest Consideration for himself is, that the *Disinterested,* who rather over-pays than wrangles; . . . is everywhere the Darling of the Company: Whereas the Man of Sense and Knowledge . . . is seldom so well beloved as a weaker Man less Accomplish'd. (1:342, emphasis added)

Mandeville uses the word "Disinterested" ironically here. By restricting it to mere politeness, even flattery, he separates the qualities—politeness and good sense—that Shaftesbury, Horatio's model and philosophical hero, meant it to join. The "Disinterested" individual is "the Darling of the Company" because he "over-pays" or flatters the pride of his fellow conversationalists; "the Man of Sense and Knowledge," because he does not hesitate to "wrangle" with or criticize his fellows, is ostracized. In his usual, paradoxical way, Mandeville finds evidence that conversation cannot be disinterested in the obvious interest that those who like to talk take in the polite (or disinterested) flatterer. As he reiterates here, when we do "converse," "we only endeavour to *strengthen* our Interest" (1:343, emphasis added), either materially or because it flatters our pride to appear disinterested, polite, and sociable. Why should his own conversations be any different?

At the very least, one might expect that Mandeville's dialogues would promote a sort of grudging acceptance of dissimulation, as well as vice in general, as necessary to the functioning and prosperity of the commonwealth. This is, in fact, the reason Mandeville gives for writing the *Fable.* He objects to those who vociferate against private vice (in his day, the members of the Societies for Reformation of Manners), and the problem that besets "The Grumbling Hive" is just that, not vice: the bees are not "content" with the bustle that makes their hive so prosperous but curse, cry, rail, and *grumble* at the moral imperfections, the desires, that account for that bustle (1:26–27). Just as Tory polemicists like Roger L'Estrange, before the revolution of 1688, railed at the "meddling" of ordinary citizens in public affairs supposedly too sophisticated for them, Mandeville tells his bees, in the moral of the poem, to "leave Complaints: Fools only strive / To make a Great an Honest Hive" (1:36). If Horatio were a moral reformer who tried to remedy that from which he reaped, one might expect Cleomenes to show him where his own hypocrisy lies, as Mandeville shows the philanthropists in part 1's "An Essay on Charity, and Charity-Schools" who conceal the "Satisfaction" that they take in doing good (1:280). If part 2 followed the plan of part 1, that is, Mandeville's dialogues would not necessarily be like Restoration comedy; they would resemble Augustan satire, with Cleomenes mocking Horatio's pretensions to virtue.

But part 2 of the *Fable* is not satiric, or at least it is much less satiric than part 1: if there is a mocking voice in the dialogues, it belongs to Horatio,[13] not to Mandeville's spokesperson, Cleomenes, whose usual tone is gently explanatory. Horatio is not a moral reformer but one of Shaftesbury's "moralists," not a bourgeois philanthropist or tradesman but a member of the beau monde, on the order of Shaftesbury himself. In his sketch of Horatio's character in the preface to part 2, Mandeville tells us that he is one of those fashionable young men who, although they "have very little Religion, . . . are extremely fond of the amiable [and fashionable] sound" of "Virtue" (2:11–12). As such, he errs not by thinking too lowly of humankind (and grumbling) but by thinking too highly, and this, as Mandeville discerns, makes him more difficult to deal with than a "lowly" moral reformer: "[T]he more exalted the Notions are, which Men entertain of their better part, their reasoning Faculty, the more remote and averse they'll be from giving their Assent to any thing that seems to insult over or contradict it" (2:15).

How is a Mandevillian like Cleomenes to command the "Assent" of such an exalted reasoner as Horatio? The same way, ironically, as Shaftesbury's Theocles attempted to win over the fashionably skeptical Philocles: not by lying to him or mocking him but by talking to him politely. At one point in their dialogue Cleomenes tells Horatio that however "convincing" an argument may be "that had all its Force from the Vehemence it was made with," he prefers the present "Fashion" in

England, which is "speaking low," for "when a Man addresses himself to me in a calm manner . . . he gives me the Pleasure to imagine, that he thinks me not influenc'd by my Passions, but altogether sway'd by my Reason" (2:291–92). This "unaffected manner of speaking" (2:292) is clearly being displayed in their own discourse; it is the style of dialogue. Despite the irony of Cleomenes, who scorns fashion in general, now saying that he prefers the "Fashion" of talking politely, it seems that this is the way Mandeville really thinks of dialogue: as a disinterested or at least dispassionate use of reason. In part 2 of the *Fable*, virtue, at least the virtue of politeness that would-be opponents exhibit toward one another in conversation, is a reality, not the sham "Political Offspring" of pride. Mandeville's dialogues propose not that conversation aims to drive commerce or even to mock hypocrisy but that it aims to discover truth.

On the one hand, Mandeville's turn to dialogue, in part 2 of the *Fable* and elsewhere, is entirely consistent with his desire to demystify what passes for "virtue" among his contemporaries. Part 1, especially with the addition of the charity-school essay in 1723, had been condemned by those philanthropists, politicians, and divines who preached the ethic of public over private good: in many ways, Mandeville's dissection of the self-interest that motivates most (if not all) human actions made him the same sort of whipping boy for eighteenth-century moralists that Hobbes had been for those in the seventeenth century. As Mandeville pleads his case in the preface to part 2, such criticism is simply the result of misunderstanding. He thus writes part 2 (published in 1729), he says, to "illustrate and explain several Things, that were obscure and only hinted at in the First," and he uses the dialogue as "the easiest way of executing" this "Design" (2:7). Like the other figures in this study, Mandeville is attracted to the dialogue as an "easy and familiar" (Shaftesbury, 1:41) and especially accessible form.

On the other hand, Mandeville's dialogical turn, though hardly *re*mystifying, is antithetical to the persistently practical concerns that the *Fable* justifies and (in part 1) represents. When, in part 2, Cleomenes proposes that human beings first associated because of "the common Danger they were in from wild Beasts" and Horatio objects "that Providence should have no greater regard to our Species, than it has to Flies, and the Spawn of Fish,"[14] Cleomenes evades the theological point and, as Mandeville does the misunderstandings of the *Fable* itself, attributes Horatio's objection to human pride and the usual bustle: "[W]e are so full of our own Species, and the Excellency of it, that we have no *Leisure* seriously to consider the System of this Earth; I mean the Plan on which the OEconomy of it is built, in relation to the living Creatures, that are in and upon it" (2:251, emphasis added). If Horatio thought about Cleomenes' theory harder—more important, if he had the *time* to think about it—he would come to share Cleomenes' evolutionary view. Presumably, Horatio does not have time to think because he is caught up in the satisfying bustle—as in the busy hive of the poem—that keeps society going: to be "full of" one's own species is to be a consumer rather than curious. What Cleomenes neglects to mention is that thinking hard about the subject of human evolution, not to mention the subsequent development of language, religion, ethics, and government, in approximately that order, is precisely what he and Horatio are doing in these dialogues. In the realm of dialogue they *do* have the leisure that it takes to think successfully, a philosophical leisure that is severely at odds with the practical bustle happening elsewhere. If Mandeville's commerce is a kind of conversation, the leisureliness of the conversation that makes up the dialogues of part 2 of the *Fable* suggests that it is not a kind of commerce.

That dialogue is leisurely and commerce is bustling is just a formal difference between the two, however. Dialogue differs from commerce in at least three other, more substantial ways. The first is that dialogue explains rather than dissimulates. Mandeville, after all, concedes that there were obscurities in part 1 that he will "illustrate" and "explain" in part 2, and that statement is earnest and even apologetic. He seems genuinely dismayed that the *Fable* has been misunderstood and genuinely determined to right that misunderstanding. When, for example, at the end of the first dialogue Horatio, at Cleomenes' request, actually condescends to read the *Fable* (part 1) and comes back at the beginning of the second with the mistaken impression that in it Mandeville "speaks in Favour of Duelling" and "shews the Necessity of keeping up that Custom, to polish and brighten Society in general," Cleomenes asks outright,

> Don't you see the Irony there?
> HOR. No indeed: he plainly demonstrates the Usefulness of it, gives
> as good Reasons as it is possible to invent, and shews how much

Conversation would suffer if that Practice was abolished. . . . [Cle-
omenes then asks Horatio to read aloud a passage from the *Fable*
in favor of dueling. Horatio does and admits:] That indeed seems
to be said with a Sneer: but in what goes before he is very serious.
CLEO. He is so, when he says that the Practice of Duelling, . . . contributes to the Politeness of Manners and Pleasure of Conversation,
and this is very true; but that Politeness itself, and that Pleasure, are
the Things he laughs at and exposes throughout his Book. (2:101–2)

Cleomenes, after Mandeville, finds the humor of a deadly serious activity like dueling in the matter that it provides for polite conversation.
Horatio eventually finds it too, but not without even further explication by Cleomenes. Philosophical dialogue, it seems, is less ironic,
and thus less ambiguous, than ordinary speech, and it is especially
less ironic than the mocking, sarcastic, and sometimes puzzling prose
of part 1 of the *Fable*. Irony, as any satirist knows, can easily be misunderstood; if one's interlocutor fails to understand what one is saying
in dialogue, however, one can always, as Cleomenes does here for
Mandeville, explain it again. If the dialogues of part 2 of the *Fable* are
to explain part 1, irony is a disguise that must be dropped.

The second way that dialogue differs from commerce is that it commands assent with logical argument rather than deceitful eloquence
or even violence. Because Horatio is already civilized (and because
Cleomenes is no politician), Cleomenes does not have to use "cunning
Management"—either "Persuasion" or "Superior Force"—to draw
him "from his Savage State" and make him "a Disciplin'd Creature"
(1:347); because Cleomenes himself is uninterested in commercial
exchange with Horatio, neither does he have to dissimulate his real
interests, or tell lies in his own defense. Instead, Cleomenes abides by
the liberal faith in logical dialogue that Mandeville expresses in *Free
Thoughts on Religion, the Church, and National Happiness* (1720): "'Tis
by *Discourse* and *Reason*, not by *Blows, Insults* or *Violence*, that Men are
to be inform'd of Truth, and convinc'd of Error."[15] To show his friend
"how small the Difference is between us, which you imagine to be so
considerable," he will "demonstrate" (2:57), not deceive or threaten.
Such logical argument, as even the optimist Horatio begins to detect
halfway into their dialogue, goes against the grain of most conversations: "Where Men are certain that the Truth of a Thing is not to be
known, they will always differ, and endeavour to impose upon one

another." "Whilst there are Fools and Knaves they will," Cleomenes assures him. "But I have not impos'd upon you" (2:167). Only "Fools and Knaves," either through eloquence or through violence, impose their opinions on one another. Cleomenes has merely "discover'd" the truth to Horatio (2:147), and that is what reasonable people do.

Horatio's conversion from Shaftesbury's to Mandeville's system is virtually complete by the end of the second dialogue, when he exclaims to Cleomenes, "You have almost conquer'd me." Cleomenes' answer, "I aim at no Victory, all I wish for is to do you Service, in undeceiving you" (2:96), reveals the third and most important way that dialogue differs from commerce: it enlightens. People grumble about the vices of others, according to Mandeville, because they do not know their own propensities to vice. If human beings are constantly deceiving one another about their virtues and their goods, they are also, and primarily, deceiving themselves. How, Horatio wonders, can a person of sense "be ignorant of his own Heart, and the Motives he acts from"? Because, Cleomenes answers, to be enlightened is to be appalled at one's own self-interest. "[E]nquiring within, and boldly searching into ones own Bosom," he says, "must be the most shocking Employment, that a Man can give his Mind to, whose greatest Pleasure consists in secretly admiring himself" (2:79–80). Most avoid enlightenment— and the dialogue that provides it—because they fear "dragging the lurking Fiend from his darkest Recesses into a glaring Light, where all the World shall know him" (2:81). Cleomenes, who begins part 2 confessing his own lack of virtue, achieves his most important "victory," not by explaining or demonstrating Mandeville's system to Horatio, but by getting him to admit him that despite his tendency to think of himself as a distinctive, virtuous Shaftesburean, he is really as self-interested as everyone else. And he succeeds: Horatio returns from their first dialogue conceding that "I don't remember, I ever look'd into myself so much as I have done since last Night after I left you" (2:62). Drawing Horatio away from Shaftesburean virtues like honor, Cleomenes attempts to convince him that the only reliable virtue is honesty.

Mandeville is careful not to call such honesty or the desires to explain himself and to argue logically "disinterestedness." One can, after all, tell the truth without being disinterested, just as Cleomenes confesses without claiming any special virtue. Yet, the philosophical

search for truth in which he and Horatio are engaging clearly transcends the normal, dissimulative exchanges that drive commerce and
keep society going.[16] In addition, Mandeville occasionally claims a
sort of disinterestedness for his philosophical project, such as when,
in the preface to part 2 of the *Fable*, he declares that he will use "the
same unbiass'd Method of searching after Truth and enquiring into
the Nature of Man and Society" that he used in part 1 (2:22–23). Being
"unbiass'd" would have seemed impossible for one of Mandeville's
merchants or even for one of the moralists whose false virtue he so
enjoys exposing. And how is it that Horatio can so easily compliment
Cleomenes—at the conclusion of part 2, before he tells him that "I
am your Convert, and shall henceforth look upon the *Fable of the Bees*
very differently than what I did"—not only for "aim[ing] at Truth" but
also for being "entirely impartial" while he did it (2:355–56)?

Mandeville's Contradiction

It is only mildly inconsistent of Mandeville to claim the disinterestedness of the truth-teller while simultaneously asserting that true disinterestedness is impossible. It is another matter for Mandeville to pursue
a "disinterested," demystifying search for truth in part 2 of the *Fable* (or
anywhere else) while maintaining that dissimulation keeps the rest of
society going. To put it bluntly, if everyone were as enlightened as
Cleomenes and Horatio, commerce—even society itself—would cease
to function, or at least to function as well: people would see through
the veil of dissimulation to the self-interest underneath and refuse to be
taken advantage of. In society, this would make everyone as skeptical
about the reality of virtue as Mandeville is himself, and no one would
strive to emulate his or her "betters." In commerce, it would make
everyone distrust the claims that merchants make for their commodities—including their most important claim, that their products actually help people to emulate the virtue of the upper class—and no one
would desire anything more than he or she needed to survive.

At least some of Mandeville's contemporary critics noticed that he
was giving away the knowledge that, if truly received, would alert average persons to the depth of their benightedness and mean the death
of his dissimulative system. The anonymous author of the proministry
paper *The Tea-Table* even objected on such grounds, calling Mandeville's conclusions "pretty right" but his book "a very wrong and perni-

cious thing, and the greatest Breach imaginable upon Society . . . to spread abroad indifferently, and without distinction, . . . among the common People." If "Men of Sense" understood among themselves that they must cheat and lie to the "common people" to maintain their advantage over them, this writer complained, they knew better than to tell them about it. Less obviously partisan was this observation by the anonymous author of *The True Meaning of the Fable of the Bees* (1726): "Suppose every body knew as much as the Author of *The Fable of the Bees* and that Virtue and Vice were but Bugbears invented for the uninterrupted indulging of the Appetites of some certain Persons, or suppose they had made the Discovery that it was in the Essence of the *Politician* to consult nobody but himself. How would you keep People in awe?"[17] Because of their more polite, less ironic stance—their clear intention *to* enlighten—Mandeville's dialogues make this inconsistency explicit, but it is a problem in all of his writings.[18] If commerce is to continue to function as he has described it, Mandeville must presume either that his readers will disregard the information that he is giving them and (if they are among the enlightened few) continue to dissimulate or that they will fail to understand it at all and (if they are among the many) continue to be ignorant.[19]

Mandeville seems to realize his own inconsistency at two places in the *Fable,* one outside and one inside the dialogues. In part 1, heading off criticism that his system is "immoral" because it promotes private vice, he gives the right answer to the wrong question: "Now I cannot see what Immorality there is in shewing a Man the Origin and Power of those Passions, which so often, even unknowingly to himself, hurry him away from his Reason. . . . What hurt do I do to Man if I make him more known to himself than he was before?" (1:229). Mandeville's answer here might satisfy the moralists among his critics, but the inconsistency in his philosophy is an economic, not a moral, one: making a person "more known to himself than he was before" does not necessarily encourage him or her to take advantage of others, but—because knowing oneself is knowing others—it *does* make that person less likely to be taken advantage of. Enlightenment, that is, is not immoral but counterproductive. Surprisingly, in part 2 it is Horatio who perceives this difference. When Cleomenes argues that because most virtue is an artificial quality—what flattery begot upon pride—those who hold high places in government (and who are proclaimed "virtuous") need be no greater than anyone else (or really virtuous), Horatio raises an objection like that the author *The Tea-Table* raised, but about the leaders of society, not the followers:

> I don't believe you have an ill Design in advancing these Notions; but supposing them to be true, I can't comprehend that divulging them can have any other Effect than the Increase of Sloth and Ignorance; for if Men may fill the highest Places in the Government without Learning or Capacity, Genius or Knowledge, there's an End of all the Labour of the Brain, and the Fatigue of hard Study.

For the moment, Horatio realizes that if Cleomenes' notions were widely "divulged," the economic (and moral) structure of society would fail. Enlightened leaders, like enlightened economic agents, would see through the lies of those whom *they* were trying to emulate and attain their places through similar means, without hard "Labour" and "Study." But Horatio's insight has no lasting impact on the course of the dialogue: rather than answering the question that he implies, that is, Why advance such notions, or write at all? Cleomenes simply denies that he has made any "such general Assertion" (2:340).

Given Mandeville's insight into the dissimulative nature of commerce, it is possible to see the inconsistency in his philosophy as what in Marxist social theory is termed a *contradiction*.[20] As William C. Dowling explicates it, "Contradiction . . . is what occurs when the underlying forces of material production begin to outstrip the system of social relations to which they earlier gave rise."[21] In Mandeville's case, the "underlying forces of material production" would be dissimulative commerce, and the "system of social relations" would be the literary conventions that dictate that dialogue is disinterested and that writers write to enlighten their audiences, not deceive them.[22] Mandeville, that is, cannot enlighten us about commerce without betraying the system—civil society—that supports it. He betrays it not by lying about it but by telling the truth.

Other writers of Mandeville's day who attempted to justify early capitalist society (e.g., Daniel Defoe) escaped this contradiction not by evading the same conventions but by failing to notice that commerce —the underlying forces of material production—*is* dissimulative. They employed variations on the language of civic humanism, insisting that commerce was in fact a "virtuous" way of life or accusing those who opposed the "vices" of capitalism of being "corrupt" themselves.[23] But Mandeville justified commerce by "asserting both that [it] was beneficial and that luxury and vice were necessary to it."[24] Conventional apologists like Defoe manifested the false consciousness that Marxist critics think endemic among persons "subjected" to capitalism, deluding themselves that the system is both beneficent and virtuous. But Mandeville, who was not blind to at least the hypocrisy of the system, manifested a kind of false consciousness too: he falsely assumed that an enlightened populace would still be an exploitable one. From this angle, what makes Mandeville's dialogues interesting is that by showing a naive participant in the system (Horatio) being liberated (by Cleomenes) from the foolishness of his existing justifications, they dramatize the contradiction that all his writings about commerce present. If ignorance is bliss (or a "great" hive), why aim at enlightenment? Why, as Horatio implies, write at all?

Dialogue and the History of Reason

There is a sense, however, in which Mandeville's philosophy already encompasses (if it does not resolve) the contradiction between interested commerce and disinterested dialogue. If dialogue, including the dialogue that Mandeville has with his reader, is understood as an exercise in persuasion rather than pure (i.e., wholly disinterested) enlightenment, then it can be interested (and thus more like commerce) without calling for continuing dissimulation (and thus still like dialogue). Cleomenes and Mandeville, that is, can ask their hearers both to regard the information that they dispense (not to disregard it and continue to dissimulate) and to acknowledge that they have a stake in the conversation, including an "interest" in converting the other to their point of view. Mandeville, or Cleomenes, has already informed us that speech was first "intended for the use of him who made it," and he equates such interested speech with persuasion, not —as Horatio proposed—with the enlightened goal of making one's thoughts perfectly "laid open and seen through by others." Yet, in using speech to persuade, a certain kind of enlightenment *is* achieved, the enlightenment that occurs when two or more discussants agree on what is rational.

Mandeville has consistently argued, as Stephen H. Daniel puts it, that "rationality is essentially social: it is the ability to *persuade* oneself and others to act in socially beneficial ways, especially when this means acting contrary to one's own self-interest."[25] And if rationality is essentially social, it is not a timeless, absolute fact, as it is in some versions of the Enlightenment, but a useful fiction, like Mandeville's vision of commerce itself.[26] Mandeville's "final turn to dialogue," as Daniel continues, thus "make[s] explicit the *cooperative exchange* which goes on in . . . philosophy between author and reader" (605, emphasis added). Or, I may add, between Cleomenes and Horatio, who exchange opinions in an atmosphere that is as self-aware (and thus unlike commerce) as it is necessarily cooperative (and thus like it). Mandeville's dialogists, that is, are committed not just to getting along for the greater good of each other, as the participants in society's dissimulative commerce are; they are committed to understanding itself, which, they come to understand, consists *in* their "getting along," in their consensus or agreement. Persuasion, which, however it may begin in the speaker's interest in converting the other, ends by demonstrating that some mutual settlement is in the interests of everyone involved, may be all, or everything, that enlightenment can mean for Mandeville.

In a sense, all of part 2 of the *Fable* is devoted to persuading Horatio that reason is a useful fiction, but a particular exchange can serve to illustrate the point. When Horatio asks Cleomenes whether "Notions of Right and Wrong" are natural, Cleomenes replies with an answer that at first seems to say yes and thus to accord with an idea of reason as timeless and absolute, at odds with commerce: "A Man of Sense, Learning and Experience, that has been well educated, will always find out the difference between Right and Wrong in things diametrically opposite; and there are certain Facts, which he will always condemn, and others which he will always approve of" (2:221). But the catch in this response is that Cleomenes' "Man of Sense" must be "well educated": our moral sentiments, a large part of what we call "reason," as Cleomenes goes on to explain, are not given naturally or a priori, as Horatio's Shaftesburean sensibility would have it, but are acquired a posteriori, through conversations like the one that he and Horatio are now having. "[T]here are things, which are commonly esteem'd to be eternal Truths," Cleomenes adds, that not only a "Savage" but "an hundred or a thousand People of fine Sense and Judgment, could have no Notion of." The only way that we can know our notions of right and wrong, such as the general notion that it is better to mind the public rather than to mind our private interest, is through "our *Commerce* with others, and the Experience of Facts" (2:223, emphasis added).

To say that reason is not timeless or absolute but acquired a posteriori is to say that it has a history. One of the reasonable things that Horatio learns from his commerce with Cleomenes is that our notions of right and wrong are acquired and that innumerable similar instances of commerce over time have fined and refined the useful fiction that keeps society going. Because he is only tapping into the wisdom of the ages, Cleomenes refuses to take full credit for the thinking and the talking that convert Horatio to his point of view. "Among the things I hint at," he acknowledges,

> there are very few, that are the Work of one Man, or of one Generation; the greatest part of them are the Product, the joynt Labour of several Ages. . . . The Wisdom I speak of, is not the Offspring of a fine Understanding, or intense Thinking, but of sound and deliberate Judgment, acquired from a long Experience in Business, and a Multiplicity of Observations. (2:321–22)

In short, as Cleomenes summarizes the same thought in *An Enquiry into the Origin of Honour* (1732), Mandeville's sequel to the *Fable*, "Human Wisdom is the Child of Time."[27] Such a historicized view of reason makes it a less remarkable quality, for example, than the "very bright Parts and uncommon Talents" that Horatio, replying in the *Fable*, says are necessary for the governing of a commonwealth. Rather, the "Laws and establish'd Oeconomy of a well-order'd City," as Cleomenes draws the analogy, are like a "Clock": "[W]hen once they are brought to as much Perfection, as Art and human Wisdom can carry them, the whole Machine may be made to play of itself . . . ; and the Government of a large City, once put into good Order, the Magistrates only following their Noses, will continue to go right for a great while, tho' there was not a wise Man in it" (2:321–23). Perhaps, Mandeville seems to aver here, a reasonable politician does not have to be so "skilful" after all.[28]

Such a historicized view of reason also makes Cleomenes a less "uncommon" reasoner than his skillful conversion of Horatio would imply. Cleomenes himself is nothing if not modest about his own abilities. He not only refuses to take full credit for his reasoning but also quite freely confesses, contrary to Mandeville's other statements about the disinterestedness of philosophical conversation, to his own "interestedness." Mandeville establishes his spokesperson's character in the preface to part 2, where he says that "*Cleomenes* seemed charitable, and was a Man of strict Morals, yet he would often complain that he was not possess'd of one Christian Virtue, and found fault with his own Actions, that had all the Appearances of Goodness; because he was conscious, he said, that they were perform'd from a wrong principle" (2:18). The "wrong principle" is that of self-interest, and that Cleomenes knows and confesses his own propensity to act from it makes what he says about the propensity of others all the more believable. In his way, Cleomenes is a *post*-Enlightenment philosopher, one who has exploded the myth that a historically situated observer can be an impartial observer of history: he knows, as Victoria Kahn abstracts the perspective of certain twentieth-century critical theorists, that "Interestedness is unavoidable, but superior interest will at least be self-critical."[29] Indeed, for Cleomenes as for Mandeville, disinterestedness would mean the very dissolution of "truth" since truth itself is the product of various interests.

But what if a reasoner is not as honest as Cleomenes? And what if persuasion is not the mutually cooperative exchange to greater understanding that Cleomenes and Horatio partake of but the sort of "coaxing and wheedling" that Cleomenes warns Horatio "Persons of mean Parts and weak Understandings" are susceptible to (2:297)? To understand dialogue as persuasion rather than enlightenment may help to encompass the contradiction between commerce and dialogue in Mandeville's philosophy, but it does nothing to solve the problem that results when the enlightenment (or persuasion) that Mandeville pursues in all of his writings is made "common" knowledge. It may, in other words, resolve Mandeville's contradiction for himself and his fellow dialogists—for those whose honesty can be relied on—but it does not resolve it outside the privileged realm of dialogue. Knowing that reason is a fiction, if a useful one, might persuade people to act in socially beneficial ways, or it might not. It might, instead, persuade them to use reason for their *own* good. If it is put into the wrong hands—the hands of less honest, or less wise, reasoners than Cleomenes and Horatio—enlightenment may still be counterproductive.

The Ignorant Many versus the Enlightened Few

Mandeville attempts to solve, or at least anticipates, this problem by claiming that the ignorant—he says nothing specifically about the dishonest—are not the audience for which he writes. He criticizes those who would educate the poor in charity schools because he thinks that enlightenment there would mean economic chaos: it may be diverting for those whom the poor call virtuous to know that virtue is a sham, but it would be a disincentive for the poor (who must labor for the virtuous) themselves to know it. Where "Ignorance" becomes "low Learning," Mandeville asserts in the charity-school essay, "Self-Love turns Knowledge into Cunning, and the more this last Qualification prevails in any Country the more the People will fix all their Cares, Concern and Application on the Time present, without regard of what is to come after them, or hardly ever thinking beyond the next Generation" (1:320). In order to show that *he* does not want to make learning "low" by disseminating it promiscuously, he concludes part 1 by publicly vindicating the inaccessibility of his style: "[I]f I had wrote with a Design to be understood by the meanest Capacities, I would not have chose the Subject there treated of; or if I had, I would have amplify'd and explained every Period, talked and distinguished magisterially, and never appeared without the Fescue in my Hand" (1:402). He would, in short, have written less like a philosopher and more like an orator. If widespread enlightenment is chaos, Mandeville insists that widespread ignorance is "a necessary Ingredient in the Mixture of Society" (1:249).

Rather than for the ignorant, Mandeville protests, the *Fable of the Bees* was designed "for the Entertainment of People of Knowledge and Education, when they have an idle Hour which they know not how to spend better." Ingeniously, he skirts the problem of enlightenment by restricting the knowledge that the *Fable* provides to the *already* enlightened few. Countering the charge, as Horatio recounts it in part 2, that the *Fable* "is wrote for the Encouragement of Vice, and to debauch the Nation" (2:103), he maintains instead that "It is a Book of severe and exalted Morality" (1:404–5). Most virtue is a sham, but the only ones who need know that fact are those who can practice real virtue as the *Fable* defines it: an absolute selflessness that is "contrary to the impulse of nature."[30] "I write not to many, nor seek for any Well-wishers, but among the few that can think abstractly, and have their Minds elevated above the Vulgar," Mandeville confirms. "If I have shewn the way to worldly Greatness, I have always without Hesitation preferr'd the Road that leads to Virtue" (1:231). If only the virtuous can be enlightened, then enlightenment will remain restricted, and not a problem.

Despite his protests to the contrary, however, the *Fable* has a leveling, even democratic effect that Mandeville's critics, at least, perfectly understood. Cleomenes demonstrates his creator's democratizing impulse when he commends self-interest for being the most common and therefore most reliable passion on which to base a social order. In contrast, a "Social System" like Shaftesbury's, which must be guided by an elite, is, Cleomenes implies, the strongest argument against it: "[T]he Advantage that is justly expected from his [Shaftesbury's] Writings can never be universally felt," he tells Horatio, "before the Publick Spirit, which he recommended, comes down to the meanest Tradesmen" (2:50–51). By shifting the ground of consensus in society from rational dialogue to dissimulative commerce (shifting it away, that is, from the previous dialogue writers in this study), Mandeville widens the scope of those responsible for it: society functions not because of the distinction of an enlightened few but because of the acquisitive desires—the vices—of many, including the ignorant. Like Addison and Steele's Mr. Spectator at the Royal Exchange, he makes material interest the basis of the social bond and, true to the logic of political economy, shows how commerce promotes "civilized intercourse . . . amongst persons with otherwise incommensurable habits and beliefs."[31]

But to widen the scope of society is not necessarily to widen the scope of the public sphere. Mandeville may delight in commerce, but there is no room in his philosophy for the critical public that in Habermas's version emerges simultaneously in bourgeois society with private, commercial capitalism. Private property and the limited protection from state intervention afforded by private societies may have freed individuals to mingle among themselves and create a "public," but the private realm is not *itself* the public. Whatever those private citizens exchange in the public sphere, that is, is not economic but philosophical (or speculative) and political; they talk about matters of common concern, not merely about how to get their own needs met. To compare the bargaining (or Mandeville's "bartering") that is the life of commercial exchange with the discourse that is the life of the public sphere, then, is both to narrow the rationality of the public sphere and to obliterate the public in it.[32] The "sphere" of commerce may be democratic—it may even be open in the sense of accessible, if not honest—but it is not critical. It cannot, by its very definition, be critical because the goal of both the trader and the politician is to keep those with whom they bargain in the dark about the real nature of their transaction.

Mandeville, then, inadvertently reinforces the divide between politics and philosophy that Hobbes opened when he separated public duty from private conscience, a divide that widened when Shaftesbury retreated from politics for a life of pure philosophy. Shaftesbury widened the gap because he found the negotiation of interests that politics involves to be distasteful; before him, Harrington and Neville widened it because they found the distance between their speculation and that negotiation necessary to be able to think about it more clearly. But Mandeville finds himself assenting to that division because he really does not want his philosophically informed sphere of conversation—his public sphere, as modeled by Cleomenes and Horatio—to contravene the dissimulative nature of commerce. In Mandeville's vision of the commonwealth, one can practice critical speculation in a diminutive public sphere or one can practice dissimulation in a dominant private sphere. The discrepancy between philosophical speculation and practical dissimulation is what I have been calling Mandeville's contradiction, but his reluctance to disabuse the public of its illusions is part of the oddly democratizing impulse—the real commonness—of his philosophy.[33] Mandeville may, as the philosophical author of the *Fable*, meddle in the governing of the commonwealth, but he does not grumble.

5

BERKELEY
Dialogue as Catechism

THERE IS a moment very near the beginning of George Berkeley's polemic against freethinking entitled *Alciphron, or the Minute Philosopher* (1732) when the title character, having just inveighed against the clergy for being motivated by "ambition, avarice, and revenge," temporarily departs the scene of conversation with his fellow freethinker Lysicles. Berkeley's spokesperson Euphranor, who remains on the scene, wants to refer Alciphron's outburst to a prior resentment, but Berkeley's other spokesperson, Crito, sees it as something more deliberate:

> I . . . have often observed those of his sect run into two faults of con-
> versation, declaiming and bantering, just as the tragic or the comic
> humour prevails. Sometimes they work themselves into high passions,
> and are frightened at spectres of their own raising. In those fits every
> country curate passes for an inquisitor. At other times they affect a sly
> facetious manner, making use of hints and allusions, expressing little,
> insinuating much, and upon the whole seeming to divert themselves
> with the subject and their adversaries. But, if you would know their
> opinions, you must make them speak out and keep close to the point.[1]

The "two faults of conversation" that Crito detects in Alciphron could, if one were extending Berkeley's polemic, be applied to the typical rhetorical strategies of his most notable freethinking opponents in *Alciphron*. The "tragic" humor of "declaiming" could be the strategy of Shaftesbury, who worked himself into "high passions" of enthusiasm to reach the truths of natural religion (and to defeat the "spectre" of religious orthodoxy). The "comic" humor of "bantering" could be the strategy of Mandeville, who insinuated that priests were among those who benefited from the artful management of human passion. If freethinkers like Shaftesbury and Mandeville, or Alciphron (who stands for Shaftesbury in Berkeley's dialogue) and Lysicles (who stands for Mandeville), have scored any points with their criticisms of the clergy, Berkeley implies, it is due to the perverse attractiveness of their conversational styles.

Somewhat later, after the two have returned and Lysicles has smugly asserted that freethinkers are the only human beings to be "above prejudice," Euphranor challenges him directly: "How doth it appear that you are the only unprejudiced part of mankind? May not a minute philosopher, as well as another man, be prejudiced in favour of the leaders of his sect? May not an atheistical education prejudice towards atheism? What should hinder a man's being prejudiced against religion, as well as for it?" (3:81). Rather than asserting his own lack of prejudice, Euphranor argues that no one, certainly not a freethinker but also not a religious apologist like himself or Crito, can be above it. Some sort of bias, possibly for religion but also possibly against it, is inevitable in any education.

Improper—and proper—conversation, the inevitability of prejudice, and the connection between the two are the subjects of this chapter. As Berkeley's freethinkers go on to explain, a large part of their claim to be "above prejudice" rests on their cultivation of polite, philosophical conversation. Such conversation supposedly delivers what Shaftesbury assumes of the participants in his disinterested, philosophical realm and what Mandeville, for all that he does to show it untenable, similarly aspires to[2]—enlightenment—which, as Kant famously defines it, is the ability "to use one's own understanding without the guidance of another." What inhibits that ability for Kant is precisely those "Dogmas and formulas" that keep humankind enchained in intellectual immaturity,[3] but for Berkeley it is impossible, and even undesirable, to be "above" prejudice. Indeed, it is prejudice, not enlightenment, that holds a political community together. In *Alciphron* Berkeley uses the dialogue form not to engage in disinterested philosophical speculation, as does Shaftesbury, nor to enlighten his readers to the artful management of skillful politicians (and priests), as does Mandeville, but to rehabilitate a preconscious respect for authority and tradition that can only be called prejudice. Berkeley aligns himself with the "vulgar" public *against* an elitist "enlightenment"—

and keeps his freethinking opponents "close to the point"—by practicing dialogue as catechism.

Freethinking and Polite Conversation

In Berkeley's polemical dialogue freethinkers are simply atheists (like the "sceptics and atheists" against whom he directed his earlier *Three Dialogues between Hylas and Philonous* [1713]), and some—namely, Mandeville—probably were. But most of those whom Berkeley lumped together as freethinkers—Shaftesbury, John Toland (author of *Christianity not Mysterious* [1696]), Anthony Collins (*Discourse on Free-thinking* [1713]), and Matthew Tindal (*Christianity as Old as the Creation, or the Gospel a Republication of the Religion of Nature* [1730])—were in fact deists, who questioned not religious truth per se but only the truth of religious revelation, the idea that God grants knowledge not otherwise discoverable by human reason. Such freethinking opinions, as Crito implied by criticizing their manners and now says outright, "are best learned from conversation with those who profess themselves of it" (3:32), and the freethinkers agree. Lysicles declares "the reign of pedantry" to be "over" because freethinking "philosophers . . . are of a very different kind from those awkward students who think to come at knowledge by poring on dead languages and old authors, or by sequestering themselves from the cares of the world to meditate in solitude and retirement" (3:47), and Alciphron, substituting a rougher verb for the "polishing" that Shaftesbury says occurs in polite company, adds: "Proper ideas or materials are only to be got by frequenting good company. I know several gentlemen who, since their appearance in the world, have spent as much time in rubbing off the rust and pedantry of a college education as they had done before in acquiring it" (3:48). The freethinkers draw the now familiar contrast between the "pedantry" of a college education and the politeness of conversing in clubs and coffeehouses and maintain that polite conversation is both a more efficacious and a more inviting way of learning than what Crito, sarcastically agreeing, calls the "dry academical way" (3:48).

It may be more inviting, but Berkeley has serious reservations about the efficacy of polite conversation. It is not, as Berkeley says directly of freethinking in the preface to *Hylas and Philonous*, a "close and methodical application of thought" but a "loose, rambling way" enjoyed "by certain libertines in thought, who can no more endure the restraints of *logic,* than those of *religion,* or *government"* (2:168). Freethinkers, that is, extend their desire for freedom or liberty in politics (and apparently morals) to reasoning itself, learning through conversation that is "without rule or design," Lysicles admits. As Euphranor replies to Lysicles, however, learning without "rule" is not learning at all: "I always thought that some order was necessary to attain any useful degree of knowledge; that haste and confusion begat a conceited ignorance; that to make our advances sure, they should be gradual, and those points first learned which might cast a light on what was to follow" (3:48). In short, Euphranor charges, polite conversation attracts persons—usually the young and restless followers of fashion—to free-thinking "who are too much employed to think for themselves" (3:297), a conclusion that exactly opposes it to Kant's definition of enlightenment.

But even if they reason poorly, freethinkers are nothing if not "conversable," and their easiness with the style of dialogue and conversation raises the question why Berkeley would choose to stage his polemic against them on their own ground. One reason, as I have maintained throughout this study, is that the dialogue has just as rich a history in disputation, especially religious disputation, as in "polite" philosophy, and the form allows Berkeley to damn Alciphron and Lysicles out of their own mouths while he shows two conversationalists—Crito and Euphranor—who both reason better and treat their opponents more fairly, if not more politely. But Berkeley cannot merely satirize his opponents either. As a comment from Crito indicates, the freethinkers' reasons may not be good, but they are influential: "Arguments, in themselves of small weight, have great effect when they are recommended by a mistaken interest, when they are pleaded for by passion, when they are countenanced by the humour of the age; and above all, with some sort of men, when they are against law, government, and established opinions" (3:96). Freethinkers may reason poorly, but they actually gain from being outside the mainstream of public opinion. If Berkeley refuses to "talk" with them, they become even more appealing. Imitating the manner of polite conversation, then, he actually uses the dialogue form to converse *less* freely, making his advances "sure" and logical by making them "gradual."[4]

The Problem of Diversity and the Force of Language

If polite conversation and freethinking go hand in hand, it is because what conversation—and dialogue—always circulates is opinion, of all ideological shapes and sizes. "[B]eing able to embrace in one comprehensive view the several parts and ages of the world," explains Alciphron, freethinkers "have observed a wonderful variety of customs and rites, of institutions religious and civil, of notions and opinions very unlike and even contrary one to another—a certain sign they cannot all be true" (3:39). Hobbes, who took his radical empiricism to similar extremes, argued that the sight of such "discord" should lead one to submit to a truth defined by an absolute, if arbitrary, authority, but Alciphron, like all "thinking men," concludes from it "that all religions are alike false and fabulous" (3:41). If one opinion succeeds another, freethinkers "[know] how to suit [themselves] to occasions, and make the best of every event" (3:101), and they figure, as does Mandeville—indeed, as Mandevillians—that this natural circulation of opinions is good for the commonwealth anyway.

For Berkeley, however, this casual view of diversity, especially in religion, is anathema. In 1712, reviving the controversial doctrine of "passive obedience" to the sovereign authority,[5] Berkeley warns in Hobbesian fashion that unless "several independent powers [are] combined together, under the direction (if I may so speak) of one and the same will: I mean the law of society," there is "no politeness, no order, no peace, among men, but the world is one great heap of misery and confusion" (6:25). Also like Hobbes, and like his more immediate predecessor Locke, Berkeley had tried to solve the "problem" of ideological diversity at the source, with words. In *An Essay Concerning Human Understanding* Locke went as far as to say that "The knowing precisely what our Words stand for, would . . . quickly end" most "dispute[s]" and that "*Men* who abstract their Thoughts, and do well examine the *Ideas* of their own Minds, *cannot much differ in thinking*" (180). Early in his career Berkeley seemed to agree, recalling in his notebooks (entitled by his editor A. A. Luce the *Philosophical Commentaries*) that time "in History," presumably before the revolution of 1688, when "fears & jealousies, Privileges of Parliament, Malignant Party & such like expressions of too unlimited & doubtfull a meaning were words of much sway" and how even now "the Words Church,

Whig, Tory etc. contribute very much to Faction and Dispute" (1:75).
In the introduction to *A Treatise concerning the Principles of Human
Knowledge* (1710), Berkeley thus vows, like Locke, to separate the
ideas that he considers from "all that dress and encumbrance of
words which so much contribute to blind the judgment and divide
the attention" (2:40).

But Locke himself, Berkeley realizes even from the time of the
Principles, was confused by the ambiguity of language to assert the
existence of so-called abstract ideas. In the *Principles* and elsewhere,
Berkeley explains that we are led to believe that such ideas actually
exist—ideas signified by words like "extension," "motion," "humanity
or human nature," or, infamously for Berkeley, "matter"—by our ability
to generalize about the qualities that a number of concrete particulars
have in common (2:28, 44).[6] Tending to think, like Locke, that the
ability to generalize about a quality means that it actually exists, as a
"thing" on its own, we formulate abstract ideas to account for those
things. But abstract ideas, as Berkeley says over and over again in his
writings, do not exist: we cannot perceive "matter" in the abstract, but
only concrete particular things with concrete particular qualities.
This does not mean, however, that abstract *language* does not have its
uses. In the *Principles,* after denying "the doctrine of abstract ideas,"
he continues:

> Besides, the communicating of ideas marked by words is not the chief
> and only end of language, as is commonly supposed. There are other
> ends, as the raising of some passion, the exciting to, or deterring from
> an action, the putting the mind in some particular disposition; to
> which the former is in many cases barely subservient, and sometimes
> entirely omitted, when these can be obtained without it, as I think
> doth not infrequently happen in the familiar use of language. . . . May
> we not, for example, be affected with the promise of a *good thing,*
> though we have not an idea of what it is? (2:37)

A "good thing" is surely both vague and abstract, but that does not
diminish its capacity to move us emotionally. Its promise affects us even
"though we have not an idea of what it is." In *Alciphron,* Euphranor
reiterates that words have "another use . . . besides that of marking
and suggesting distinct ideas, to wit, the influencing our conduct and
actions, which may be done either by forming rules for us to act by, or

by raising certain passions, dispositions, and emotions in our minds" (3:292). Such influencing can be negative as well as positive. After all, Euphranor does not call Alciphron and Lysicles "minute philosophers" because it is a more precise (or less abstract) appellation than *freethinkers* (3:46); taking the term from Cicero, "who understood the force of language,"[7] he calls them that because it is a more disagreeable one. The "force" of language that Cicero understood is not its capacity to confuse us with abstractions or to use language more carefully to avoid such confusion. The real force of language is its capacity to convey emotive meaning.[8]

On closer inspection, the speaker mouthing Lockean sentiments in *Alciphron* is the freethinker Alciphron, not Crito or Euphranor. Like Locke's freethinking disciples Toland and Collins, he applies to religious mysteries what David Berman calls Locke's "extreme cognitivist view on meaning, according to which a word can have meaning only if it stands for, or communicates, an idea."[9] Alciphron insists that the only use of words "is to raise those ideas in the hearer which are in the mind of the speaker" and that a word like *grace*—"the main point in the Christian dispensation"—which has no "clear and distinct idea" annexed to it, is therefore "nothing . . . but an empty name" (3:287–90). Appropriating Locke's dictum about "the shortest way to end disputes" for a freethinking end, he asserts that "it is an allowed method to expose any doctrine," such as the Trinity or the dispensation of grace, by "stripping them [*sic*] of the words, and examining what ideas are underneath, or whether any ideas at all" (3:289).

But Berkeley is now unsure that disputes about religion or any other public matter can be absolutely avoided, because human beings are not the dispassionate reasoners that Alciphron wants them to be, but will be stirred by even "empty" language if it conveys emotional force. A person "may believe the doctrine of the Trinity," Euphranor replies, if "this doctrine . . . produc[es] therein love, hope, gratitude, and obedience, and thereby becomes a lively operative principle, influencing his life and actions" (3:297), and "grace may, for ought you know, be an object of our faith, and influence our life and actions, as a principle destructive of evil habits and productive of good ones, although we cannot attain a distinct idea of it" (3:296). Berkeley's dialogue is itself a battle over the uses of passionate—or, better, emotive—language. His freethinkers use words to move us, however confusedly, toward the negative "ends" of atheism and skepticism; Berkeley hopes to move us toward the "good things" of God and faith. "[A]fter all," replies Crito to the freethinkers' usual position that the real fact of religious diversity should encourage the "unprejudiced" philosopher to be skeptical about all belief,

> if men are puzzled, wrangle, talk nonsense, and quarrel about religion, so they do about law, physic, politics, and everything else of moment. . . . And yet this doth not hinder but there may be many excellent rules, and just notions, and useful truths, in all those professions. In all disputes human passions too often mix themselves in proportion as the subject is conceived to be more or less important. (3:194.

To the Berkeley of *Alciphron*, diversity *and* disagreement are inevitable, and not just because of the language—the useless abstractions—that people use. They are inevitable because matters of moment come up for discussion in the public sphere, and defending such matters— here, the just notions and useful truths of religion—takes the real and whole force of language, the language of emotive meaning.

Utility as the Test of Truth

In *Alciphron* Berkeley is almost reluctant to make his language, or the language of his apologists, signify distinct ideas, preferring them to focus their arguments on the good things that religion promises and the feelings that it evokes. Early in the dialogue, for example, in reply to Alciphron's claim that he can disprove, with logic alone, the truth of religion, Euphranor says:

> O Alciphron! I do not doubt your faculty of proving. But, before I put you to the trouble of any farther proofs, I should be glad to know whether the notions of your minute philosophy are worth proving. I mean, whether they are of use and service to mankind.
> ALCIPHRON. . . . [T]ruth is truth, whether useful or not, and must not be measured by the convenience of this or that man, or party of men.
> EUPHRANOR. But is not the general good of mankind to be regarded as a rule or measure of moral truths, of all such truths as direct or influence the moral actions of men?
> ALCIPHRON. That point is not clear to me. I know, indeed, that legislators, and divines, and politicians have always alleged that it is

necessary to the well-being of mankind that they should be kept in awe by the slavish notions of religion and morality. But, granting all this, how will it prove these notions to be true? Convenience is one thing, and truth is another. (3:60)

By demanding that Alciphron's freethinking notions be "*worth* proving," Euphranor already injects emotive meaning into Alciphron's strictly denotative way of thinking about, and disproving, the "truth" of religion. If utility is the "rule or measure" of such truth, a philosopher must take the feelings as well as the ideas of human beings into account to prove (or to disprove) it.

Proving the utility of religion, Crito proceeds to explain, is all that he need do to prove its truth. "[T]hat one great mark of the truth of Christianity is," he says, "its tendency to do good, . . . moral or practical truths being ever connected with universal benefit" (3:178). As Crito summarizes in *Alciphron*'s fifth dialogue, devoted, according to Berkeley's subtitle, to "The Utility of Christianity," "whatever evil is in us, our principles certainly lead to good; and, whatever good there may be in you, it is most certain your principles lead to evil" (3:190). Against the principle that, as he is saying it, nearly causes Alciphron to choke on his own egotism—"The happiness of other men, making no part of mine, is not with respect to me a good"—Berkeley has Euphranor generously reply that "man ought . . . to consider himself . . . as the part of a whole" and that "the general happiness of mankind" is a "greater good than the private happiness of one man, or of some certain men" (3:62–63, 61).[10]

The nature of Berkeley's utilitarianism is both less and more extreme than one would suppose, given his position as a defender of the faith. On the one hand, Berkeley never suggests, as do the more secular philosophers in this study, that truth itself is the consensual product of various interests. Berkeley's religious truth is revealed by God, not arrived at by committee or in conference. On the other hand, and in a remarkable move for an orthodox eighteenth-century clergyman, Berkeley does refer to the reason, as well as the health and well-being, of the greatest number of people to determine what is true. In a devastating critique of Shaftesbury's nominally common *sensus communis,* Berkeley even claims that "virtue," as well as reason, is the province of the vast middle class rather than of the select aristocratic class. Naming him "Cratylus," Crito asserts that Shaftesbury, "having talked himself, or imagined that he had talked himself, into a stoical enthusiasm about the beauty of virtue, did, under the pretence of making men *heroically* virtuous, endeavour to destroy the means of making them *reasonably and humanly* so" (3:132, emphasis added). Berkeley thus dismisses Shaftesbury's attempt to unite (or replace) a differently "reasonable" Christian sense of virtue with his own preferred, classical one. Heroic, stoical virtue may be the province of Shaftesbury's aristocratic elite, but "humane" virtue and common sense belong to those whom Euphranor names the "plain untutored" middle (3:315).

In this work of Christian apologetics Berkeley's utilitarianism and his sense of the common are, ultimately, the same, for it is usually the common people who are most in need of religion's useful truths. The exchange at the end of the third dialogue is typical. In reply to Alciphron's usual contention that truth is not measured by "convenience" or "consequences," Euphranor directs a series of rhetorical questions: "What! Would you undeceive a child that was taking physic? Would you officiously set an enemy right that was making a wrong attack? Would you help an enraged man to his sword?" Nearly defenseless, Alciphron makes an uncommon (for him) appeal to "common sense," agreeing that "In such cases" it "directs one how to behave," that is, to leave well enough alone. Euphranor, however, will not allow his opponent's uncommon appeal to sneak by unremarked: with an air of triumph, he concludes that Alciphron has conceded that "Common sense . . . must be consulted whether a truth be salutary or hurtful, fit to be declared or concealed." Alciphron can stomach the conclusion but not the corollary:

> ALCIPHRON. How? You would have me conceal and stifle the truth, and keep it to myself? Is this what you aim at?
> EUPHRANOR. I only make a plain inference from what you grant. As for myself, I do not believe your opinions true. And, although you do, you should not therefore, if you would appear consistent with yourself, think it necessary or wise to publish hurtful truths. What service can it do mankind to lessen the motives to virtue, or what damage to increase them? (3:140)

It actually *is* better, Euphranor acknowledges, to keep certain truths concealed. It will not do to wonder what those "hurtful truths" are; to publish them is already to reveal them. We can infer, however, whom they are being concealed from: those for whom they would be most hurtful, the common people.

It is possible to accuse Berkeley of manufacturing a logical tautology here—"Useful abstract ideas lead to Christian behavior; Christian behavior . . . generates useful abstract ideas" (Prince, 128)—that avoids the necessity of demonstrating the truth of religion for the presumably easier task of showing its utility. But given that "moral or practical truths" are "ever [or always] connected with universal benefit," logic, or demonstration, is not really the issue. We cannot abstract the principles for governing our lives from the lives, even the bodies, that they are to govern, and even if we could, demonstrating the truth of those principles in some theoretical proof would be useless to the bulk of the persons who must live by them. From the time of the *Philosophical Commentaries,* Berkeley "Question'd whether we are capable of arriving at Demonstration about . . . Moral Actions" (1:82), and as his career progressed he grew even less confident about that possibility.[11] For example, when Alciphron, noting the historical obscurity of Christianity, asks how it is "possible, at this remote distance, to arrive at any knowledge, or frame any demonstration about it," Crito answers,

> Knowledge, I grant, in a strict sense, cannot be had without evidence or demonstration: but probable arguments are a sufficient ground of faith. Who ever supposed that scientifical proofs are necessary to make a Christian? Faith alone is required; and provided that, in the main and upon the whole, men are persuaded this saving faith may consist with some degrees of obscurity, scruple, and error. (3:280)

For Berkeley, truth is absolute, but we can only believe on faith. And faith itself can only be probably, not absolutely, true. "Faith," summarizes Crito by way of definition, "is not an indolent perception, but an operative persuasion of mind, which ever worketh some suitable action, disposition, or emotion in those who have it" (3:301).

This is not to say that faith is irrational, or unreasonable; on the contrary, the good things that religion promises are among the reasons for believing in it. Thus, when Lysicles tires of Crito's constant criticism of his freethinking tenets and complains, "I can never hope, Crito, to make you think my schemes reasonable. We reason each other right upon his own principles, and shall never agree till we quit our principles, which cannot be done by reasoning" (3:212), what he says is both correct and, as usual, irrelevant.[12] One's primary aspiration should not be to make one's schemes reasonable, in the sense of demonstrating them, but to make them probable or persuasive, and making one's schemes persuasive means, at the least, showing how the average person has an interest in believing them. In the *Philosophical Commentaries,* jotting down notes for a projected treatise on ethics, Berkeley asserts, "I'd never blame a man for acting upon Interest. he's a fool that acts on any other Principle. the not understanding these things has been of ill consequence in Morality" (1:68). In *Alciphron,* defending a religious tradition that would stabilize the commonwealth as it saves individual souls, Euphranor argues that it is our self-interested "hope of reward and fear of punishment" that "cast the balance of pleasant and profitable on the side of virtue, and thereby very much conduce to the benefit of human society" (3:119). Recognizing that our true interests lie in the next world, in pursuing its hope of reward and avoiding its threat of punishment, "very much" helps us in this one, making us fitter for one another and for the greater community. "[C]an there be a stronger motive to virtue," Euphranor concludes, "than the shewing that . . . it is every man's true interest?" (3:120). The "element of rational calculation" that Berkeley, in contrast to Shaftesbury, puts back into ethics and politics makes it all the more persuasive, at least for the plain, untutored middle, whom he wants to persuade.[13]

The "Vulgar" Dissemination of Freethinking

By speaking up for common sense in religion—the sort of common sense that rationally calculates what a believer can get out of it— Berkeley's spokespersons in *Alciphron* could say of themselves what Philonous declares at the end of Berkeley's better-known dialogue: "I do not pretend to be a setter-up of *new notions.* My endeavors tend only to unite and place in a clearer light that truth, which was before shared between the vulgar and the philosophers" (2:262). If Berkeley's critics tend to doubt that Philonous is ultimately so trusting of common sense in epistemology as he says he is—the idea that matter (Locke's "substance") does not exist independently of its being perceived is a most uncommonsensical one[14]—there can be no doubt that Crito and Euphranor are. With respect to religion and all the practical, mundane fields associated with it (i.e., ethics and politics), the lower class that eighteenth-century literati designated as the "vulgar" do have the right ideas. This is why when Alciphron claims that the "tenets of our philosophy have this in common with many other truths in metaphysics, geometry, astronomy, and natural philosophy, that vulgar ears cannot bear them," Euphranor thankfully agrees (3:53–54). The common sense of the vulgar immediately dismisses such esoteric notions as outrageous and absurd.

But if he trusts the sense of the vulgar in religion, why is Berkeley so distrustful that they will be able to resist the progress of freethinking notions among them? Crito asks Lysicles why he needs "professors and encouragement" when freethinking "needs no teaching," and claims that "An acquaintance of mine has a most ingenious footman that can neither write nor read, who learned your whole system in half an hour" (3:97). When Berkeley has Lysicles boast that "These [freethinking] discoveries are published by our philosophers, sometimes in just volumes, but often in pamphlets and loose papers for their readier conveyance through the kingdom" (3:52), the same adjective that he used to describe the sloppy thinking of the freethinkers now describes the promiscuous reception of their notions among the common people: for a clergyman concerned with public morals, freethinking is too "loose."

The answer seems to lie in a favorite maxim of Berkeley's, first voiced in the *Principles:* "[W]e ought to *think with the learned, and speak with the vulgar*" (2:62).[15] In the *Principles,* the maxim signals Berkeley's intention, consistent with his emotive-language position, to retain common phrases when "they excite in us proper sentiments, or dispositions to act in such a manner as is necessary for our well-being, how false soever they may be, if taken in a strict and speculative sense." In that overhauling of "received opinions" in epistemology (2:63),[16] as well as in the dialogue that could be considered its "vulgar" sequel, *Hylas and Philonous,* Berkeley tends to tolerate language that is false in a "strictly speculative sense" (e.g., "sensible things do really exist") in order to get to truer ideas (sensible things do exist, but only in the mind of God [2:212]). In *Alciphron,* however, which, as it treats religion rather than epistemology, deals with more reliable opinions, the weight of the maxim is less on thinking, or ideas, than on speaking. There Berkeley's reason for trusting the language of ordinary believers is not to think his way through to newer, truer opinions but to teach, through his own proper speaking, the received, conventional ones.

As they do with so much else that he advises, freethinkers invert Berkeley's maxim.[17] What speaking they do with the vulgar is a speaking *at* them: Crito lumps freethinkers in with orators—those who specialize in "speaking at"—when he complains that it is "needless to establish professors for the minute philosophy in either university while there are so many spontaneous lecturers in every corner of the streets" (3:101). The only class whom freethinkers speak *with* is themselves, in polite conversation. Instead of speaking with the vulgar, they attempt to *think* with them, just as they think with one another in their clubs and coffeehouses, and this is why, even though freethinking notions "*sound* strange and odd among the vulgar" (3:54, emphasis added), the vulgar are susceptible to being corrupted by them. Vulgar speaking may be trustworthy, but not vulgar thinking.

By criticizing the too easy dissemination of freethinking, Berkeley is not necessarily, or not primarily, recommending the concealment of uncomfortable (or inutile) truths. He realizes that religion, as a persuasion rather than perception of the mind, must be openly argued for, among the vulgar as among any other class. But truly speaking with the vulgar requires more attention to conversational decorum than freethinkers are willing to pay. It does not mean to disrespect their intelligence, by speaking at them, or to respect it too much, by attempting to think with them as one would with the learned. Truly speaking with the vulgar means to "translate," as Peter Walmsley puts it, the freethinkers' "self-indulgent talk . . . into the vulgar and specific," reasserting "the integrity of public usage over the esoteric meanings of the club."[18] But it also means to attend to the formal aspects of conversation, delivering those simple, "vulgar" words through the methodical, sometimes resolutely slow process that I will refer to as "catechism."

Dialogue as Catechism

When Crito faults the "declaiming" and "bantering" of freethinkers early in Berkeley's dialogue, he declares his own (and Euphranor's) intention to keep Alciphron and Lysicles "close to the point." For Berkeley, such close reasoning can best be conducted in an incremental practice of question and answer that he models on the Socratic method of *elenchus*. Elenchus begins in *Alciphron* when Euphranor examines Alciphron about his thesis that "For a thing to be natural . . . it must be universally in all men" (3:55). Through a series of particular questions, Euphranor pokes a hole in Alciphron's thesis by emphasizing the natural particularity of languages:

> EUPHRANOR. Answer me, Alciphron, do not men in all times and places, when they arrive at a certain age, express their thoughts by speech?
> ALCIPHRON. They do.
> EUPHRANOR. Should it not seem, then, that language is natural?
> ALCIPHRON. It should.
> EUPHRANOR. And yet there is a great variety of languages?
> ALCIPHRON. I acknowledge there is.
> EUPHRANOR. From all this will it not follow a thing may be natural and yet admit of variety?
> ALCIPHRON. I grant it will. (3:57)

Rather than propounding his own theory or providing counterevidence, Euphranor closely examines that of his opponent. And although he would not do so in a more speculative conversation, Euphranor so directs his questions that Alciphron cannot elaborate but can only assent to—or in rare and ultimately reversible instances, dissent from—them. The eventual purpose of Berkeley's elenchus is to force the freethinkers against whom it is directed to contradict their original theses. The overall effect is progressive and cumulative, the discussants never moving to the next step in the argument until they have well understood the preceding one.[19] "Throughout this whole inquiry," asks Euphranor after a later instance of elenctic reasoning, "have we not considered every step with care, and made not the least advance without clear evidence? You and I examined and assented singly to each foregoing proposition: what shall we do then with the conclusion?" (3:147).

Elenchus, however, can only force the respondent into a contradiction; it cannot teach revealed truths.[20] For that reason, a better—more inclusive—parallel for Berkeley's question-and-answer method in *Alciphron* is religious catechism.[21] Many of the more didactic, and popular, dialogues of the late seventeenth and early eighteenth centuries, like Defoe's *Family Instructor* (1715), do in fact resemble a type of catechism: while they leave as little room for creative reply as elenchus, they begin with positive assertions—statements of belief—rather than end in doubt and confusion.[22] *Alciphron* is not usually as strict as that because Berkeley has little hope of converting the freethinkers whom he would instruct. Unlike the untutored child usually instructed by religious catechism, they have already gone wrong, and unlike the usual catechumen, they are unwilling to be set right again. Like Telesilla, the freethinking woman "who was good for nothing so long as she believed her catechism," they "now [shine] in all public places" (3:70), and they are not likely to give up that acclaim. When I call Berkeley's dialogue a "catechism," then, it is not because it aims to convert, or even to instruct, the freethinkers but because it demonstrates the need, through their obstinacy if nothing else, for the proper instruction of those less hardened in the faith.

Berkeley's catechismal dialogue includes more than elenchus, too, because the freethinkers do not appreciate being endlessly contradicted. Alciphron's complaint before he and Lysicles leave the dialogue for good is final, but typical: "It is now time to set out on our journey: there is, therefore, no room for a long string of question and answer" (3:313). When, tiring of elenchus *before* they leave for good, the freethinkers attempt to change the subject or the method of inquiry, they unwittingly open the real battleground of *Alciphron* and allow Berkeley to exhibit another aspect of catechism. For then both freethinkers—no longer answering questions—and Berkeley's spokespersons—no longer asking them—are forced to provide, and to describe in a fashion not permitted by the strict progression of elenchus, their competing visions of the good, their different ends. Euphranor, who calls these lengthier descriptions his "summary way," apologizes for being in them "more *dogmatical* than became me" but also asks to be "excuse[d]" by what the freethinkers "occasioned, by declining a joint and leisurely examination of the truth" (3:317, emphasis added). Somewhat partially, what Euphranor calls a "joint and leisurely examination of the truth" is elenctic reasoning; what he offers in contrast, and excuses as "dogmatic," is dialogue, along with catechism, as teaching. In addition to reasoning via elenchus, Berkeley's catechists teach the good things that religion promises.

Although elenchus is certainly a more demanding form of reasoning than polite conversation, teaching as Berkeley conceives it is not as rigorous as the usual contrast with polite conversation might suggest. It is Alciphron, not either of Berkeley's spokespersons, who demands that religion be taught, or demonstrated, as rigorously as a science if it is to command assent. Elaborating on his points that the only use of words "is to raise those ideas in the hearer which are in the mind of the speaker" (Locke's extreme cognitivist view on meaning) and that a word like *grace,* which has no "clear and distinct idea" annexed to it, is therefore meaningless, Alciphron now triumphantly concludes that "there can be no assent where there are no ideas: and where there is no assent there can be no faith" (3:291). Taking Berkeley's hint in the *Principles* that language has an emotive as well as a denotative function, however, Euphranor replies,

> There is, if I mistake not, a practical faith, or assent, which sheweth itself in the will and actions of a man, although his understanding may not be furnished with those abstract, precise, distinct ideas, which, whatever a philosopher may pretend, are acknowledged to be above the talents of common men. . . . What should hinder, therefore, but that doctrines related to heavenly mysteries might be taught, in this saving sense, to vulgar minds, which you may well think incapable of all teaching and faith, in the sense you suppose? (3:299–300)

Euphranor as much as admits that "vulgar minds" are not suited to the rigors of scientific demonstration but counters that "teaching and faith," which use language that moves the "will and actions of a man" more than his mind, are so suited. Again, all that a catechist need do is to show that religion *may* be true (or is probable); he or she does not have to demonstrate that it *is* true (or certain). The good things that religion promises, like the dispensation of grace, will do the rest.

The Rehabilitation of Prejudice

It is characteristic of the practice that we commonly designate as catechism to assume that human beings come to it like children—and often *as* children—with already formed, if inadequate, notions of a God and a will to believe. Even freethinkers grant as much: as Alciphron concedes, "the confused notion of a Deity, or some invisible power," is "of all prejudices the most unconquerable" (3:143). If Berkeley often, as Robert E. Sullivan observes, "seem[s] to be refuting arguments which none of his contemporaries had ever published,"[23] he at least represents the freethinkers' attack on "prejudice" accurately. Toland, for one, consistently lumps together "prejudice," "superstition," and "mystery" as a trio of "vulgar errors" inhibiting the progress of reason in human affairs.[24] The vulgar, however, are not responsible for them. Prejudices, Toland says in *Reasons for Naturalizing the Jews* (1714), actually originate not from the vulgar but from the "Priests" and "Politicians" who seek to control them, and in *Christianity not Mysterious* he proclaims that mysteries in religion were "calculated" by those in power "to stop the Mouths of such as demand a Reason where none can be given, and to keep as many in Ignorance as Interest shall think convenient."[25] In Kantian terms, freethinkers would describe prejudice as "a leash to control the great unthinking mass" (Kant, 54–55). It embodies the *un*examined understanding of someone else, of authority and tradition, and is invariably wrong.

In Berkeley's dialogue the freethinkers attribute the pervasiveness of prejudice to the hegemony of Christian belief, and especially Christian education, in early-eighteenth-century society. The Shaftesburean Alciphron complains that "the main points of Christian belief have been infused so early, and inculcated so often, by nurses, pedagogues, and priests, that, be the proofs ever so plain, it is a hard matter to convince a mind, thus tinctured and stained, by arguing against revealed religion from its internal characters" (3:258). He even admits "that I, like the rest of the world, was once upon a time catechised and tutored into the belief of a God or Spirit" (3:144). Berkeley's spokespersons, however, propose a more fundamental reason for the pervasiveness of prejudice. "[I]s it not possible," Euphranor asks after Alciphron criticizes the banality of Scriptural accounts of divine revelation, that "some men may shew as much prejudice and narrowness in rejecting all such accounts as others might easiness and credulity in admitting them?" (3:240). Prejudice, as Berkeley's spokespersons redescribe it, is not only the presence of religious (or any other) belief but also the absence of it, or at least the sort of active disbelief that prevents skeptics from listening to arguments that might show their opinions to be wrong. "Atheism, and a wrong notion of Christianity, as of something hurtful to mankind," maintains Crito, "are great prejudices, the removal of which may dispose a man to argue with candour, and submit to reasonable proof" (3:220). Freethinkers, in short, are just as "prejudiced" as believers, and Crito's suggestion that prejudices can be "removed,"

while technically true, is more difficult than this, an ironic accommo-
dation to the language of his opponents, implies.

We know just how difficult it is from the definition of prejudice
that Berkeley provides in a later essay that "concludes his campaign
against the free-thinkers,"[26] *A Discourse Addressed to Magistrates and Men
in Authority* (1738):

> Prejudices are notions or opinions which the mind entertains without
> knowing the grounds and reasons of them, and which are assented to
> without examination. The first notions which take possession of the
> minds of men, with regard to duties social, moral, and civil, may there-
> fore be justly styled prejudices. The mind of a young creature cannot
> remain empty; if you do not put into it that which is good, it will be
> sure to receive that which is bad.
>
> Do what you can, there will still be a bias from education; and if
> so, is it not better this bias should lie toward things laudable and use-
> ful to society? (6:203–4)

That a young mind is unable to "remain empty" means that no mind
is ever a tabula rasa; one can only "suppose [the] mind white paper"
as a thought experiment, as Euphranor proposes it to Alciphron to ask
what "you would write thereon" (3:321). A mind will always "entertain" opinions before it knows the "reasons of them"; before, indeed,
it knows how to "reason" at all. A good "judge," as Crito anticipates
this argument in *Alciphron*, will thus "check that disposition of his
mind to conclude all those notions groundless prejudices, with which
it was imbued before it knew the reason of them" (3:283). All notions
"imbued" before the age of reason, as Berkeley signals by the adjective
"groundless," are prejudices, groundless or no. There is no absolute
"ground" of opinion and no—to extend, with Alciphron, the metaphor
up rather than down—"sublime soul, who can raise himself above
popular opinions" and stand "above the reach of prejudice" (3:220–21).
The issue is not who is unprejudiced but whose prejudices—believers'
or freethinkers'—are better for the commonwealth. A good judge
will weigh all notions—whether new- or old-fashioned—and conclude
that they have a "ground" if they are "laudable and useful to society,"
if they have utility.

Berkeley is not saying that all prejudices are justified. In *Alciphron*
the freethinkers are prejudiced against religion, and in *Hylas and*

Philonous Hylas is prejudiced against Philonous's immaterial way of viewing the world.[27] But what makes a prejudice false is not the lack of some abstract, speculative truth content but its ill effects on the general good. Thus, when Lysicles brags that freethinkers have "freed the minds of our fellow-subjects" of "many prejudices, errors, perplexities, and contradictions," specifically here the "prejudice" against suicide, Crito reacts in horror:

> I say, with respect to these great advantages of destroying men and notions, that I question whether the public gains as much by the latter as it loseth by the former. For my own part, I had rather my wife and children all believed what they had no notion of, and daily pronounced words without a meaning, than that any one of them should cut his throat, or leap out of a window. Errors and nonsense, as such, are of small concern in the eye of the public, which considereth not the metaphysical truth of notions, so much as the tendency they have to produce good or evil. Truth itself is valued by the public, as it hath an influence, and is felt in the course of life. (3:105–6)

This does not, at first glance, seem like the sentiment of a philosopher who trusts the common sense of the populace, in morals or any other matter. It does not turn wives and children into a synecdoche of the public as much as it turns the public into wives and children, whom Berkeley conceives as entirely dependent on paternal reason. At the same time, Berkeley's vulgar public is usually right, or at least has the right to be wrong, and the thinking person should accept what he calls "the authority of the public" (3:159) for the sake of the general good. Accepting their prejudices is part of "speaking with" the vulgar. Thus, even though a thinking person—the kind who "knows the reason" for the public's prejudices—may judge them to be "metaphysically" wrong, or groundless, it is better for the public to believe them. Crito is quick to add that he is not implying that freethinking notions are true (3:106) or that a notion could be "practically wrong and speculatively right" (3:74), but his defense of wrong but useful prejudices, like the general turn from truth to utility from which it derives, does more than open the possibility that a notion could be practically right and speculatively wrong: it essentially concedes it. Berkeley buries such notions under the weight of so much utility, however, that it makes it difficult to imagine, cognitively, *where* they go wrong.

Berkeley's rehabilitation of prejudice in *Alciphron* and the *Discourse to Magistrates* makes him one of the few philosophers of the Enlightenment period to escape what Hans-Georg Gadamer, performing a similar rehabilitation in his hermeneutical masterwork, *Truth and Method,* calls its "fundamental prejudice," "the prejudice against prejudice itself."[28] Strictly speaking, says Gadamer, a "prejudice" is simply "a judgment that is rendered before all the elements that determine a situation have been finally examined," and we are always "judging" a situation at the same time that we are "examining" it (270). We cannot, in Joel Weinsheimer's words, "present ourselves as a blank slate ready to be inscribed" with the meaning of a text.[29] More important, we would not *want* to do away with all prejudices even if we could, because prejudice, says Gadamer, can have "either a positive or a negative value" (270). False, or negative, prejudices will adversely affect subsequent interpretations, but some prejudices may be confirmed in the course of fully examining a situation, the prejudices that turn out to be true. For Gadamer, these "legitimate" or "just" prejudices constitute what is right about authority and tradition,[30] and the Enlightenment's prejudice against prejudice, tending "to accept no authority and to decide everything before the judgment seat of reason," "denies tradition its power" (272, 270). Berkeley's subject is religious belief, not textual interpretation, but his spokespersons in *Alciphron* similarly dispute the project that all the figures in this study, even the cynic Mandeville, have been engaged in: the fundamental Enlightenment project, supported by the freethinkers Alciphron and Lysicles, of gaining an unprejudiced, disinterested perspective on the pursuit of knowledge. They deny that Alciphron's claim to have a soul above the reach of prejudice is either possible or desirable.

Indeed, to be *for* prejudice, at least when a prejudice is true, is to be *against* enlightenment itself, or at least against too much of it. Heavily influenced by Locke and eager to make a name for himself as a philosopher, the young Berkeley of the *Philosophical Commentaries* (written between 1707 and 1708, when he was twenty-two and twenty-three years old) boasted like Alciphron of being above the reach of prejudice: "I am young, I am an upstart, I am a pretender, I am vain, very well. . . . But . . . I act not out of prejudice & prepossession. I do not adhere to any opinion because it is an old one, a receiv'd one, a fashionable one, or one that I have spent much time in the study and cultivation of" (1:58). The largely negative reaction to his immaterialism indicates that Berkeley was not afraid to disturb received opinions.[31] As his career progressed, however, and as he shifted his attention from epistemology to religion, where received opinions were more reliable, Berkeley grew suspicious of the practice and the promise of enlightenment, of "publishing hurtful truths."[32] If there is enlightenment to be had, it comes (as Crito says) from an "eternal source, the Father of Lights," not philosophy, and yet even individuals who defer to authority and tradition can only see that light through a glass darkly because, "with respect to us, it is variously weakened and obscured, by passing through a long distance or gross medium, where it is intercepted, distorted, or tinctured, by the prejudices and passions of men." Rather than lamenting this fact, however, Berkeley is confident that "he that will use his eyes may *see enough* for the purposes either of nature or grace" (3:280–81, emphasis added). "Seeing enough," not absolute enlightenment, is all that human beings need to be saved.[33] For the sake of a well-ordered commonwealth (as Euphranor acknowledged), it *is* better to keep certain truths concealed.

The Purpose of Dialogue

If to be for prejudice is to be against enlightenment, then to be against enlightenment is to be against dialogue as the Enlightenment idealizes it: as a disinterested pursuit of speculative truth. The closest thing to speculative conversation in *Alciphron* is the lengthier descriptions, or "conferences," that alternate with the periods of elenctic reasoning, but even in conference Berkeley's discussants are driven to offer their competing visions of the good and demand a practical benefit from speculation that would sound discordant in Shaftesbury's polite, disinterested conversation. Berkeley's opinion of the Enlightenment ideal can be gleaned from Euphranor's derisive comments on Shaftesbury's essay *Soliloquy,* in which—it is to be remembered—Shaftesbury proposes to rid himself of interest through a philosophical regimen that is a kind of dialogue with the self. "You must know," enthuses Alciphron of Shaftesbury, that "this great man hath (to use his own words) revealed a *grand arcanum* to the world, having instructed mankind in what he calls *mirror-writing, self-discoursing practice,* and *author practice* . . . [H]e hath found out that a man may argue with himself; and not only with himself, but also with notions, sentiments, and vices." But when Alciphron attempts to demonstrate his enthusiasm for his hero by reading a passage from *Soliloquy*, a passage that Berkeley parodies by printing it verbatim as blank verse, Euphranor listens only long enough to get a sense of the overabundant style and then exclaims, "What! . . . why should we break off our conference to read a play?" (3:199–200).

If Euphranor is demanding more "realism" from the philosophical dialogue than the enthusiastic writer Shaftesbury is willing, or able, to give it (Prince, 63), it is only as a consequence of the primary purpose of this passage, which is to ridicule the philosopher's pretence that this "self-discoursing practice" is any kind of dialogue. Shaftesbury, Berkeley intimates, would be better off putting his interests—his prejudices—into play in "conference" with others than trying to eradicate them in a soliloquy with himself. Such a conference is not a dialogue as Shaftesbury understands it, not because its antagonists are not talking with one another but because they cannot talk without their interests clashing and their real values conflicting. Euphranor rudely interrupts Alciphron when he senses that conflict; he does not continue to listen, politely. And whereas in an idealized dialogue the truth would prevail on its listeners without coercion, Euphranor corrects his listener *to* the truth.

To recall, Berkeley's freethinkers want to spread their notions indiscriminately throughout the populace. Universal enlightenment might damage the interests of priests and politicians, but it would ultimately —by removing the power of prejudice—benefit the commonwealth of ordinary citizens. But what holds a political community together for Berkeley is prejudice, not enlightenment. "[A] religious awe and fear of God," says Berkeley in the *Discourse to Magistrates*, a superstitious "awe and fear" that is antithetical to enlightenment and to dialogue, is "the centre that unites, and the cement that connects all human society" (6:219). In a supposedly enlightened age, when civil philosophers, most notably Locke, had exerted themselves to discover the "origin" or absolute ground of civil society and had at least begun to remove God from its governing, Berkeley reverts to the idea that a reverence for superiors, not a voluntary contract among equals, "unites" and "cements" the commonwealth.[34]

It is no wonder that he regards freethinking in religion to be, not a matter of inculpable speculation, but a clear and present danger to the political order. As Euphranor explains in *Alciphron,* "[W]hen the fear of God is quite extinguished the mind must be very easy with respect to other duties, which become outward pretences and formalities, from the moment that they quit their hold upon the conscience; and conscience always supposeth the being of a God." Because freethinkers think nothing sacred in religion, admits Lysicles, "we are too wise to think there is anything sacred either in king or commonwealth" (3:52). Theism is for Berkeley the linchpin of all belief, in politics as well as religion, and nothing but a deliberately anachronistic, not enlightened, education—one that inculcates notions "*before* their grounds and reasons are apprehended or understood" (6:203, emphasis added)—can put the "fear of God" in humankind. Catechism as Berkeley practices it in *Alciphron* is education, but because it is directed at those who have forgotten the good things that religion promises rather than at those who have not yet learned them, it is not *that* kind of education. At its best Berkeley's catechism in *Alciphron* only confirms old notions, it does not create new ones. It only rehabilitates prejudice, it does not habituate it.

Put another way, Berkeley's catechism knows whom it can reach and whom it cannot. In *Hylas and Philonous,* Berkeley's spokesperson Philonous does reach Hylas, persuading him that, in Berkeley's famous formulation from the *Principles,* the "esse," or being, of physical objects is their "percipi," or perception (2:42), not their existence independent of (or "outside") the senses. "I have been a long time distrusting my senses," concludes Hylas in language that delivers the Pauline illumination that Berkeley, in *Alciphron,* finds far less likely in the here and now: "methought I saw things by a dim light, and through false glasses. Now the glasses are removed, and a new light breaks in upon my understanding" (2:262). In *Alciphron,* however, Berkeley's spokespersons never fully reach their freethinking adversaries. Crito does list the several opinions that he and Alciphron come to the dialogue *already* agreed on (such as that "the reasonable legal liberty of our constitution" is a good thing [3:215]), and near the end of their conversation he produces several other points of agreement that would be more significant were they less qualified: "You are . . . a downright sceptic. But, sceptic as you are, you own it probable there is a God, certain that the Christian religion is useful, possible it may be true, certain that, if it be, the minute philosophers are in a bad way"

(3:322). Dion, the rather shadowy narrator of Berkeley's dialogue, even holds out the hope that the adversaries will "come to an entire agreement in the end" (3:220).

But believers and freethinkers never do come to that "entire agreement": Alciphron and Lysicles walk away, unpersuaded. There is, in Walmsley's words, a "dissolution of community" and a "failure of dialogue" at the end of *Alciphron* (134), a failure registered by Lysicles' parting shot: "Every one hath his own way of thinking; and it is as impossible for me to adopt another man's as to make his complexion and features mine" (3:323).[35] While all the affected participants are still assembled, Berkeley's last word on the subject is that consensus among them, much less consistently rational dialogue, is impossible. "Had men reasoned themselves into a wrong opinion, one might hope to reason them out of it," Crito grumbles after the freethinkers leave. "But this is not the case"; the freethinkers' "infidelity" is due not to "thought and reason" but to such motives as "inclination" (3:326). No matter what one does, or what one talks about, Berkeley concludes, there will be some who will never agree. Controversy is irradicable, given the diverse passions and interests of humankind.

In a way that none of Berkeley's critics have realized, however, the dialogue that is *Alciphron* is even more interesting after Alciphron and Lysicles leave. Crito and Euphranor do not say anything particularly important to the point of Berkeley's polemic as they review their conversation with the freethinkers and why it failed, but they do continue talking—for what amounts in T. E. Jessop's edition to seven pages—without there being anyone left to catechize. The scene mirrors the moment that I discuss at the beginning of this chapter, when the freethinkers temporarily depart the scene of conversation, and it gives a glimpse of what Berkeley's dialogue might be without a polemical purpose, without a freethinker (or a freethinking reader) to convert. Crito and Euphranor do not change the subject, continuing to talk about the good things that religion promises, but the relaxed, expansive way in which they do so suggests that Berkeley has his own idea of what polite, speculative conversation should be.[36] Such speculative conversation, imply Berkeley's spokespersons, can only be engaged in by those who, like themselves, are already confirmed in the faith. "[A]n infidel can have no right to argue from one side of the question" in "points disputed between Christians," or doctrinal matters,

Crito states. He will "contend" with the freethinkers for "the general faith taught by Christ and his apostles, and preserved by universal and perpetual tradition in all the churches down to our own times," but he will not dispute with Alciphron or Lysicles "This or that tenet of a sect, this or that controverted notion" (3:276). The distinction between the two, between arguing "points disputed" and contending for "the general faith," is important because Alciphron would use "the multiplicity of religious opinions and controversies" as "an argument *against* religion in general" (3:275, emphasis added). But Crito effectively draws a ring around the endeavors for which a religious believer is accountable to the unbelieving world and implies that pure speculation, the kind that attempts to claim "adventitious" (3:276) notions rather than reclaim tried and true prejudices, is not one of them. Believers can and will "contend" for the faith against unbelievers—the entire dialogue *Alciphron* is an example of that—but the arguments they have with their unbelieving adversaries will not really be speculative in nature, or even, in a restricted sense, controversial. They will only defend, from evidence already at hand, the usefulness of religion; not advance, from evidence yet to be determined, the truth of this or that particular doctrine. One must already be a Christian to "dispute," or to refine, its truth. Only believers can engage in speculative conversation.

As a consequence of its being confined to a believing few, such speculative conversation does not take place in public. Shaftesbury, expressing confidence in the power of philosophy to change the world, proposed to bring it "upon the publick *Stage*," but Berkeley recommends that speculative philosophy retreat to the very same "Colleges and Cells" from which Shaftesbury said that he wanted to remove it. Drawing a Shaftesburean contrast between the ancient Greeks and the "northern rough people"—the British—Crito draws an un-Shaftesburean conclusion about the capacity of the latter to engage in *public* speculative conversation:

> Greece produced men of active and subtle genius. The public conventions and emulations of their cities forwarded that genius; and their natural curiosity was amused and excited by learned conversations. . . . Our genius leads to amusements of a grosser kind: . . . and that curiosity which was general in the Athenians, and the gratifying of which was their chief recreation, is among our people of fashion treated like

affectation, and as such banished from polite assemblies and places of resort; and without doubt would in a little time be banished the country, if it were not for the great reservoirs of learning, where those formalists, pedants, and bearded boys, as your profound critic [i.e., Shaftesbury] calls them, are maintained by the liberality and piety of our predecessors. (3:201)

Learning needs not only "curiosity" to "amuse" and "excite" it but also religion to keep it on the straight and narrow, and only the universities have the "liberality *and* piety" to support speculative conversation. Berkeley may here be defending existing British colleges (like his own Trinity College, Dublin) from the assaults of those moderns who criticized them as bastions of illiberalism and pedantry, or he may be looking forward to founding his own college in Bermuda, where, he proposed, the native or "savage *Americans*" he hoped to teach were "fitter to receive" the truth of Christianity because "if they are in a State purely natural, and unimproved by Education, they are also unincumbred with all that Rubbish of Superstition and Prejudice, which is the Effect of a wrong one."[37] Because they are "unimproved" by the wrong sort of education, that is, native Americans are capable of being improved by the right sort, including the *proper* prejudice that is Christianity. "A Christian," Crito explains a bit earlier, "is for confining reason within its due bounds," as "is every reasonable man" (3:182), and in addition to limiting the public use of reason to strict elenctic reasoning and conferences that talk only about preordained good things, confining reason in its due bounds means confining speculative conversation—and philosophical dialogue—to those pious "formalists" who know how to use it. We do not really get such conversation in *Alciphron*, just as we would not get it in Bermuda: the freethinkers have abdicated their right to it, and the native Americans who would have been Berkeley's students have not yet assumed theirs.

What we are left with, then, is a rather uninspiring reason for Berkeley's use of the dialogue form. Dialogue as catechism is not the stirring call to liberality in conversation that is Shaftesbury's dialogue as distinction nor even the paradoxical call to enlightenment that is Mandeville's dialogue as commerce. It is not even as ambitious as Hobbes's dialogue as counsel, looking not to reconstitute the commonwealth but merely to contend with a few freethinkers while still inviting them to believe. Lowering expectations even further, Euphranor draws an elaborate metaphor between catechism and medicine that recalls Harrington's greater ambition to be a proper physician of the commonwealth while it demotes the physician to a mere apothecary. Granting Lysicles' premises that the "clergy pass for physicians of the soul, and that religion is a sort of medicine which they deal in and administer" and that "men should judge of a physician and his physic by its effect on the sick," he nevertheless maintains that "if great numbers refuse to take the physic, or instead of it take poison of a direct contrary nature, prescribed by others," the physician should not be blamed. "[R]eligious doctrines," therefore, "ought to be judged of by the effects which they produce, not upon all who hear them, but upon those only who receive or believe them" (3:180–81). Although a freethinker could rightly protest that this is a blatant example of begging the question, that a doctrine judged only by those who have already been confirmed in it is not being judged at all, Euphranor's metaphor does draw a definite line between dialogue as persuasion and dialogue as speculation. No doubt those believing few (those catechists) who administer the "medicine" of religion do debate among themselves which doctrines are best and why, but their patients— including "great numbers" of freethinkers—never hear the results of these speculative conversations. They are only persuaded to take their medicine and like it.

Off in Bermuda, and famous for an immaterialist philosophy that no one but him seems to have really believed, Berkeley might seem to be an idiosyncratic figure on which to end this study of the dialogue form in early-eighteenth-century England. In fact, Berkeley's politics, if not his philosophy, are entirely representative of the mainstream of English society. In addition, Berkeley's *Alciphron* represents very well a general tendency in the intellectual prose of the period. If one reads, as I do throughout this book, the philosophical dialogue as a simulacrum of the public sphere, then the public sphere that this philosopher's late dialogue imagines is one denuded of speculation, if not entirely of persuasion. Berkeley's restriction of philosophical speculation to the already believing few—the believing many, secure in their common sense, would have little need of speculation anyway—may itself be restricted to matters of religion,[38] but religion is such a key to all mythologies for Berkeley that restricting it there is tantamount to restricting it everywhere, at least in every matter that might have a bearing on the public good. More overtly than Shaftesbury, Berkeley assumes that there will be ideological factions in the commonwealth —here, believers and freethinkers—that may try to convert, but cannot ultimately commune, with one another. Shaftesbury tried to enthuse such factions away; Berkeley concedes that they are likely to stick and invites the other faction to convert or leave. Berkeley's catechism may teach the good things that religion promises, but it is not the free and open dialogue that one expects from a truly public sphere. It only calcifies the commonwealth's factions; it does not mutually enlighten them.

CONCLUSION
The Idea of a Perfect Commonwealth

IN THE *Discourse to Magistrates,* just before he states the doctrine that "Religion is the centre which unites, and the cement which connects, the several parts or members of the political body," George Berkeley commits a remarkable error of historical criticism. As if to frustrate his belief that a political community is constituted by prejudice, here "a religious awe and fear of God" (6:219), Berkeley complains that

> Too many in this age of free remarks and projects are delighted with republican schemes; and imagine they might remedy whatever was amiss, and render a people great and happy, merely by a new plan or form of government. This dangerous way of thinking and talking is grown familiar, through the foolish freedom of the times. (6:210)

With this comment, Berkeley extends his obsession with freethinking from religion to politics, spying a republican behind every tree where in *Alciphron* he spied an atheist. The problem that he diagnoses is the same in both religion and politics: too much "freedom" and—because departing from "established opinions" (6:211) or useful prejudices— too much speculation.

In actuality, as T. E. Jessop notes, the "republican schemes" that Berkeley fears "sprang up in the preceding century. . . . Such other republicanism as there was in Berkeley's day would have to be sought, so far as I know, in petty and forgotten pamphlets" (6:210). Jessop himself overstates the historical absence of republican "schemes"— there is not much difference between the thought of Harrington and that of the "old Whigs" John Trenchard and Thomas Gordon, who issued another call for the balance of property and power after the collapse of the South Sea Bubble in 1720 in their popular *Cato's Letters* (1724)—but I suspect that Berkeley's real target is less republicanism, or even Whiggery, than it is "free remarks and projects," or speculation. Not much more than a decade after Berkeley's essay, David Hume, in his essay "Idea of a Perfect Commonwealth" (1752), views speculation about politics as an object more of mirth than of apprehension. Indeed, although the "subject" of "what [government] is the most perfect of all" is "surely the most worthy curiosity of any the wit of man can possibly devise," Hume realizes that he must "revive" the subject for "speculation." Because even "the common botched and inaccurate governments seem to serve the purposes of society," and because it is "not so easy to establish a new system of government, as to build a vessel upon a new construction," the subjects of the present English commonwealth are perfectly content with the government that they have. Hume thus decides to "deliver my sentiments [his own 'idea of a perfect commonwealth'] in as few words as possible." The eighteenth-century reading public, he goes on to say, would regard anything longer "both as useless and chimerical" (Hume, *Essays*, 513–14).

For Jürgen Habermas, the early eighteenth century in England marks the height of the influence of the political public sphere. When the Licensing Act was allowed to expire in 1695, governmental censorship was effectively ended and the press was able to bring "rational-critical arguments" about public affairs "before the new forum of the public" relatively unmolested by the authorities. Politicians like Robert Harley employed journalists like Defoe to persuade (or propagandize) the public that their policies promoted the public good (or, in Bolingbroke's case, did it themselves) and make "the 'party spirit' a 'public spirit'" (Habermas, *Structural Transformation*, 58–59). Expelled from power, Henry St. John, viscount Bolingbroke, articulated a theory of opposition from this new tribune of "public opinion," and even though he argued (in his *Dissertation on Parties* [1733–34]) that the best government was a united government, without faction or party, he was instrumental in legitimating the idea "that an organized opposition might play a constructive role in political life."[1] Even (or especially) Robert Walpole, the constant target of Bolingbroke's opposition, recognized the power of the press to advance or impede his political program, and he marshaled his own army of journalists and writers to defend it, and himself.[2]

All of this is true. But perhaps because "compared to the press in the other European states, . . . the British press enjoyed unique liberties" (*Structural Transformation,* 59), Habermas's enthusiasm for the early-eighteenth-century English public sphere causes him to downplay the dark side of these developments. There is more public discourse, both oppositional and establishment (or ministerial), than ever before, but the sense of the opposition, at least, is that their voices are not being heard. This is hardly an unusual complaint for any party out of power to make, but the shrillness of the complaints, as well as their persistence, is notable. Like the disparagement of "speculation" in politics, the complaint implies that political argument, while vigorously "critical," is not necessarily productive or even "rational." The minor poet Bezaleel Morrice, paying Alexander Pope the flattery of imitating his most openly political satire, *One Thousand Seven Hundred and Thirty Eight* (the two "dialogue" poems published as the *Epilogue to the Satires*), writes that same year in *The Present Corruption of Britons:*

> Not only Now, Dissimulation reigns,
> Encumb'ring gallant Minds, with Cloggs and Chains;
> Our gen'ral Practice, like a Fog surrounds,
> And all the Paths of Probity confounds;
> Not only now, t'Extremity are brought
> Meanness of Soul, and Impotence of Thought;[3]

What is worth noting here is not only how a "gen'ral" political "Practice" is enveloped in a Mandevillian cloud of "Dissimulation," but also how that dissimulative practice "confounds," and overwhelms to the point of "Impotence," all possible "Probity" and "Thought." Whatever complaint writers have about the character of public discourse in late-seventeenth-century England, it is not that thought and speculation are impotent to influence it. Like Hobbes midway through *Leviathan* (making the plea to "a Sovereign" that I quote in chapter 1), they make a clear, if not always consummated, connection between "convert[ing]" the "Truth of Speculation, into the Utility of Practice" (408).

Indeed, it might be said that while there was much more talk about the "Utility of Practice" in mid-eighteenth-century political discourse, there was much less confidence in the "Truth of Speculation." By the 1730s or 1740s, as Hume allows, it was difficult to find the equivalent of a Hobbes, a Harrington, a Filmer, a Locke, or even a James Tyrrell (the author of *Bibliotheca Politica* [1702], a massive series of fourteen dialogues on the English constitution). There were political tracts, by Bolingbroke as well as by Cato and other "eighteenth-century commonwealthmen," but in general, political thought did not advance beyond where it was at the end of the seventeenth century.[4] It was not until the pressure of revolution was felt in America and on the Continent that Edmund Burke, Mary Wollstonecraft, William Godwin, and others were forced to examine the foundations of English civil society again, offering new solutions or reaffirming the old. Political speculation flourishes in times of political instability.

And so, I have argued, does the political dialogue. Perhaps it is not surprising, then, that along with speculation or theory about politics, the political dialogue experienced a decline in eighteenth-century England. The dialogue remained a popular form, although not nearly as popular as in the seventeenth century, but its primary concerns changed from politics, including the politics of religion, to religious and practical instruction and matters of taste.[5] Shelley Burtt has noticed the relative absence of dialogues, once so popular, in the ministerial press,[6] and I have found that most of the dialogues written in opposition are satiric, not serious or speculative, in tone. This seemingly minor fact of literary history takes on a greater significance if, as I have argued all along, the dialogue can tell us something about the condition of the public sphere, something that Habermas's necessarily schematic history overlooks. In order for it to be vital, the public sphere needs to have the sense that individual minds and collective opinion can be *changed* in the course of debate. Speculation—even if it is not rigorous enough to be called "philosophical"—is the means to that end. In the middle decades of the eighteenth century that sense of possibility about ideological change, and the faith in speculation that sustained it, receded. If this is not quite what Habermas means by the "structural transformation" of the public sphere,[7] it certainly indicates a transformation of sorts because it makes the actual practice of politics seem resistant to rational persuasion. What might be the reasons for this "transformation," and for the decline of the political dialogue that accompanies (and registers) it?

The most obvious explanation for the decline of dialogue (and for speculation *in* dialogue) is simply that there was less "work" for it to do. The political controversies that the form both reflected and (I have argued) existed to resolve were less of a problem in the middle of the eighteenth century than they had been in the decades before. Most historians agree with J. H. Plumb's thesis that with the assumption of power by Walpole in 1721 and the consolidation of the Whig oligarchy, England achieved a "political stability" that lasted for the next few decades. This stability, writes Plumb, possessed "adamantine strength and profound inertia" and allowed both rulers and ruled to concentrate more on the practice than on the theory of power. Even J. C. D. Clark, the most notorious recent revisionist of eighteenth-century English history, says that "the minds of leading Whigs" at mid-century "were dominated not by a canon of Whig doctrine drawn from the great seventeenth-century tradition—Harrington, Tyrrell, Moyle, Trenchard, Toland, Sidney and the rest—but by the practical details and daily techniques of their trades as politicians" and that "the Tories were even less given to political theorizing."[8] After the ascension of Walpole there was, in short, a stability in English politics, supported by ideological consensus and practical politics and resulting in the lack of speculation about government that Hume noted.

As an example of ideological consensus, consider Mandeville's and Berkeley's respective positions on the principle of liberty, a principle associated, at least during the later seventeenth century, exclusively with the Whigs. In *A Letter to Dion* (1732), the pamphlet he wrote to protest what he saw as Berkeley's manhandling of his views in *Alciphron*, Mandeville complains that a fairer opponent "would not have suffer'd such lawless Libertines as *Alciphron* and *Lysicles*, to have shelter'd themselves under my Wings," and that, by quoting Mandeville's own words in the *Fable* that the practitioners of vice should be "punish'd for them when they grew into Crimes," Berkeley could have exposed Alciphron and Lysicles' "Liberty" as "Licentiousness" (3–4). It is predictable that Mandeville, a Whig interested in reaching readers of all political persuasions, would want to dissociate himself from the more extreme interpretations of his own party's principle. Less predictable is the desire of Berkeley, closer in spirit (if not openly) to the Tories, to associate himself with a moderate interpretation of that same principle. Yet, in *Alciphron* Berkeley has Euphranor state, in the course of a tirade against extremism in politics, that

> I am and always was a sincere lover of liberty, legal English liberty, which I esteem a chief blessing, ornament, and comfort of life, and the great prerogative of an Englishman. But is it not to be feared that, upon the nation's running into a licentiousness which hath never been endured in any civilised country, men feeling the intolerable evils of one extreme may naturally fall into the other? (3:109)

What is significant here is not just Berkeley's move toward the "great prerogative" of liberty, a prerogative that had belonged exclusively to the opposing party, but his choice of the same word—*licentiousness*—to demarcate the extreme that he wants to avoid.[9] If the sign of liberty for Mandeville is an unrestrained commerce (or laissez-faire), and for Berkeley the restraints of law and religion, by 1732 Mandeville and Berkeley could agree on at least the principles of a perfect commonwealth.

No consensus is seamless, and the relative absence of ideological differences cannot be the only reason for the decline of dialogue at this time. A second, more important one is that in political discourse the state came to be seen less as a ship to be guided (or, in Hobbes and Harrington's metaphor, a body to be cured) and more as a "machine" to be wound up and left alone. Governing was too prosaic (or too vast) a subject to be described any longer as an art or a science and became merely a technical skill. Walpole is famous for preferring "experience" to "speculation" and "theory" in public life,[10] but even philosophers attribute the growth of political stability in England to a happy accident rather than, as might Hobbes or Harrington, to any kind of conscious design. Adam Ferguson, for example, in *An Essay on the History of Civil Society,* published in 1767, a few decades after the period discussed here, states:

> Every step and every movement of the multitude, even in what are termed enlightened ages, are made with equal blindness to the future; and nations stumble upon establishments, which are indeed the result of human action, but not the execution of any human design. . . . [T]he most refined politicians do not always know whither they are leading the state by their projects.[11]

Compared with seventeenth-century philosophers like Hobbes and Harrington, Ferguson is both more secure that the state is in good order and less secure that philosophy could, or did, have anything to do with it. He sees political stability as a gradual rather than a sudden achievement (a "growth," in Plumb's apt metaphor) and thus credits a kind of evolution, not speculation, with achieving that stability.

Ferguson's thoughts are shared by Mandeville. There is cause to wonder, for example, how "skilful" the politicians that artfully manage society for Mandeville really are, or how seriously one should regard his use of the traditional analogy of the politician as a good, or skillful, physician. On the one hand, Mandeville concludes the first part of the *Fable* by stating that "Sound Politicks are to the Social Body what the Art of Medicine is to the Natural" (1:322). On the other hand, he tags that conclusion a "Rhapsody of Thoughts" (1:322), a Shaftesburean phrase that suggests that he may not be entirely serious in what he says there. Mandeville's more sincere sentiments about the skill of politicians may be the ones contained in the passage previously quoted, spoken also by Cleomenes in the second, more earnest part of the *Fable,* that "the Laws and establish'd Oeconomy of a well-order'd City" are like a "Clock": "[W]hen once they are brought to as much Perfection, as Art and human Wisdom can carry them, the whole Machine may be made to play of itself" (2:322–23). If Mandeville's politicians may or may not be skillful, however, they are certainly not speculative. "Is it probable," Cleomenes asks,

> that amongst the Bees, there has ever been any other Form of Government, than what every Swarm submits to now? What an infinite Variety of Speculations, what ridiculous Schemes have not been proposed amongst Men, on the Subject of Government; what Dissentions in Opinion, and what fatal Quarrels has it not been the Occasion of! And, which is the best Form of it, is a Question to this Day undecided. (2:187)

Amazingly, Mandeville here blames the same philosophical "Speculations" and systematic "Schemes" that Hobbes, Harrington, and the like hoped would resolve "Dissentions in Opinion" and "fatal Quarrels" over politics for *creating* those same dissensions and quarrels. In all the "Orders" and "Regulations" of government, Cleomenes states, "there is a Stability, no where to be met with in Things of human Contrivance and Approbation" (2:187). Historians may be in some doubt about the relative "stability" of eighteenth-century politics, but Mandeville is not, and while that stability may have something to do with the skill of politicians, it has nothing to do with the "skill" of philosophers.

Since Berkeley is concerned to vindicate a practical wisdom against Mandeville's cynical relativism, one might assume that he would look to philosophy for the stability that Mandeville says it cannot provide. It is true that Berkeley has great faith in the power of philosophy to reform our "vision" in epistemology; to show us, for example, that what we think of as independently existing physical objects are really just associations of individual sensations, held together by a God who wants the world to cohere. When the subject of his philosophical inquiries changes from epistemology to more popular matters of religion and politics, however, Berkeley is less sure that philosophy can, or even should, enlighten ordinary believers. He is far more likely to trust notions early imbued than those lately thought on, more likely to trust even "vulgar" prejudices than philosophical speculations. According to Crito in *Alciphron,* "[T]he Christian religion is . . . an institution fitted to ordinary minds, rather than to the nicer talent, whether improved or puzzled, of speculative men; and our notions about faith are accordingly taken from the commerce of the world, and practice of mankind, rather than from the peculiar systems of refiners." Although philosophy would eventually discover the same truths that religion already possesses, Berkeley questions why a philosopher interested in maintaining political stability would want to encourage such speculation. Idle speculation—which all speculation is that attempts to discover what most people already know—as Crito continues, only creates controversy: "Certainly one that takes his notions of faith, opinion, and assent from common sense, and common use, and has maturely weighed the nature of signs and language, will not be so apt to controvert the wording of a mystery, or to break the peace of the church [or, one infers, of the commonwealth] for the sake of retaining or rejecting a term" (3:301–2). Like Mandeville, Berkeley eventually blames speculation for religious and political controversy.

The kind of speculation about politics that Hobbes, Harrington, and other earlier writers engaged in emerged from a "perfect union" of political instability and philosophical confidence. Given the new political problem of factionalism spawned by the civil wars—what I have been calling the problem of diversity—Hobbes and others turned to philosophy and dialogue to reconcile opinion. With the growth of political stability in the middle of the century, however, this union began to fall apart. Politics, as Hume noted, seemed to serve the purposes of society no matter how imperfect, and speculative dialogue no longer did. It should be remembered that although the "commerce" that Mandeville relies on to bring society together is a kind of conversation, it is not *speculative* conversation. In fact, Mandeville's own exercises in disinterested enlightenment, the dialogues that make up part 2 of the *Fable,* are antithetical to the dissimulative conversations that keep society going. It should also be remembered that whatever Berkeley is doing with the dialogue form in *Alciphron*—disputing with freethinkers, teaching readers about the good things that religion promises, or persuading readers (and those freethinkers who want to listen) to give up their fashionable skepticism and believe again in the religious truths that they were catechized in when young—it is not reconciling opinion. If the elements of political community are not already present, Mandeville and Berkeley both conclude, dialogue can do nothing to create them. Shaftesbury, of course, left practical politics behind a long time ago, preferring to speculate about the natural order of things, not an artificial, political one.

Dialogue did not fare well in the practical politics of the time either. What, for example, was the place of dialogue in Bolingbroke's theory of opposition? At times it seems that he is as intent on reviving Shaftesbury's "amicable Collision" of opposing minds in dialogue as he is on reviving the "country" values of the civic-humanist ideology that inspired it. His *Remarks on the History of England,* originally published as a series of "letters" in his newspaper *The Craftsman* in 1730 and 1731, for example, opens as a conversation among "a company" of gentleman who meet regularly to apply the lessons of English history to the present, corrupt situation of English politics. As Bolingbroke describes this company, it resembles nothing so much as Neville's group of disinterested gentleman, gathering to debate the public good: "They dispute without strife, and examine as dispassionately the events and characters of the present age, as they reason about those that are found in history."[12] What this company of men are looking to history for is evidence that the "ancient" English constitution, which protected the rights of freeholders such as themselves, predated the usurpation of those rights by William I and several monarchs (and prime ministers) since.[13] As Alexander Pettit observes, Bolingbroke "promoted the illusion" that his *Remarks* were "transcribed from the discussions of a lively and inquisitive coterie"; they might be said to fulfill the civic-humanist dream, as Pocock would put it, of a "conversation with the ancients which results in knowledge" transmuted into a "conversation among citizens which results in decision and law."[14]

The only problem with this dream is that what little "conversation" actually exists in the *Remarks* trails off by the fourth letter: by then, the narrator is simply transcribing the thoughts of the "ancient venerable gentleman" to whom the rest of the company silently defers (1:294). It is not quite a speech, but it is even less a dialogue or discussion. Bolingbroke's preferred mode of address, in fact, *is* the speech: in *A Letter on the Spirit of Patriotism* (1736) he admires the "famous orators of Greece and Rome," such as Demosthenes and Cicero, "who harangued oftener than they debated." "The nature of the governments, and the humor of those ages," as Bolingbroke draws the obvious parallel between those classical oligarchies and Walpole's England, "made elaborate orations necessary" (2:366).[15] Frustrated by his exclusion from power, Bolingbroke cannot imagine compromise (or dialogue) with what he labels as "corruption": he can only depose it with his own ideal of a disinterested (and eloquent) "patriot king," who embodies a unified "spirit of liberty" against a divisive "spirit of faction."[16]

The polemicists whom Walpole employed to defend his ministry had even less use for dialogue. One of Walpole's most energetic supporters, William Arnall, argued in a kind of Mandevillian fashion that what the prime minister's opponents called corruption was simply the way business was transacted in a commercial society and that if corruption meant putting one's private interest ahead of the public good, then everyone, in all times and places, was so "corrupt."[17] I have already noted the relative absence of the dialogue form in the ministerial press (an absence that would have mystified that establishment polemicist and inveterate dialogue writer L'Estrange), but in one of the few dialogues written to promote this view, published in Walpole's *London Journal* in 1727 and possibly by Arnall himself (Burtt, 114), the ministerial spokesperson "Mr. Hopewell" attempts to persuade a "Mr. Sullen" that with regard to the specific issue of bribing the electorate, "the End"—in this case, "the present Enjoyment of our Liberties, and the Preservation of the Constitution"—"justif[ies] the Means." Hopewell's defense even includes the stunning insinuation that the real reason Sullen is upset with political corruption is that "no Body bribes us." [18] This is hardly an argument that inspires compromise with, much less devotion to, the government that Sullen finds so unpalatable, but the most remarkable thing about this "dialogue" is that Hopewell seems not to regard *how* Sullen regards the government. He neither repudiates his interlocutor's case against corruption in a satiric manner nor attempts to persuade him of the justice of his own in an earnestly inclusive one. There is neither victory nor consensus at the end of this dialogue: Sullen simply walks away even more sullen than before. One is left wondering how Arnall (or whoever wrote this dialogue) could think that this failed conversation might persuade anyone except the already converted of the ministry's benignity, and left to conclude that he did not much care.

The decline of political speculation in mid-eighteenth-century England, and the decline of political speculation in dialogue,[19] is summed up in a remark near the end of Berkeley's *Alciphron*. After the freethinkers Alciphron and Lysicles have left the scene of conversation for good, Euphranor proposes to his fellow believer Crito that

> it would much conduce to the public benefit if, instead of discouraging free-thinking, there was erected in the midst of this free country a Dianoetic Academy, or seminary for free-thinkers, provided with retired chambers, and galleries, and shady walks and groves, where, after seven years spent in silence and meditation, a man might commence a genuine free-thinker, and from that time forward have licence to think what he pleased, and a badge to distinguish him from counterfeits.

"[T]he present age," Crito nods in assent, needs more "thinking" (3:328). By logical extension, Euphranor's proposal and Crito's assent mean also that the present age needs less conversation, at least the sort of occasionally political but always speculative conversation that occurs among Berkeley's freethinkers. If the present age needs more thinking, that is, it is only the sort of thinking, or speculation, that occurs in private, in "silence and meditation." The union of speculative philosophy and practical politics that had invigorated the public sphere in late-seventeenth-century England (and that also produced the wealth of speculation in the political dialogue) has collapsed by Berkeley's "present age": philosophy has retreated to "retired chambers, and galleries," and "the forms of society," according to Mandeville and Berkeley and in the words of Ferguson, "arise, long before the date of philosophy, from the instincts, not from the speculations, of men" (122).

NOTES

Introduction: Conversation and Political Controversy

1. Dryden, 26. The description of the *Essay* as a "skeptical" discourse comes from Dryden's *Defence of "An Essay of Dramatic Poesy,"* in Dryden, 124. Phillip Harth has shown conclusively that when Dryden compares the *Essay* to "that way of reasoning which was used by Socrates, Plato, and all the Academics of old, which Tully and the best of the Ancients followed, and which is imitated by the modest inquisitions of the Royal Society" (124), he is applying to literary criticism the same method that his friend Robert Boyle applied to his scientific investigations, that of unsettling received opinion so as to be surer of a final truth. Surveying Dryden's religious and political opinions, Harth concludes that the orthodox Anglican (later Catholic) and Tory loyalist was not skeptical at all. Harth, *Contexts of Dryden's Thought,* 14, 32.

2. Shaftesbury, *Characteristicks,* 2:215–16.

3. Hume, *Dialogues Concerning Natural Religion,* 128.

4. Zwicker, 231.

5. Lawson, *Examination,* 133.

6. Conal Condren discusses Lawson's influence on the history of political theory, and especially on Locke, in the introduction to his edition of Lawson's *Politica Sacra et Civilis,* and in his *George Lawson's "Politica" and the English Revolution.*

7. Wieseltier, 18.

8. Hill, 163.

9. Cressy, 47 and n. 19.

10. Ahrens, 42–43.

11. *Dialogue Between Tom and Dick,* 1–2.

12. Crawford, 602. The figure 2,000 comes from Purpus, 54. I draw the data about the surges in dialogue activity from Crawford. (There were similar surges during 1641–42 and 1660.) In years of relative calm the "average production" of dialogues was fewer than ten (601–2).

13. Schwoerer, 206, 218. The quotation is from L'Estrange, *Toleration Discuss'd,* 107.

14. Knights, 243.

15. Habermas, *Structural Transformation,* 52.

16. As Peter Laslett declared in the introduction to his edition of the *Two Treatises*, "Its origin belongs to the autumn and winter of 1679–80, exactly a decade earlier than it is traditionally supposed to have been written. *Two Treatises* is an Exclusion Tract, not a Revolution Pamphlet" (61). Similarly placing Locke's philosophical work in its immediate context, Richard Ashcraft reads the polemical literature of the Exclusion Crisis as serious and continuous with the *Two Treatises* (181–227).

17. *Honest Hodge and Ralph,* 3.

18. [Onslow], 12.

19. Y[arranton], 1.

20. L'Estrange, *Citt and Bumpkin,* 19.

21. Similarly, in "Habermas, Machiavelli, and the Humanist Critique of Ideology" Victoria Kahn criticizes the value placed on consensus in Habermas's theory of "communicative action" (for which the public sphere provides the rules) from the perspective of Machiavelli's antihumanist emphasis on the creative force of conflict.

22. After surveying the objections of other historians, Steven Pincus reaches the same conclusion about "a public sphere in the Habermasian sense" as it was realized in the coffeehouses of seventeenth-century England. The emergence of such a public sphere, writes Pincus, was "precipitated largely by a thirst for political discussion and a desire to preserve English liberties" (811).

23. *Dialogue at Oxford,* 4.

24. For Michael Prince's *Philosophical Dialogue in the British Enlightenment,* see below. For other histories of the dialogue form, see Hirzel, Merrill.

25. McKeon, 107, 103–5. Scholars of the form have distinguished between the "periastic," or speculative, dialogues of Plato's later period, which would be more dialectical, and the "eristic" ones of his earlier period, in which Plato's philosophical hero, Socrates, in a spirit of disputation rather than dialectic, drives his hapless respondent into an "*elenchus,* or self-contradiction." Such eristic dialogues, as K. J. Wilson points out in a study of their Renaissance equivalents, furnish "*training* in controversy." They seek eventually to end a conversation rather than sustain it indefinitely and are thus more likely models for Restoration polemicists than the formal practice of dialectic that McKeon discusses (Wilson, 47–49). For more on elenchus, see chapter 5.

26. This is the tradition to which George M. Logan, Robert M. Adams, and Clarence H. Miller assign More's dialogue in their edition of *Utopia,* xxiii.

27. J. A. W. Gunn maintains that "public opinion" emerges in England during the eighteenth century rather than the seventeenth, but his later dating may result from his focus on the expression rather than the political force (*Beyond Liberty and Property,* 260–315). The marquis of Halifax as early as

1689 warned that a prince risked being "undo[ne]" by acting "contrary to reason it selfe, or to the universall Opinion of his subjects" (1:187), and there are occasions in other late-seventeenth-century texts where the writers refer to the concept of public opinion, if they do not use the precise expression. See also Habermas, "Public Opinion—*Opinion Publique*—Öffentliche Meinung: On the Prehistory of the Phrase," in *Structural Transformation*, 89–102.

28. "I replied very modestly, I was not so well vers'd in our Court-affairs as to be able to give him any account thereof, only I have heard some say he had none," the narrator slyly answers, whereupon his interlocutor "smilingly . . . began some other matter of discourse" (*Conference Between a Bensalian Bishop and an English Doctor*, 2).

29. Milton, 336.

30. *Brief Discourse Between a Sober Tory and a Moderate Whigg*, 1.

31. L'Estrange, quoted in *Dictionary of National Biography*, 1917, s.v. "L'Estrange, Sir Robert."

32. Of orthodox doctrine Phillip Harth says, "The notion that sermons were an indispensable means of buttressing the civil order was already a century old at the time of the Restoration, and accepted as a matter of course by the Anglican clergy" (*Pen for a Party*, 6).

33. That is to say, I have found only one Nonconformist dialogue—John Bunyan's *The Life and Death of Mr. Badman* (1680)—from the years for which my survey can claim to be comprehensive (1679–81), and it mentions preaching only in passing, when the character Wiseman lists the "wicked ways" that Mr. Badman had "to hinder himself of hearing . . . the best Preachers" (41). N. H. Keeble, in *The Literary Culture of Nonconformity*, mentions Nonconformist autobiography, letters, and even romance but not dialogue.

34. Eachard, 39.

35. Eagleton, *Function of Criticism*, 11.

36. Prince, 149, 256.

37. Thus, when Prince first mentions rhetoric, it is in reference to Richard Hurd's praise of how Plato brought "the tumour of poetic composition into discourses of philosophy," and it is opposed to "dialectic," or pure argument (17–18). For Prince, rhetoric is the fiction that surrounds the argument of a dialogue: it is what turns dialectic into dialogue.

38. For the history of this dispute, see Vickers, 247–66.

39. "How . . . superior . . . is the recreation that a man finds in words, when he discourses about justice and the other topics you speak of," says Phaedrus, to which Socrates replies, "But far more excellent, I think, is the serious treatment of them, which employs the art of dialectic" (Plato, *Phaedrus* [trans. R. Hackforth] 276e). The gloss of Lucian's praise of dialogue is from Peter Gay (172).

40. Locke, 508. Wilbur Samuel Howell's *Logic and Rhetoric in England, 1500–1700* is still the best source on the complementary relationship between philosophy (or logic) and rhetoric in the Renaissance.

41. "In practice," asserts Richetti, "what philosophy has offered is a controlled rhetoric that often begins with the old rhetorical turn of denying rhetoric and then goes on to establish its own forms of persuasion within its logical structures" (6).

42. Michael Walzer, by way of critiquing the "idealizations" of such philosophers of dialogue as Habermas, John Rawls, and Bruce Ackerman, contrasts philosophical conversation to "real talk."

43. Hobbes, *Leviathan*, 111, 213.

44. Neville, *Plato Redivivus*, 177.

45. Mandeville, *Fable of the Bees*, 1:349.

46. Hobbes, *Elements of Law*, 150.

47. Harrington, 171.

48. *Modest Attempt*, 8.

49. Habermas, *Knowledge and Human Interests*, 301–2. See also Kahn, "Habermas, Machiavelli, and the Humanist Critique of Ideology," 465–66.

50. Albert O. Hirschman tells how the idea of interest became a new "paradigm" for explaining human action in the seventeenth century (42–48). Hobbes's and Harrington's doubt about the "rightness" of an absolute standard of reason accords with the finding of several scholars that the search for certain knowledge in many fields evolved during the seventeenth and eighteenth centuries into a search for *probable* knowledge, a knowledge that is often consensual and produced through conversation. See also Struever.

51. Strictly speaking, Koselleck's is a "public sphere" only by analogy. His philosophes retreated from politics because in the absolutist state that they inhabited there was no avenue like the one that Habermas describes for communicating their opinions to the government.

52. Plato, *Gorgias* (trans. W. D. Woodhead) 500c.

53. White, 79, 4. Even Thomas Sprat, the chronicler of the Royal Society, insisted that natural philosophers should not apply its skeptical method to moral or political questions. "This *doubtfulness* of thoughts, this *fluctuation*, this *slowness* of concluding, which is so usefull" in science, says Sprat, "is most destructive in *matters of State*, and *Government*" (104).

54. Glanvill, sig. A4v.

55. Thus, Koselleck's book is subtitled "Enlightenment and the Pathogenesis of Modern Society." Elsewhere, he explains that the Enlightenment philosophers he discusses kept their criticism "aloof from the State so that later, through that very separation it could, seemingly neutrally, extend its reach to the State and subject it to its judgement." Their "ostensible neutrality"

from politics is exactly the stance that Shaftesbury assumes in his philosophical writings (98).

1. Hobbes: Dialogue as Counsel

1. Hobbes, *Peloponnesian War,* 584–85.
2. de Certeau, 183.
3. Hobbes, *Behemoth,* 52.
4. *Elements of Law,* 150. For this quotation, as well as a discussion of this point, see the introduction.
5. Hobbes, *Common Laws,* 84.
6. "A LAW OF NATURE," according to Hobbes, "is a Precept, or generall Rule, found out by Reason," that dictates what we should do, and not do, to preserve our lives (*Leviathan,* 189).
7. Aristotle, *Nicomachean Ethics* 1138b.
8. S. A. Lloyd's objection to the "standard philosophical interpretation" of Hobbes, which holds that the fear of death is enough to motivate people to submit themselves to the sovereign authority, is that it fails to account for such passionately held opinions, or "ideals" (6–47).
9. Kahn, *Rhetoric, Prudence, and Skepticism in the Renaissance,* 164.
10. I take this "shortsightedness" account of conflict from Hampton, 81.
11. The adjective is Leo Strauss's (159).
12. Aristotle, *Rhetoric* 1355b; Hobbes, *Briefe of the Art of Rhetorique,* 40, emphasis added. Hobbes would thus appear to be adopting the antirhetoric stance of seventeenth-century educational reformers like Peter Ramus. Ramus had dissociated logic from rhetoric in the attempt to create a dialectic, or method of argument, that would produce propositions of absolute certainty. On the other hand, as Aristotle's first English translator, Hobbes reinstated ethos (ethical proof) and pathos (emotional proof) as modes of persuasion and, like Aristotle, recognized that rhetoric has its own "logic" of probabilities (Zappen, 74, 79–80). Ramus, in other words, narrowed the scope of rhetoric to mere eloquence, or fine speaking; Hobbes broadened it again to include the study of human character and passion.
13. Hobbes, *De Cive,* 154.
14. Zappen, 66.
15. The only one who does, as far as I can tell, is Gary Shapiro, who asserts that "what Hobbes distrusts is not so much opinion and discourse in general as the ambiguities and irresolution of spoken language and conversation" (156). What Hobbes's use of the dialogue form proves, however, is that he distrusts not "spoken language" in general but oratory and disputation in particular and that he even relies on "conversation," such as that between

Hobbes the counselor and his reader, to check the "ambiguities and irresolution" of all (spoken and written) discourse. Conversation and dialogue, in other words, are more properly "philosophical" kinds of speech than oratory and disputation.

16. As Laurie M. Johnson notes in the only full-length study of Hobbes's translation of Thucydides, Hobbes thus cannot account for a figure like Pericles, an orator who is *not* a demagogue (161).

17. "In Demonstration, in Councell, and all rigorous search of Truth, Judgement does all; except sometimes the understanding have need to be opened by some apt similitude; and then there is so much use of Fancy" (*Leviathan*, 136–37).

18. Curtis, 88.

19. Rogow, 50–51. Disputation was practiced throughout a student's academic career. During his third and fourth years at Oxford, for example— where, he told his friend and biographer John Aubrey, he "thought himself a good Disputant" (Aubrey, 229)—Hobbes would have been required to participate in four disputations, two upholding the affirmative side and two the negative (Rogow, 51).

20. My point here is influenced by Quentin Skinner, who claims that Hobbes's political science is a reaction to "the entire rhetorical culture of Renaissance humanism" (9). I elaborate on Skinner's claim in "The Reader as Sovereign," below.

21. For more on the difference between teaching and persuasion in Hobbes, see Zappen, 80–82.

22. Hobbes, *De Homine*, 39. I have cast the word *command* in this sentence as a verb, but Hobbes uses it both as a verb and, along with the gerund *commanding*, as a noun. I shall follow Hobbes's convention in using the word.

23. David Johnston finds that Hobbes writes more accessible texts—in effect, uses more rhetoric—as he becomes more interested in shaping public, not just sovereign, opinion. Skinner, in a brilliant study of Hobbes and the rhetorical tradition, divides his career into three stages—an early humanist period, a turn toward science, and a final attempt to reconcile reason and rhetoric—and explains, through an exhaustive formal analysis of Hobbes's rhetoric, how, in *Leviathan*, Hobbes makes good on that attempt. Three others who might be mentioned here, and whose insights I draw on in this chapter, are Kahn, Shapiro, and Tom Sorell. The quotation is from Skinner, 12 n. 61. For a useful summary of Hobbes's ambivalence toward rhetoric, see Silver, "Hobbes on Rhetoric."

24. Other critics describe Hobbes's political science as a form of counsel. Sorell compares it to counsel to "resolve the tension" that exists there between reason and rhetoric (350–51). Skinner does the same, after noting that Hobbes

initially rejected the dialogical nature of counsel for contributing to conceptual instability (69–70, 10). Frederick G. Whelan calls counsel one of the proper "uses" of language in Hobbes and connects it to teaching and science (67–71).

25. Johnston, 62, 26, 89, 91.

26. Both *Behemoth* and the *Common Laws* dialogue were published posthumously, in 1682 and 1681, respectively. *Behemoth* was completed in manuscript about 1668 (Holmes, vii), and the *Common Laws* dialogue about 1665 (Cranston, 383). Their publication was delayed for different reasons. Stephen Holmes speculates that Charles II refused to license *Behemoth* earlier because of its "outspoken, but politically awkward, anticlericalism" (vii). Hobbes himself objected to the publication of the *Common Laws* dialogue because he was dissatisfied with what he called its "imperfect" ending. For the speculation on this point, see Cropsey, 5–7; and Rogow, 217.

Behemoth is mentioned, more often than the *Common Laws* dialogue, in many of the works already cited. The *Common Laws* dialogue was influential enough in its day, however, to incite a refutation from Matthew Hale, chief justice of the King's Bench from 1671 to 1676. Richard Peters discusses the dialogue's contribution to the seventeenth-century controversy between the advocates of absolute sovereignty, such as Hobbes, and those of the common law, such as Hale (213–21), as does Enid Campbell.

27. This is not to say, with Tracy B. Strong, that "the sovereign is in each of us, not differentiated from the others, but me and you insofar as we have been able to read or acknowledge the text of *Leviathan* by ourselves" ("When Is a Text Not a Pretext?" 176). To my mind, Strong gives *too* much sovereignty to readers. Hobbes may respect them enough to think that they can be persuaded to submit their right to the sovereign authority—to be persuaded of the truth of his text—but they must still be *persuaded* of it, by a counselor or teacher with the "authority" of the truth. Thus the need for an "aggressive system of education" in Hobbes (Lloyd, 219), and the reason why his own counseling, of his civil philosophy, is so directive. I agree with Victoria Silver that unsupervised acts of reading "def[y] agreement" among individuals and that Strong neglects "the related issues of interpretation and suasion" that are raised, say, when Hobbes declares that right reason does not exist in nature ("A Matter of Interpretation," 166; Silver is responding to Strong's original article, "How to Write Scripture").

28. Holmes says that what makes *Behemoth* significant for students of Hobbes is its "explicit rejection" of the idea that human motivations can be "reduced to self-preservation or the rational pursuit of private advantage" (x–xi).

29. Hobbes, *English Works,* 7:184.

30. Skinner, 299, 9. Skinner thus argues that Hobbes reacts not to the general "current of 'sceptical relativism'" in Renaissance humanism but to the rhetorical culture "within which the vogue for scepticism had developed" (9).

31. Hill, 193. But William Holdsworth supposes that, led by Hobbes, "political speculation" at this time "was tending in the direction of the supremacy of a sovereign person or body which was above the law" (5:480).

32. Holdsworth, 5:215.

33. The lawyer is quoting Coke in the previous sentence. The editor Joseph Cropsey notes the quotation (*Common Laws*, 55) but does not cite the source, which is Coke's *Commentary upon Littleton*, fol. 97v.

34. Francis Bacon, quoted in Cropsey, 12.

35. By way of defining the common law, James R. Stoner Jr. says that it exists "whenever precedents have the force of law" (6).

36. Shapiro, 151.

37. I encountered the idea that Hobbes's political science is "ultimately prudential" in nature in Kahn, *Rhetoric, Prudence, and Skepticism in the Renaissance*, 235.

38. Aristotle, *Rhetoric* 1356a. Zappen observes that Hobbes effects a "tenuous reconciliation between . . . rhetoric and science" with this appeal to pathos. Even as a passion, it becomes the "starting point and foundation" of *Leviathan*, "his most mature work of political science" (82).

39. Hobbes himself never uses the term, but his understanding of the concept is summed up in the maxim that "the safety of the People, is the highest Law." As J. A. W. Gunn points out, no concept of the public interest has any substance for Hobbes unless it is concretely embodied in a person (the sovereign) or persons (*Politics and the Public Interest in the Seventeenth Century*, 59–66).

40. Hanna Fenichel Pitkin, who called my attention to this passage and classifies Hobbes's as an authorization theory, actually says that authorization supplements the contract-making process. It supposedly explains how the sovereign authority can legitimately continue to impose his or her will on the populace after the original contract has been forgotten, but, as Pitkin discusses, it does not do so very well (11, 14–37, esp. 34–37). Following Pitkin, Johnston calls authorization "essential to the revised account" of the social contract that Hobbes gives in *Leviathan* (81).

41. Habermas, *Structural Transformation*, 7.

42. The quotation is from Okin, 51; the point from Stoner, 129–30.

43. Pitkin, 35.

44. I say "fall back" on because, as Ernst H. Kantorowicz shows, the distinction was a recurring one in English (and Continental) legal history. For the English context, see esp. 20–23.

45. Hobbes probably considered the end of the dialogue to be "imperfect" because this discussion is a digression from the ostensible topic, "Of Punishments."

46. For Cropsey, there is an important "difference in emphasis" between the dialogue and Hobbes's earlier works: Hobbes is now proposing that "the true rationality of the law inheres not simply in the reason of the sovereign doctrinairely insisted upon but in the endurability of the laws as that is signified or imparted to them through the assent of the people in Parliament" (13–14). His view reminds us that for Hobbes, rationality, even if it is "doctrinairely insisted upon," is artificial, something made rather than found, and those who challenge it challenge only whom Hobbes allows to do the making. Pocock, agreeing with Cropsey, says that in his concessions to the lawyer and to the role of Parliament in that making, Hobbes's philosopher sounds like none other than James Harrington, the political theorist who imported the ideology of civic humanism to England in the seventeenth century in part to challenge Hobbes's doctrine of absolute sovereignty (*Ancient Constitution and the Feudal Law*, 165). But Susan Moller Okin, although she agrees that Hobbes places a new emphasis on the monarch's need to consult with Parliament, to compensate for the possible deficiencies in his or her "natural intelligence," concludes that this difference "does not constitute a radical break with Hobbes's theory of absolutism," for Hobbes continues to insist that the monarch is the ultimate judge in the commonwealth (71). And Stoner, even more skeptical of the "change" that the dialogue is supposed to indicate, maintains that Hobbes's monarch has always had to consult with Parliament because he or she has always had to seek good counsel for his or her actions. If Hobbes's philosopher does concede a point here and there to the lawyer and to Parliament, it is only because he has come to see Parliament as a counselor writ large (123–30).

47. But shifting the responsibility for knowing the law is not the same as shifting the authority to interpret the law (or Scripture) to the individual subject (or believer). Again, I agree with Silver, in "A Matter of Interpretation," that Hobbes wants to supervise individual acts of interpretation (166).

48. As Stoner would have it.

2. Harrington and Neville: Dialogue and Disinterestedness

1. Woodmansee, 11, 32. Jerome Stolnitz traces a lineage of the concept that begins with Shaftesbury and other eighteenth-century British writers on aesthetics, and Elizabeth A. Bohls follows the migration of the concept into eighteenth-century moral and political theory, where the subject of aesthetics, contemplating an object of art disinterestedly, becomes the "paradigmatic"

figure for the abstractly equal individual entering into a social contract and the impartial spectator exercising a sympathetic morality (17). What I do in this chapter is reverse the lineage traced by Stolnitz and Bohls, finding an alternative origin of disinterestedness in civic-humanist political theory, a concept that the civic-humanist Shaftesbury later *makes* aesthetic. Although he begins with Shaftesbury, John Barrell makes much the same move.

2. For his use of the term *cultural capital*, see Bourdieu.

3. J. G. A. Pocock defines the "style of thought" that he and others have termed *civic humanism* in *Politics, Language, and Time*, 85. In *Machiavellian Moment* and again in *Virtue, Commerce, and History* Pocock traces the evolution of the civic-humanist concept of virtue from sixteenth-century Florence to eighteenth-century America. The central dynamic for Pocock in this evolution is the antinomy between virtue, which depends (as I discuss below) on the possession of real property to resist appeals to private interest, and commerce, which accumulates mobile property by seeming to succumb to those appeals. This antinomy is a central concern of chapter 4.

4. Robbins, introduction to *Two English Republican Tracts*, 48.

5. Pocock explains the necessary connection between civic humanism and a republican form of government in *Politics, Language, and Time*, 80–103. Elsewhere, Pocock expresses the relationship between civic humanism and republicanism thus: civic humanism "denote[s] a certain formulation of republican consciousness and its problems" (*Machiavellian Moment*, 58).

6. According to C. B. Macpherson, this insight, which Neville takes directly from Harrington, is Harrington's singular contribution to political theory: he "discovered a relation between property distribution and political power that had only been glimpsed by earlier writers, had formulated it systematically, and used it successfully to explain political change" (160).

7. For the importance of property to civic humanism, see Pocock, *Machiavellian Moment*, pt. 3; and idem, *Virtue, Commerce, and History*. For a discussion of Harrington's Agrarian Law, see Blitzer, 226–33. For the Agrarian Law itself, see Harrington's *Oceana*, in Harrington, 230–41. All further page references for Harrington's works, cited in the text and notes by their individual titles (e.g., *Valerius and Publicola*), are to his *Political Works*, ed. Pocock.

8. That said, it is worth noting that the composition of the commons was still greatly restricted to property holders. Although Harrington and Neville wanted to extend the franchise to inject more of the "many" into government, they and their fellow republicans, as Caroline Robbins notes, "were in no sense democratic" (*Eighteenth-Century Commonwealthman*, 49). In *Plato Redivivus* the Englishman warns that admitting into government "the meaner sort of people"—that is, the ones who have no property—is "anarchy" (102). And in response to the Doctor's allegation that his reforms smell like "a common-

wealth, or democracy," he insists that "I abhor the thoughts of wishing, much less endeavouring, any such thing, during the circumstances we are now in" (173).

9. For the best discussion of this critical passage from *Oceana,* see Pocock's historical introduction to Harrington's *Political Works,* 64–67.

10. Hume, *Essays,* 99, 106–7.

11. [Neville], *Parliament of Ladies,* 12.

12. Pocock, historical introduction to Harrington, *Political Works,* 115.

13. In *Valerius and Publicola,* for example, Publicola asserts that "every proposition to the people" that is debated in the senate "is to be promulgated, that is, printed and published to the whole nation, six weeks before the time that the representative is to assemble and give the vote of the commonwealth without which no such proposition can be any law." As Valerius surmises, "By this means it must follow that the whole people, both by discourse and letters, debate six weeks together upon the matter," and he wonders of Publicola, "How is it then that you say the representative of the people must not debate?" Harrington's spokesperson replies that the publication of proposed laws may constitute debate "*of* the representative" but "not unto any debate at all *in* the representative" (799–800, emphasis added). He means that the debate that takes place among the people is already distanced enough to count as "resolution" rather than debate.

14. In his elaborate description of the debating function in *Oceana,* Harrington similarly aligns it with the ability to "divide," or judge. Imagine two "girls" given the task of distributing "a cake yet undivided" fairly between them. In such a situation, Harrington exclaims, one girl will naturally "divide" the cake and the other, just as naturally, will elect to "choose" between the halves the first girl has divided. If one girl both divides and chooses, the distribution of the cake will not be fair: it is the separation of powers that ensures distributive justice." Immediately after this illustration Harrington defines the debating function as the ability "to discern, or put a difference between things that being alike are not the same, or . . . separating and weighing the reason against that and that reason against this, which is dividing" (172–73).

15. On Neville's parliamentary career, see Cotton, 54–55; and Von Maltzahn. Pocock says that Neville "was a leader of debate" in Richard Cromwell's 1659 Parliament ("James Harrington and the Good Old Cause," 45).

16. Pagden, 8.

17. In her introduction to *Two English Republican Tracts* Robbins identifies some possible models for the characters in *Plato Redivivus.* The English Gentleman is obviously Neville himself. The Noble Venetian "has not been identified," but he may be modeled after Neville's friend Cosmo III, the grand duke of Tuscany (1643–1723). The Doctor, Robbins claims, is Richard

Lower (1631–91), known as the "Aesculapius of his age," although others have suggested that he may be John Locke (71, 13–19).

18. The party of opposition to the king, which came to be known in early 1681 as the Whigs, began in 1678 to gain in public opinion by stirring fears, through the so-called Popish Plot, of "popery and arbitrary government." In 1681, however, Charles dissolved the Oxford Parliament and arrested the leader of the opposition, the first earl of Shaftesbury, and the tide turned back to the king and his party. For the complex struggle between the loyalist and opposition parties (Tories and Whigs) for political power and public opinion in the years 1678–81, see Jones, Knights.

19. Pocock notes that the dialogue "bears the date 22 October, ten days after the Army dissolved the rump, and contains several of what may be allusions to that event" (historical introduction to Harrington, *Political Works*, 114).

20. Von Maltzahn, 41.

21. Hutton, *British Republic, 1649–1660*, 128; see also ibid., 124–30, and Hutton, *Restoration*, 67, 70–71.

22. Then again, Neville may have contributed his share of the writing too: Hobbes was among those who suspected that he "had a finger in that pye," that is, the writing of *Oceana* (Aubrey, 208).

23. That fear became hysteria over the Popish Plot should not, according to its historians, prevent us from taking that fear seriously. For a detailed account of the Plot, see Kenyon. For the place of the Plot and the Exclusion Crisis in the rise of political parties in England, see Jones.

24. Pocock, *Machiavellian Moment*, 406. Pocock treats Neville only in passing. The most detailed analysis of Neville's contribution to republican thought is in Robbins's introduction to *Two English Republican Tracts*, 5–20; Robbins also has a bibliography of Neville's works. Other discussions of Neville can be found in Fink, 123–48; and Robbins, *Eighteenth-Century Commonwealthman*, 32–41.

25. Robbins takes this phrase from a tract, entitled *The Armie's Dutie: or, Faithful Advice to the Souldiers*, that various Harringtonians, most likely including Neville, published to influence parliamentary opinion in May 1659 (introduction to *Two English Republican Tracts*, 10).

26. Another republican, Algernon Sidney, actually justified rebellion in his *Discourses Concerning Government* (posthumously published in 1698) and was executed in 1683 for his real or supposed role in the Rye House Plot (Neville, *Plato Redivivus*, 167 n. 1).

27. Fink, 70.

28. Robbins quotes a letter from Anthony Hammond to Walter Moyle, two of her "eighteenth-century commonwealthmen," in which Hammond, referring to Neville, declares that "the late Happy Revolution has brought

such a change in our Constitution in those several branches which he only wished and proposed to King Charles II." Among other reforms, the revolution limited the monarch's right of making war and peace (Robbins, *Eighteenth-Century Commonwealthman*, 36). In her introduction to *Plato Redivivus*, however, Robbins herself concludes that such measures "by no means carried the recommendations put forward in *Plato Redivivus*" (*Two English Republican Tracts*, 15).

29. W. W., 29, 34, 31, 34–35. Robbins lists the replies to *Plato Redivivus*, many of which, like *Antidotum Britannicum*, were also cast as dialogues, in her introduction to *Two English Republican Tracts*, 17–18.

30. In actual fact, Harrington is somewhat more solicitous of those with "hereditary rights" than Neville. In *Oceana* Harrington assumes that the wiser few who compose the senate will be aristocratic as well as meritorious: "There is something first in the making of a commonwealth, then in the governing of her, and last of all in the leading of her armies, which, though there be great divines, great lawyers, great men in all professions, seems to be peculiar unto the genius of a gentleman" (183).

31. Pocock, historical introduction to Harrington, *Political Works*, 116.

32. Valerius quotes Harrington's own words to Publicola—that "the people cannot see, but they can feel" (798)—as a way of expressing his skepticism that Publicola's proposals for reform will ever be heeded by an emotional, not rational, populace. The words Valerius quotes are from Harrington's *Aphorisms Political* (762).

33. Robbins, introduction to *Two English Republican Tracts*, 11; Aubrey, 209. The Rota disbanded when George Monck made his move to restore the king in February 1660.

3. Shaftesbury: Dialogue and Distinction

1. Lawrence E. Klein notes that Shaftesbury actually delivered this, his "maiden speech" in Parliament, in January 1696 (*Shaftesbury and the Culture of Politeness*, 136).

2. Shaftesbury, "Sketch of the Life of the Third Earl of Shaftesbury," xxi.

3. In defense of his more generous interpretation of Shaftesbury's philosophy and politics, one that sees him as more interested in giving voice to real ideological differences than I consider to be the case, Prince asks, "Are we not, as members of different 'classes' . . . simultaneously involved in various structures of power, articulations of authority, constructions of identity?" (28). I would answer that of course we are but that to be "involved" in various structures of power is not the same as "constructing" one, and my claim in

this chapter is that the structure of power—distinction—that Shaftesbury constructs and the philosophy of dialogue that is contained within it suppress rather than give voice to difference.

4. This skepticism about bringing an ideological consensus out of diversity is not the rejection of rational grounds for belief that is labeled Pyrrhonian skepticism, and yet many scholars place Shaftesbury in that tradition. See, e.g., Aldridge, 353; Grean, 14–18; and especially Norton. Shaftesbury was certainly a deist in religion and thus, at least to an orthodox divine like Berkeley, a freethinker or skeptic himself, but, as Prince points out, in *The Moralists* he gives the "Pyrrhonian commonplaces" that were used against the argument from design to Philocles, his representative skeptic (59), and favors the Neoplatonic theist Theocles.

5. Norton, 3–4. Another way of phrasing this distinction, as I have already done, is to say that Shaftesbury doubts the certainty of opinions but not of manners.

6. For Shaftesbury as a civic humanist, see Barrell, 3–10; and Solkin, 1–26. For Shaftesbury as a republican, see Robbins, *Eighteenth-Century Commonwealthman*, 128–32.

7. Klein, *Shaftesbury and the Culture of Politeness*, 198.

8. Eagleton, *Ideology of the Aesthetic*, 34.

9. Voitle, 58. "Politics," says Klein, was for Shaftesbury "the exemplary arena of inauthenticity" (138).

10. Shaftesbury, *Life, Unpublished Letters, and Philosophical Regimen*, 115.

11. Jerome Stolnitz, in his groundbreaking article, states that Shaftesbury "is the first philosopher to call attention to disinterested perception" (132); see also above, ch. 2, n. 1. Although one of my conclusions in chapter 2 is that disinterestedness should be understood as originating in political theory rather than in aesthetics, Shaftesbury is certainly the first to theorize, or "philosophize" about, the concept and to give it a specifically aesthetic tinge.

12. Stanley Grean discerns that both factionalism—"having an excess of social affection"—and corruption—"having an excess of self-directed impulses"—are political problems for Shaftesbury (176), and his analysis is unique in even identifying factionalism as a problem. It is clear, however, that Shaftesbury's real concern is with factionalism rather than corruption, for by stressing that natural sociability is stronger than self-interest he can draw the contrast with Hobbes most sharply.

13. This is where Shaftesbury fits the thesis of Ernest Lee Tuveson, in *The Imagination as a Means of Grace*, that he and other "pre-Romantics" make "the very absence of rational activity" into "a virtue of the imagination" (94).

14. As R. L. Brett perceives, the most crucial moments in *The Moralists*, the moments in which Theocles attempts to convince Philocles of the truth

of his "final convictions," are based "on presuppositions which he does not argue" (65).

15. Swift, 108. Klein discusses Shaftesbury's rehabilitation of enthusiasm in the context of his critique of Anglican orthodoxy in *Shaftesbury and the Culture of Politeness*, 160–69.

16. These statements of Philocles', coming as they do at the end of *The Moralists*—Philocles' first statement, which comes at the beginning of the dialogue, is written to Palemon in retrospect—lead me to doubt Prince's conclusion that Philocles "holds himself aloof from any determination" and that his dialogue with Theocles "does not result in any binding conclusion, least of all in a rhapsodic apprehension of unity" (51). Prince seems to hold that Shaftesbury's dialogue remains open, not closed or conclusive, because of two interpretive commitments: that a dialogue "structured . . . as a confrontation between two senses of dialogue . . . seems an odd way of staging" a conversion from skepticism to theism (51) and that Philocles the skeptic consistently "annexes" Theocles' enthusiastic rhetoric "to suspect temporal interests" (52), specifically the latter's landed estate. Any initial disparity in their positions, or their "senses of dialogue," however, would only make Philocles' conversion more dramatic, not less likely, and I see no evidence that Philocles ever seriously calls attention to the material wealth that enables Theocles to transcend skepticism.

Enthusiasm is the central concept in Grean's *Shaftesbury's Philosophy of Religion and Ethics:* he discusses it in particular on pages 19–36. For more on enthusiasm in general, see Knox.

17. The title of the first draft of *The Moralists* is *The Sociable Enthusiast;* the subtitle of *The Moralists* is *A Philosophical Rhapsody*. Two copies of *The Sociable Enthusiast* survive in the Shaftesbury papers at the Public Record Office. See Whitaker; and Voitle, 313–14. For more on the meaning of rhapsody (and enthusiasm) in Shaftesbury, see Rogers.

18. Prostko, 60.

19. Shaftesbury wrote that Locke's denial of innate ideas "struck at all fundamentals, threw all order and virtue out of the world" (Shaftesbury, *Life, Unpublished Letters, and Philosophical Regimen*, 403).

20. Several critics have made the point that Shaftesbury seeks in taste, and in the discourse of aesthetics that his discussion of it initiates, a unity that he finds no longer possible in the factionalized world of postrevolutionary politics, and I would strongly agree. Eagleton, for example, asserts that for Shaftesbury and the moral-sense philosophers who followed him, "the beautiful is just political order lived out on the body" (*Ideology of the Aesthetic*, 37). Elizabeth A. Bohls says even more forcefully that for the same group of philosophers, "the aesthetic sphere emerges as an alternative site for a harmony

perceived to be slipping away in other areas of life, notably the political" (18). And part of Prince's argument about Shaftesbury is that he displaces his dislike of extreme political positions "onto the more tractable plane of a 'criticism of authors'" and genres (32).

21. As John Andrew Bernstein explains, Shaftesbury "attempted to demonstrate that what is truly beautiful is what *ought* to please after the fashion of a moral norm, and that what is morally good provides the truest forms of pleasure and satisfaction" (23).

22. Shaftesbury uses a gamut of terms to describe the sense or faculty that resolves controversy at the end of *The Moralists,* but I have settled on the term *distinction* in order to evoke Pierre Bourdieu's critique of the aesthetic enterprise. In *Distinction,* a vast survey of contemporary aesthetic attitudes, Bourdieu reveals how "art and cultural consumption are predisposed . . . to fulfill a social function of legitimating social differences" (7). I discuss the social differences that Shaftesbury's distinction legitimates, and therefore the essentially private character of the sphere of dialogue that he depicts as public, in the last section of this chapter.

23. Williams, 281.

24. I have been significantly influenced in this section, indeed throughout this chapter, by two articles on Shaftesbury by Robert Markley, "Style as Philosophical Structure" and especially "Shaftesbury, Sterne, and the Theatrics of Virtue." Although Markley's palpable dislike for Shaftesbury seems motivated by his own anachronistic yearnings for a more egalitarian eighteenth century, he does expose the exclusive principles that lie behind Shaftesbury's inclusive rhetoric.

25. For this reason, David S. Shields cautions us not to understand even Shaftesbury's "sensus communis" as "'common sense,' either in its guise as conventional wisdom or a generally apprehended experience" (xviii). Ernst Cassirer does the same: "It is a certainty which reveals itself only to the nobler and finer nature" (162).

26. Prostko makes much the same point as I do when he questions Shaftesbury's "sleight of hand" in using the Socratic dialogue as his "model" for "the conversation that one should have with oneself before participating in public discussion" and then avoiding the "freewheeling rational debate" that such a model would suggest (54).

27. This is Markley's more cynical view of Shaftesbury's rhetoric. He draws his notion of "dialogic" discourse (and the "monologic" discourse that opposes it) from, of course, Mikhail Bakhtin ("Shaftesbury," 214–15).

28. Shaftesbury's anxiety about overt persuasion explains his derision of the way dialogue writing is usually practiced in eighteenth-century England.

Because most dialogues are polemical, not philosophical (and disinterested), most dialogue writers are like the "poor Pencil-man" who, writing for hire, is both engaged and too engaging, and contemporary "*Dialogue* is at an end" (1:110).

29. See, e.g., Price, 90.

30. Shaftesbury declined William's offer to become secretary of state in 1701 because he thought that "I could best serve Him & my Country in a disinterested Station" (quoted in Voitle, 212).

31. In other words, Shaftesbury reserves his dialogue for like-minded individuals and talks *at* the public. When he imagines what it would be like to talk to the undifferentiated, undistinctive public, as in the following passage from the *Miscellaneous Reflections,* Shaftesbury manifests the disdain for rhetoric and its usual audience that Jasper Neel traces back to Shaftesbury's philosophical heroes the Greeks. "Classical Greek thought," says Neel, "as it has come down to us in the texts of Plato and Aristotle, is structured on a notion of social order in which the philosophical, ennobled few are simply better than the rhetorical, degraded many" (73).

32. Prostko (60) calls attention to this passage, as well as to the gentleman's retreat.

33. Hohendahl, 52. This is why Habermas says that the public sphere originated in the literary realm, where the judgments are more "subjective." The middle class took what it had learned from criticizing what had been absolute standards in art and literature and exposed as similarly subjective the more stubborn absolutist justifications in politics.

34. Fraser, 6.

35. Douglas, 68, 86. Reinhart Koselleck criticizes the philosophes that he discusses in *Critique and Crisis* for a similar stance of critical nonengagement.

In calling Shaftesbury's skepticism a luxury, I am aware that I am placing a modern, or at least Mandevillian, "spin" on a word that Shaftesbury's contemporaries—in particular those (like Bolingbroke) who followed him and reinterpreted the language of civic humanism in opposition—defined quite differently. For them, luxury was a vice of the middle or lower classes, associated with the surplus wealth generated by commerce, not of "disinterested" gentlemen and their landed estates. John Sekora surveys the history of the concept, especially in the eighteenth century, and Christopher J. Berry examines what concerns about luxury throughout history reveal about ideas of social order. What I am calling a luxury, however, is not as much Shaftesbury's privileged social status as the privilege that he claims in disavowing political engagement for philosophical dialogue.

4. Mandeville: Dialogue as Commerce

1. Gorak, 5.

2. This is, needless to say, a simplified version of Mandeville's economic "theory," which I believe, with F. B. Kaye (cxxxiv–cxli) and Nathan Rosenberg, is better classified as laissez-faire than mercantilist.

3. When Mandeville looks for Shaftesbury's standard of taste, he finds that "we are puzzled and agree not always with ourselves, much less with others," and concludes, "It is manifest then that the hunting after this *Pulchrum & Honestum* is not much better than a Wild-Goose-Chace" (1:325–26, 331). Kaye, the editor of the classic, scholarly edition of the *Fable*, calls this Mandeville's "philosophical anarchism" and classifies him as a Pyrrhonian skeptic (lvi–lviii). Mandeville most fully explicates his skepticism in *Free Thoughts on Religion, the Church, and National Happiness* (1720). For an alternative (and I think seriously mistaken) view "that Mandeville's ethical theory is not at any point sceptical, relativist, or Pyrrhonist," see Maxwell, 245.

4. Mandeville's "one overtly political pamphlet," *The Mischiefs that Ought Justly to be Apprehended from a Whig-Government* (1714), justifies the Whig ascendancy in a dialogue between Tantivy, a discontented Tory, and Loveright. It is attributed to Mandeville by H. T. Dickinson in his introduction to the reprinted pamphlet (i). Dickinson further considers Mandeville's politics in "The Politics of Bernard Mandeville" and "Bernard Mandeville: An Independent Whig."

5. Given Mandeville's skepticism about conventional moral codes, I find it difficult to describe his writings as satire. He certainly mocks the moral transgressions of his day as vigorously as any satirist, but he lacks the fixed moral standard, or satiric norm, that a true satirist needs to evaluate those transgressions. Both Robert H. Hopkins and, to a greater extent, Phillip Harth, in "The Satiric Purpose of *The Fable of the Bees*," argue, as Harth puts it, that Mandeville's satire is not directed against "palpable vices" but against "the less obtrusive vice of hypocrisy" as practiced by those who decry private vices as they reap their public benefits (328). I prefer Robert W. Uphaus's view that Mandeville writes not to satirize (and thus prescribe moral terms) but merely to describe facts about human nature that, because they are disorienting, have the *effect* of satire (144–45).

6. Mandeville does not, as Irwin Primer shows, explicitly contrast his system to Shaftesbury's until the 1723 edition of the *Fable*, which contains the essay "A Search into the Nature of Society," which I quote in this paragraph. In his 1720 work *Free Thoughts* Mandeville actually approves of Shaftesbury's skepticism in religion and borrows from him in several places ("Mandeville and Shaftesbury," 126–30).

7. Copley, 69.

8. Bond, *Tatler,* 3:146.

9. Dissimulation not only divides or distinguishes the greater quality from the lesser one; it also, as Nicholas Hudson explains, favors the abstract term over the concrete one. In Mandeville's account of the origin of society, according to Hudson, politicians reject "the frank dialogue of our distant ancestors" as too specific and replace it "by a language that is vague and unspecific, but nonetheless more conducive to peaceful and stable interaction between people" ("Language," 257). See also Hudson, "Dialogue."

10. See Klein, "The Third Earl of Shaftesbury."

11. Hundert, 114.

12. The dialogue was one of Mandeville's favorite literary forms. Not only part 2 of the *Fable* but also his conduct manual for women, *The Virgin Unmask'd* (1709), his medical text *A Treatise on the Hypochondriack and Hysterick Passions* (1711), *The Mischiefs that Ought Justly to be Apprehended from a Whig-Government,* and the sequel to the *Fable, An Enquiry into the Origin of Honour* (1732), were written in dialogue form.

13. When Horatio parodies William Law's reference to the undoubtedly virtuous "Sons of *Noah*" in answer to Mandeville's account of the vicious origin of virtue, for example, Cleomenes has to ask him "Whether you intend this as a *Sarcasm* or not" (2:197–98). Richard I. Cook calls the "tone" of part 2 "far less deliberately provocative" and "less jarring" than that of part 1, "one of good-humored explication rather than one of aggressive assertion" (137–38). The change in tone is part of Mandeville's overall effort to "illustrate and explain" part 1.

14. According to F. A. Hayek, Cleomenes' theory "mark[s] the definite breakthrough in modern thought of the twin ideas of evolution and of the spontaneous formation of an order" (126).

15. Mandeville, *Free Thoughts,* 164. Primer notes that this sentence is actually one of Mandeville's "unacknowledged borrowings from Shaftesbury" and that Shaftesbury in turn borrows it from (and acknowledges) the emperor Julian's message to the Bostrens (Primer, "Mandeville and Shaftesbury," 132–33; Shaftesbury, *Characteristicks,* 2:171).

16. In particular—and just as does Shaftesbury—Mandeville distinguishes philosophical thinking from the political practice of "Those Polemick Authors" and "Party-Men" who "have a greater Regard to what will serve their Purpose, than they have to Truth or Sincerity" (*Letter to Dion,* 9). In part 2 of the *Fable* Cleomenes mentions that he and Horatio long ago "agreed . . . never to enter into Party Disputes" (2:42).

17. *Tea-Table* 25; *True Meaning of the Fable of the Bees,* 27. These examples are mentioned in Gunn, *Beyond Liberty and Property,* 108; and Hundert, 153.

18. Although I frame Mandeville's contradiction as an inconsistency between dissimulative commerce and enlightening dialogue, the same contradiction is present in all of his writings, if somewhat muted in part 1 of the *Fable*, for example, by his heavily ironic tone. Even irony is not dissimulation, because the ironic author wants the reader to get the joke, and the dialogues of part 2 only exemplify the enlightenment that Mandeville always pursues. In this sense, all of Mandeville's writings are part of an honest conversation, or dialogue, with his reader (and every reader a Horatio).

19. Steven Fuller states it best: if Mandeville is to represent public virtue as the "unintended consequence" of private vice, "then he must presume that the agents are ignorant of the consequences of their actions" (31). Mandeville cannot presume this, however, because he writes to enlighten, not to keep the people "in awe."

20. Irene E. Gorak also refers to Marx when she compares the contrast that Mandeville detects between the subjective self and the social self to the "contradictions" that Marx sees between the harsh reality of capitalism and the beneficent face that it presents to the world (7–8).

21. Dowling, 116. Dowling points out that Marx borrowed the concept of contradiction from Hegel, for whom it was an ontological concept, "a principle of the unfolding of reality," not a socioeconomic one.

22. Jonathan Brody Kramnick perceives a similar contradiction in Mandeville's attack on the charity-school movement that sought to educate the "labouring poor" to be virtuous, as well as dutiful, subjects. On the one hand, Mandeville insists that he is no "Mortal Foe to all Literature and useful Knowledge, and a wicked Advocate for Universal Ignorance and Stupidity" (1:298), and elsewhere he defies the exclusively aristocratic nature of a Shaftesburean kind of virtue by insisting "that the poor *are* educable," that they have "the same passions as anyone else." On the other hand (and to follow the logic of his own argument), to keep the capitalist system going—a system that needs workers who will accept low wages because they do not know any better—Mandeville has to keep the poor where they are: uneducated. In short, to oppose how the charity-school movement threatened, through education, to discontent the poor with their meager lot in society, Mandeville was forced to explain what would make them discontented, an explanation that itself amounted to a kind of education (170–71).

23. For Defoe, see Meier.

24. Goldsmith, 134. Malcolm Jack traces the history of the eighteenth-century debate between those who, employing the language of civic humanism, criticize "corruption" and those (like Mandeville) who, employing the language of political economy, accept commercial modernity and "progress."

25. Daniel, 606, emphasis added.

26. In saying that Mandeville thinks of rationality not as a "fact" but as a useful "fiction," I appropriate the terms of Uphaus, 143–44.

27. Mandeville, *An Enquiry into the Origin of Honour,* 41.

28. M. M. Goldsmith says that "it is not necessary to take Mandeville's skillful politicians as literally as they seem to be presented to us": they are simply a "device" to personify "the long, gradual development of social institutions" (61, 64). (For an alternative view, see Viner, 14.) If the skillful politician is, like reason itself, a useful fiction, then so is the idea that one can profitably speculate about what makes a commonwealth "well-order'd." The commonwealth will run of its own accord, no matter what a philosopher may think about it. For the implications of this point for the history of the dialogue, see the conclusion.

29. Kahn, "Habermas, Machiavelli, and the Humanist Critique of Ideology," 466.

30. Kaye calls this, Mandeville's "strict Test of Virtue" (1:405), his position of moral "rigorism," which he contrasts to his "dominant" utilitarianism (xlvii–lvi).

31. Hundert, 149–50. For Mr. Spectator at the Royal Exchange, see number 69, in Bond, *Spectator,* 1:292–96.

32. "The public sphere in Habermas's sense is . . . conceptually distinct from the official economy; it is not an arena of market relations but rather one of discursive relations, a theater for debating and deliberating rather than for buying and selling" (Fraser, 2). I would add only that "market relations" are discursive too. Even if they exchange interests rather than share opinions, Mandeville's disagreeable lawyers, physicians, divines, and tradesmen must still talk to one another (however deceitfully) in order to do so.

33. Mandeville's democratizing impulse extends to gender as well as class. Refusing to succumb to the conventional eighteenth-century distinction between reasonable men and passionate women, he frequently used female characters in his dialogues to show that women could be just as reasonable as men. For example, in the first dialogue of part 2 of the *Fable,* a woman named Fulvia, introduced as Cleomenes' cousin, makes a brief appearance to debunk the civic-humanist aesthetic of Horatio in an even harsher fashion than Cleomenes does. In the preface Mandeville says that his female readers "will find no reason . . . to suspect that she wants either Virtue or Understanding" (2:19). As both David H. Solkin and Michael Prince propose of this passage, by having a woman oppose the prevailing sentiments of upper-class culture, Mandeville calls attention to that which such sentiments customarily exclude: the reason(s) not only of women but also of the poor and those who were otherwise marginal to eighteenth-century society (Solkin, 14–16; Prince, 204–5).

5. Berkeley: Dialogue as Catechism

1. Berkeley, *Works*, 3:37.

2. One of Mandeville's more perceptive critics, Berkeley was among those who caught the contradictions in his philosophy, not only his own intent, as Crito tells Lysicles, "to sacrifice all [self-interested] regards to the abstracted speculation of truth" (3:102) but also the counterproductive implications of such enlightened speculation. If virtue is merely "a trick of statesmen," Euphranor asks Lysicles, "[w]hy then do your sagacious sect betray and divulge that trick or secret of State, which wise men have judged necessary for the good government of the world?" (3:80).

3. Kant, 54–55.

4. It is curious, then, that Prince, in his chapter on *Alciphron*, describes it as a "mess" (108). He does so, presumably, because he wants to distinguish between its conversational stretches and the terse argument of Berkeley's *Hylas and Philonous*, and for that reason he classifies the former as a Ciceronian (rather than Platonic) dialogue, noting also the greater degree of fictional representation in *Alciphron*. But his description has the effect of diminishing the contrast that Berkeley draws between the orderly reasoning of the philosophically committed believer and the disorderly reasoning of freethinkers, a contrast in style and ability that Berkeley deliberately exemplifies in the dialogue itself.

5. As G. J. Warnock shows, Berkeley could not have endorsed a doctrine called "passive obedience," which to most dictated that hereditary monarchs must be obeyed at all costs and which had been "particularly associated with the Stuart monarchy" (555), without being suspected of Jacobitism. There is evidence that such a suspicion did hurt his preferment in the church. But Berkeley recognizes an even more sovereign power—God—over whatever entity is vested with sovereign power in the state, and he argues in the conclusion to *Passive Obedience* that we must resist, if still passively (not, that is, through active rebellion), the sovereign power if it commands an action that is immoral or against an individual citizen's conscience.

6. It should be pointed out, as T. E. Jessop does in his introduction to the *Principles*, that Berkeley uses the word "'idea' . . . in a particular sense." It "meant any *sensory* object, and therefore any corporeal object, whether perceived, remembered, or imagined. It is only of 'ideas' in this sense . . . that Berkeley makes his distinctive pronouncements" (2:8). In other words, for Berkeley, saying that a word signifies an idea is the same as saying that the idea actually exists, as a physical object. For the sake of clarity, however, I have preferred to say that Berkeley denies that abstract ideas actually exist, or that abstract words actually exist as ideas, rather than simply that he denies abstract ideas.

7. Jessop notes the relevant locations in Cicero (*De Senectute* 86 and *De Divinatione* 1.62) in Berkeley, 3:46 n. 1.

8. Bertil Belfrage offers a schematic overview of Berkeley's theory of emotive meaning. Paul J. Olscamp discounts the theory's importance by concluding that Berkeley makes no clear "distinction between clearly emotive and clearly cognitive meaning" (148). David Berman both explicates the theory and shows how Berkeley uses it to defend religion in *George Berkeley*, 12–17, 143–55.

9. Berman, *George Berkeley*, 12.

10. Olscamp, George Pitcher, and C. D. Broad all point out that for Berkeley, utility only allows one to determine the truth of a rule; it does not itself *make* it true. For Berkeley, "what makes any moral precept binding on us is simply that God has ordered us to act in accordance with it," not, as a utilitarian would have it, that that precept promotes the general good (Broad, 78).

11. For Berkeley's difficulties with the idea of "demonstration" in morality, see Conroy, 211.

12. In one respect, Lysicles is entirely correct. First "principles," those imbued by both freethinkers and believers before the age of reason, cannot be gained by "reasoning." Lysicles, in fact, has voiced the philosophical rationale for Berkeley's concern with proper education, which I discuss below.

13. Conroy, 211. I take this point from Stephen R. L. Clark, 244. Olscamp (167) and Pitcher (233ff.) make the same point.

14. Pitcher, for example, decides that at least in epistemology Berkeley "had no great respect for the deliverances of ordinary common sense" (254). How far Berkeley trusts common sense in philosophy is related to how far, because he denies the existence of physical objects, he can be described as a "skeptic," for common sense is usually opposed to skepticism. Berkeley devoted his career, as the subtitle to *Hylas and Philonous* proclaims, to opposing "Sceptics and Atheists," and in the dialogue Philonous brings Hylas to "believe our senses" by recognizing that objects simply are what we perceive them to be (2:244). Yet, to David Hume and others, Berkeley's immaterialism, "in spite of all attempts to avoid it, led to skepticism too" (Popkin, 317). Berkeley's critics invariably cite the lines that conclude *Hylas and Philonous*—that "the same principles which at first view lead to *scepticism*, pursued to a certain point, bring men back to common sense" (2:263)—to sum up his paradoxical attitude toward common sense. See Richetti, 159–63; Berman, *George Berkeley*, 29–44; and Prince, 96–104.

15. The maxim, as Jessop notes, is from the sixteenth-century Italian Augustinus Niphus (Berkeley, 2:62 n. 2).

16. Because it "contradicts vulgar and settled opinion," Berkeley writes in a letter to his friend John Percival, immaterialism "had need been introduced with great caution into the world" (8:36).

17. Ironically, it is Alciphron who repeats Berkeley's maxim in *Alciphron*, approving of it as "true" even as he asserts that at present "vulgar ears cannot bear" to hear freethinking notions (3:53–54).

18. Walmsley, 128–29.

19. I am indebted, as usual, to Peter Walmsley for this account of elenchus (69). Both Jessop, in his introductions to *Hylas and Philonous* (2:155–56) and to *Alciphron* (3:3), and Michael Morrisroe Jr. (156) classify Berkeley's dialogues as Platonic. As Walmsley points out, however, neither refers to the method of elenchus to do so (68). Prince makes a persuasive case for *Alciphron* as a Ciceronian rather than a Platonic dialogue based on "the degree of fictional representation" (109), but insofar as it depends on elenchus, it must be considered Platonic as well.

20. Socrates himself recognized that the method of elenchus tends to skepticism; Plato has him describe himself, famously, as one who has nothing to teach and who does "not think that I know what I do not know" (*Socrates' Defense [Apology]*, trans. Hugh Tredennick, 8 [21d], quoted in Walmsley, 87).

21. Perhaps because the comparison is a low one, none of Berkeley's critics—as far as I have been able to determine—draw the parallel between his method of dialogue and religious catechism.

22. The *replies* might not be creative, but the questions often were. Defoe's *Family Instructor* relies on the naive questions of a child who yearns to be instructed in the ways of faith to shame his mother and father into teaching him properly, and the official Anglican catechism for most of the sixteenth and seventeenth centuries, translated from Alexander Nowell's Latin into English in 1570 by Thomas Norton, actually puts "the declaration of the matter" in the mouth of the student rather than that of the teacher. Norton explains Nowell's reason for making "the scholar" seem "wiser than the maister" thus: "[T]he maister opposeth the scholar to see how he hath profited, & the scholar rendereth to the maister to geue accompt of his memory and diligence" (sig. A2r–A3v).

23. Sullivan, 211.

24. Ibid., 141. The phrase "vulgar errors" is from Toland, *Reasons for Naturalizing the Jews*, 17.

25. Toland, *Reasons for Naturalizing the Jews*, 21; idem, *Christianity not Mysterious*, 126–27.

26. Berman, *George Berkeley*, 170.

27. Even though Berkeley does not call it a "prejudice," Hylas's predisposition is a good test of the usefulness of prejudice in general. He begins the dialogue solidly convinced that "material substance" exists (2:172), but Philonous, through speculative arguments, brings him to see the metaphysical falseness of this opinion. Indeed, because Hylas is not a member of the

vulgar—he is a thinking person who has imbued his notion of substance from other thinking people, that is, Lockean philosophers—his prejudices are less likely to be reliable. The true and truly vulgar "prejudice," Hylas is brought to see, is to trust one's senses and disbelieve that substance exists.

28. Gadamer, 270. Gadamer mentions Edmund Burke as an Enlightenment philosopher who escaped its prejudice against prejudice; he does not mention Berkeley.

29. Weinsheimer, 167. Weinsheimer paraphrases Gadamer's rehabilitation of prejudice on pages 164–84. See also Warnke, 75–82.

30. The adjective "legitimate" is Gadamer's, 270. Burke talks about "just" prejudices in *Reflections on the Revolution in France*, 138.

31. For a history of the reaction to Berkeley's immaterialism, see Bracken.

32. In a sense, Berkeley sees the problem of enlightenment that tripped up Mandeville and skirts it: Mandeville discovered truths that were counterproductive to the dissimulation that drives his economic system but published them anyway; Berkeley, suspicious of the same and other "truths" but aware that even if untrue, they are destructive to the commonwealth, keeps them concealed.

33. Berman recognizes Berkeley's antienlightenment tendencies in "Enlightenment and Counter-Enlightenment in Irish Philosophy," 161–65.

34. Berkeley is too much a product of his enlightened age, and too much an assenter to the "revolution principles" of 1688, to believe that the sovereign has a divine right to rule, but he does believe that the fear of God—a "superstition" only to those unthinking subjects who cannot rationalize it—supports the useful prejudice that we should "passively obey," or not actively resist, the sovereign.

35. See also Prince, 113–15, on the "death of dialogue" in *Alciphron*.

36. Klein makes the point that a "recognition of Berkeley's critique of [mostly Shaftesbury's] 'politeness' . . . has to be balanced with an appreciation of Berkeley's attachment to a notion of politeness" ("Berkeley, Shaftesbury, and the Meaning of Politeness," 64–65).

37. Berkeley, *A Proposal for the better Supplying of Churches in our foreign Plantations. . .* , in *Works*, 7:356. For Berkeley's Bermuda scheme, see Gaustad.

38. A later tract of Berkeley's provocatively titled *A Defense of Free-thinking in Mathematics* proves that he was not for restricting philosophical speculation absolutely. In this tract, Berkeley, an amateur mathematician, defends his right to speculate against an expert, Dr. James Jurin, and even to question Jurin's mathematical authority, Isaac Newton. To defer to Newton's absolute authority in mathematics, he writes in the *Defence*, is "converting the republick of letters into an absolute monarchy, . . . even introducing a kind of philosophic popery among a free people." In the innocent matter of mathematics,

Berkeley thus ends up defending *both* common sense—his as a mathematical layman—and freethinking, which he describes here as refusing "to fix a *ne plus ultra,* to put a stop to all future inquiries" (4:115–16).

Conclusion: The Idea of a Perfect Commonwealth

1. Burtt, 31.

2. For Walpole's management of the press, see Dickinson, "Popular Politics in the Age of Walpole"; and Harris.

3. Morrice, 9.

4. According to Nicholas Phillipson, political discourse in the early to mid eighteenth century was "shaped by the journalists of Grub Street," and while acknowledging that the questions they raised were important, he concludes that they were not "intellectually resolved." The result, he says, was "a highly eclectic and intellectually incoherent political culture" (216). Phillipson does discuss the philosophers of the Scottish Enlightenment, particularly Hume, as a notable exception but suggests that the Act of Union of 1707 was an unusual spur to their speculation. "It was here, in a political world that was remote from that of London and from English party political discourse, that the most serious contemporary attempts to develop a coherent and peculiarly *British* political culture were to be made" (235).

5. See Prince's chapter entitled "The Platonic Revival: 1730–1770," 163–89. Crawford's graph of "the production of dialogues [of all kinds] by half-decades" between 1550 and 1750 reaches its high point of 107 in 1685 and its low point of 8 in 1730, rising slightly in the decades after that (607). He also notes that when the production of dialogues rises in number, the percentage of "purely political dialogues" goes up as well (602). By way of verifying Crawford's figures, I have compared the number of works listed in the English Short Title Catalogue database with the word *dialogue* in their titles for the decade 1680–90 (the decade of the Exclusion Crisis) with the number listed for the decade 1730–40 (the last decade covered by my study). (This is, admittedly, an inexact measure of the production of dialogues because not every work that announces itself as a "dialogue" is one and because many dialogue titles do not include the word, but it does give some indication of the relative popularity of the form across decades.) Of the 22,795 titles in the catalogue published between 1680 and 1690, 284, or 12.5 percent, contain the word *dialogue.* That percentage is more than halved in the decade 1730–40: 140 titles out of 23,401, or 6 percent. Furthermore, a survey of those 140 titles yields approximately 35, or 25 percent, that could be construed as political. In contrast, Crawford says that a full 72 percent of the twenty-five dialogues published in 1681 alone were political in nature (602).

The dialogue never regained its earlier popularity as a literary form even after political speculation revived in England in the late eighteenth century. Perhaps, as Prince suggests, the energies that had been invested in dialogical speculation were transferred to the relatively new genre of the novel, or perhaps the classical aura of the form seemed increasingly anachronistic in a more romantic era. Even the exceptions, such as Jane Marcet's dialogues for women (*Conversations on Political Economy* [1816] being the most pertinent example), tend to prove the rule, since Marcet uses the form to teach what to her mind are established principles of political economy, not, as Godwin might have done, to speculate about a new kind of political justice.

6. Burtt, 114. Satiric dialogues abound at all times, and satire is an important technique of polemic. My point is merely the comparative one that such satire is not balanced, as it was in the late seventeenth century, by speculation.

7. Habermas places this "structural transformation" sometime in our own century, when the public sphere "was burdened with the tasks of settling conflicts of interest that could not be accommodated within the classical forms of parliamentary consensus and agreement; their settlements bore the marks of their origins in the sphere of the market" (198). Late capitalism, that is, shattered the trust in the power of reason that originated in early capitalism. If, however, the public sphere was always less "disinterested" than Habermas assumes, as I have maintained throughout this study, then it was already "transforming" in this sense. I would hold, instead, that the public sphere transforms when philosophical speculation separates from political engagement. Shaftesbury signifies the beginning of this transformation.

8. Plumb, xviii; J. C. D. Clark, 4. For a recent challenge to Plumb's thesis, see Roberts. In the same issue of *Albion*, Norma Landau answers Roberts and, while updating Plumb's original thesis, defends him.

9. Even at *his* most extreme, in *Passive Obedience*, Berkeley takes care to allow for liberty of conscience, and in *Advice to the Tories who have taken the Oaths* he allows for submission to the de facto sovereign, thus dissociating himself from the most extreme, Jacobite wing of the Tory Party.

10. As William Coxe, Walpole's nineteenth-century biographer, explained Walpole's indifference to literary patronage, "The truth is . . . Sir Robert Walpole neither delighted in letters, nor considered poets as men of business. He was accustomed to say, that they were fitter for speculation than for action, that they trusted to theory, rather than to experience, and were guided by principles inadmissible in practical life" (quoted in Goldgar, 10).

11. Ferguson, 122. This quotation appears in Hayek, 140.

12. Bolingbroke, 1:292.

13. They thus assume the prototypically "Whig" position in the seventeenth-century controversy named for the royalist Robert Brady, who insisted, on the

other side, that the authority of kings and ministers had long supplanted that of Parliaments and noblemen. For the applicability of the Brady controversy to Bolingbroke's *Remarks*, see Kramnick, introduction to *Historical Writings*, xli–xliv. For the controversy itself, see Pocock, *Ancient Constitution and the Feudal Law*.

14. Pettit, 40; Pocock, *Machiavellian Moment*, 62.

15. Adam Potkay draws the connection between Demosthenes and Bolingbroke, though not with this quotation (44–45).

16. For the theory of Bolingbroke's opposition, including his distrust of parties and his "idea of a patriot king," see Kramnick, *Bolingbroke and His Circle*. For particular attention to the rhetoric of opposition, see Pettit, Gerrard.

17. Horne. For more on Arnall and the other "court Whig" defenders of Walpole, see Burtt, 110–27.

18. "Hopewell and Sullen," 2. Bribery, Hopewell elaborates, is "not in itself an immoral Act" provided that the elector being bribed "does really in his private Judgment prefer me to my Antagonist." Although Hopewell insists that this "is commonly the Case in most of what they call Briberies" (2), it certainly seems like a waste of money.

19. I do not mean to claim anything about the decline of the entire genre of dialogue in the eighteenth century (which Prince has recounted), but only about the decline of dialogue in the public sphere. Indeed, my point is actually supported by Potkay's thesis that a polite, conversational style persists, even "gains ascendancy over" classically republican ideals of oratory and eloquence, in eighteenth-century discourse (1). As Potkay notes, Hume, who defines and exemplifies the polite style in his essays, letters, and his own *Dialogues Concerning Natural Religion*, describes it as "fundamentally opposed" to "the flame of politics" (81). I have said here that the continued vitality of the public sphere depends on speculation (which a polite style can accommodate); I have taken it for granted throughout that it must also accommodate political discussion, however broadly defined, to remain vital. For the public sphere, then, the exclusion of politics as a topic of discourse is precisely the problem.

BIBLIOGRAPHY

Primary Texts

Aristotle. *The Nicomachean Ethics of Aristotle*. Translated, with an introduction by David Ross. Revised by J. L. Ackrill and J. O. Urmson. Oxford: Oxford University Press, 1980.

————. *On Rhetoric: A Theory of Civic Discourse*. Translated by George A. Kennedy. Oxford: Oxford University Press, 1991.

Aubrey, John. *Aubrey's Brief Lives*. Edited by Oliver Lawson Dick. 1949. Reprint, Harmondsworth: Penguin, 1972.

Berkeley, George. *The Works of George Berkeley*. Edited by A. A. Luce and T. E. Jessop. 9 vols. London: Thomas Nelson & Sons, 1948–57.

Bolingbroke, Lord (Henry St. John). *The Works of Lord Bolingbroke*. 4 vols. 1844. Reprint, London: Frank Cass, 1967.

Bond, Donald F., ed. *The Spectator*. 5 vols. Oxford: Oxford University Press, 1965.

————. *The Tatler*. 3 vols. Oxford: Oxford University Press, 1987.

A Brief Discourse Between a Sober Tory and a Moderate Whigg. London, [1680?].

Bunyan, John. *The Life and Death of Mr. Badman: Presented to the World in a Familiar Dialogue Between Mr. Wiseman, and Mr. Attentive*. Edited by James F. Forrest and Roger Sharrock. Oxford: Clarendon, 1988.

Burke, Edmund. *The Writings and Speeches of Edmund Burke*. Vol. 8, *The French Revolution 1790–1794*. Edited by L. G. Mitchell. Oxford: Clarendon, 1989.

Chudleigh, Mary. *The Ladies Defence*. In *The Poems and Prose of Mary, Lady Chudleigh*, edited by Margaret J. M. Ezell, 1–40. Oxford: Oxford University Press, 1993.

Coke, Edward. *A Commentary upon Littleton*. . . . 5th ed. London, 1656.

A Conference Between a Bensalian Bishop and an English Doctor, Concerning Church-Government. . . . London: Tho. Parkhurst & Joseph Collier, 1681.

Defoe, Daniel. *The Family Instructor*. 1715. Reprint, with an introduction by Paula R. Backscheider, Delmar, N.Y.: Scholars' Facsimiles & Reprints, 1989.

A Dialogue at Oxford Between a Tutor and a Gentleman, Formerly his Pupil, Concerning Government. London: Rich. Janaway, 1681.

A Dialogue Between Tom and Dick, Over a Dish of Coffee, Concerning Matters of Religion and Government. London, 1680.

Dryden, John. *Essays of John Dryden.* Edited by W. P. Ker. Oxford: Oxford University Press, 1926.

Eachard, John. *Mr. Hobbs's State of Nature Considered, In a Dialogue between Philautus and Timothy.* 1672. Edited by Peter Ure. English Reprints Series, 14. Liverpool: Liverpool University Press, 1958.

Ferguson, Adam. *An Essay on the History of Civil Society, 1767.* Edited by Duncan Forbes. Edinburgh: Edinburgh University Press, 1966.

Glanvill, Joseph. *Scire/i tuum nihil est.* In *Scepsis Scientifica: Or, Confest Ignorance, The Way to Science.* 1665. Facsimile ed. New York: Garland, 1978.

———. *The Vanity of Dogmatizing: The Three "Versions."* 1661, 1665, 1676. Reprint, with an introduction by Stephen Medcalf. Hove, Sussex: Harvester, 1970.

Hale, Matthew. *Reflections by the Lrd. Cheife Justice Hale on Mr. Hobbes His Dialogue of the Lawe.* In *A History of English Law,* by William Holdsworth, 5:500–13. 3rd ed. 1945. Reprint, London: Methuen, 1966.

Halifax, George Savile. *The Works of George Savile, Marquis of Halifax.* Edited by Mark N. Brown. 3 vols. Oxford: Clarendon, 1989.

Harrington, James. *The Political Works of James Harrington.* Edited by J. G. A. Pocock. Cambridge: Cambridge University Press, 1977.

Hobbes, Thomas, *Behemoth: Or, the Long Parliament.* Edited by Ferdinand Tönnies. 1889. Reprint, with an introduction by Stephen Holmes, Chicago: University of Chicago Press, 1990.

———. *A Briefe of the Art of Rhetorique.* In *The Rhetorics of Thomas Hobbes and Bernard Lamy,* edited by John T. Harwood, 33–128. Carbondale: Southern Illinois University Press, 1986.

———. *De Cive: The English Version.* Edited by Howard Warrender. Clarendon Edition of the Philosophical Works of Thomas Hobbes, no. 3. Oxford: Clarendon, 1983.

———. *De Homine.* Translated by Charles T. Wood, T. S. K. Scott-Craig, and Bernard Gert. In *Man and Citizen,* edited by Bernard Gert, 33–85. Gloucester, Mass.: Peter Smith, 1978.

———. *A Dialogue Between a Philosopher and a Student of the Common Laws of England.* Edited by Joseph Cropsey. Chicago: University of Chicago Press, 1971.

———. *The Elements of Law, Natural and Politic.* Edited by Ferdinand Tönnies. Cambridge: Cambridge University Press, 1928.

———. *The English Works of Thomas Hobbes of Malmesbury.* Edited by William Molesworth. 11 vols. London: J. Bohn, 1835–45.

———. *Leviathan.* Edited by C. B. Macpherson. Harmondsworth: Penguin, 1968.

———, trans. *The Peloponnesian War / Thucydides: The Complete Hobbes Transla-*

tion. 1629. With notes and a new introduction by David Grene. Chicago: University of Chicago Press, 1989.

"Hopewell and Sullen: A Conversation." *London Journal,* 21 October 1727, 1–2.

Honest Hodge and Ralph, Holding a sober Discourse. . . . London: Richard Janeway, 1680.

Hume, David. *Dialogues Concerning Natural Religion.* Edited by Norman Kemp Smith. 2nd ed. London: Thomas Nelson & Sons, 1947.

———. *Essays: Moral, Political, and Literary.* Edited by Eugene F. Miller. Indianapolis: Liberty Classics, 1985.

Kant, Immanuel. *Kant's Political Writings.* Edited by Hans Reiss. Translated by H. B. Nisbet. 2nd ed. Cambridge: Cambridge University Press, 1991.

Lawson, George. *An Examination of the Political Part of Mr. Hobbs His Leviathan.* 1657. Facsimile ed. London: Routledge/Thoemmes Press, 1996.

———. *Politica Sacra et Civilis.* Edited by Conal Condren. Cambridge: Cambridge University Press, 1992.

L'Estrange, Roger. *Citt and Bumpkin.* 1680. Reprint, with an introduction by B. J. Rahn. Augustan Reprint Society, 117. Los Angeles: William Andrews Clark Memorial Library, 1975.

———. *Toleration Discuss'd.* London: Henry Brome, 1663.

Locke, John. *An Essay Concerning Human Understanding.* Edited by Peter H. Nidditch. Oxford: Clarendon, 1975.

Mandeville, Bernard. *An Enquiry into the Origin of Honour, and the Usefulness of Christianity in War.* 1732. Facsimile, with an introduction by M. M. Goldsmith, London: Frank Cass, 1971.

———. *The Fable of the Bees, or, Private Vices, Publick Benefits.* Edited by F. B. Kaye. 2 vols. 1924. Reprint, Indianapolis: Liberty Classics, 1988.

———. *Free Thoughts on Religion, the Church, and National Happiness.* 1720. Facsimile, with an introduction by Stephen H. Good, Delmar, N.Y.: Scholars' Facsimiles & Reprints, 1981.

———. *A Letter to Dion.* 1732. Reprint, with an introduction by Jacob Viner. Augustan Reprint Society, 41. Los Angeles: William Andrews Clark Memorial Library, 1953.

———. *The Mischiefs that Ought Justly to be Apprehended from a Whig-Government.* 1714. Reprint, with an introduction by H. T. Dickinson. Augustan Reprint Society, 174. Los Angeles: William Andrews Clark Memorial Library, 1975.

Marcet, Jane. *Conversations on Political Economy.* . . . London: Longman, Hurst, Rees, Orme, & Brown, 1816.

Milton, John. *Areopagetica; for the Liberty of Unlicenc'd Printing.* Edited by William Haller. In *The Works of John Milton,* vol. 4. New York: Columbia University Press, 1931.

BIBLIOGRAPHY

A Modest Attempt for Healing the Present Animosities in England. . . . London: R. Janeway, 1690.

More, Thomas. *Utopia: Latin Text and English Translation.* Edited by George M. Logan, Robert M. Adams, and Clarence H. Miller. Cambridge: Cambridge University Press, 1995.

Morrice, Bezaleel. *The Present Corruption of Britains; Being a Paraphrase on the Latter Part of Mr. P——e's First Dialogue.* . . . London: Thomas Gray, 1738.

[Neville, Henry]. *The Parliament of Ladies. Or Diverse Remarkable Passages of Ladies in Spring-Garden, in Parliament Assembled.* London, 1647.

Neville, Henry. *Plato Redivivus: or, A Dialogue Concerning Government.* In *Two English Republican Tracts,* edited by Caroline Robbins, 61–200. Cambridge: Cambridge University Press, 1969.

Nowell, Alexander. *A Catechisme or First Instruction and Learning of Christian Religion.* Translated by Thomas Norton. 1570. Reprint, with an introduction by Frank V. Occhiogrosso, Delmar, N.Y.: Scholars' Facsimiles & Reprints, 1975.

[Onslow, Richard]. *A Dialogue Between the Pope and a Phanatick, Concerning Affairs in England.* London, 1680.

Plato. *The Collected Dialogues of Plato Including the Letters.* Edited by Edith Hamilton and Huntington Cairns. Princeton: Princeton University Press, 1961.

Shaftesbury, fourth earl of. "A Sketch of the Life of the Third Earl of Shaftesbury, by His Son, the Fourth Earl." In Shaftesbury, third earl of, *The Life, Unpublished Letters, and Philosophical Regimen of Anthony, Earl of Shaftesbury,* edited by Benjamin Rand, xvii–xxxi. New York: Macmillan, 1900.

Shaftesbury, third earl of (Anthony Ashley Cooper). *Characteristicks of Men, Manners, Opinions, Times.* Edited by Philip Ayres. 2 vols. Oxford: Clarendon, 1999.

———. *The Life, Unpublished Letters, and Philosophical Regimen of Anthony, Earl of Shaftesbury.* Edited by Benjamin Rand. New York: Macmillan, 1900.

Sprat, Thomas. *History of the Royal Society.* Edited by Jackson I. Cope and Harold Whitemore Jones. St. Louis: Washington University Press, 1958.

Swift, Jonathan. *A Tale of a Tub With Other Early Works, 1696–1707.* Edited by Herbert Davis. Oxford: Basil Blackwell, 1939.

Tea-Table, 15 May 1724.

The True Meaning of the Fable of the Bees. London: William & John Innys, 1726.

Toland, John. *Christianity not Mysterious.* 1696. Facsimile ed., Stuttgart: Friedrich Frommann Verlag, 1964.

———. *Reasons for Naturalizing the Jews.* . . . London: J. Roberts, 1714.

Tyrrell, James. *Bibliotheca Politica: Or an Enquiry into the Antient Constitution of the English Government.* . . . *In Fourteen Dialogues.* London: D. Browne, 1718.

W.W. *Antidotum Britannicum: Or, a Counter-Pest Against the Destructive Principles of "Plato Redivivus."* London: Richard Sare, 1682.

BIBLIOGRAPHY

The Whigg and Tory's Friendly Dialogue, Or, Admonition to Unity, as the greatest help and inlet to peace and quietness. London: J. Deacon, 1682.

White, Thomas. *An Exclusion of Scepticks From all Title to Dispute: Being an Answer to the Vanity of Dogmatizing.* London: John Williams, 1665.

Y[arranton, Andrew]. *A Coffee-House Dialogue: Or, a Discourse between Captain Y—— and a Young Barrester of the Middle-Temple.* . . . London, [1679?].

Secondary Texts

Ahrens, Rüdiger. "The Political Pamphlet: 1660–1714: Pre- and Post-Revolutionary Aspects." *Anglia* 109 (1991): 21–43.

Aldridge, Alfred Owen. "Shaftesbury and the Deist Manifesto." *Transactions of the American Philosophical Society,* n.s., 41 (1951): 295–385.

Ashcraft, Richard. *Revolutionary Politics and Locke's "Two Treatises of Government."* Princeton: Princeton University Press, 1986.

Barrell, John. *The Political Theory of Painting from Reynolds to Hazlitt: "The Body of the Public."* New Haven: Yale University Press, 1986.

Belfrage, Bertil. "Berkeley's Theory of Emotive Meaning (1708)." *History of European Ideas* 7 (1986): 643–49.

Berman, David. "Enlightenment and Counter-Enlightenment in Irish Philosophy." *Archiv für Geschichte der Philosophie* 64 (1982): 148–65.

———. *George Berkeley: Idealism and the Man.* Oxford: Clarendon, 1994.

Bernstein, John Andrew. *Shaftesbury, Rousseau, and Kant: An Introduction to the Conflict between Aesthetic and Moral Values in Modern Thought.* Cranbury, N.J.: Associated University Presses, 1980.

Berry, Christopher J. *The Idea of Luxury: A Conceptual and Historical Investigation.* Cambridge: Cambridge University Press, 1994.

Black, Jeremy, ed. *Britain in the Age of Walpole.* London: Macmillan, 1984.

Blitzer, Charles. *An Immortal Commonwealth: The Political Thought of James Harrington.* New Haven: Yale University Press, 1960.

Bohls, Elizabeth A. "Disinterestedness and Denial of the Particular: Locke, Adam Smith, and the Subject of Aesthetics." In *Eighteenth-Century Aesthetics and the Reconstruction of Art,* edited by Paul Mattick Jr., 16–51. Cambridge: Cambridge University Press, 1993.

Bourdieu, Pierre. *Distinction: A Social Critique of the Judgement of Taste.* Translated by Richard Nice. Cambridge: Harvard University Press, 1984.

Bracken, H. M. *The Early Reception of Berkeley's Immaterialism.* Rev. ed. The Hague: Martinus Nijhoff, 1965.

Brett, R. L. *The Third Earl of Shaftesbury: A Study in Eighteenth-Century Literary Theory.* London: Hutchinson's University Library, 1951.

Broad, C. D. "Berkeley's Theory of Morals." *Revue Internationale de Philosophie* 7 (1953): 72–86.

Burtt, Shelley. *Virtue Transformed: Political Argument in England, 1688–1740.* Cambridge: Cambridge University Press, 1992.

Campbell, Enid. "Thomas Hobbes and the Common Law." *Tasmanian University Law Review* 1 (1958): 20–45.

Cassirer, Ernst. *The Platonic Renaissance in England.* Austin: University of Texas Press, 1953.

Clark, J. C. D. *The Dynamics of Change: The Crisis of the 1750s and English Party Systems.* Cambridge: Cambridge University Press, 1982.

Clark, Stephen R. L. "God-Appointed Berkeley and the General Good." In *Essays on Berkeley: A Tercentennial Celebration,* edited by John Foster and Howard Robinson, 233–53. Oxford: Clarendon, 1985.

Condren, Conal. *George Lawson's "Politica" and the English Revolution.* Cambridge: Cambridge University Press, 1989.

Conroy, Graham P. "George Berkeley on Moral Demonstration." *Journal of the History of Ideas* 22 (1961): 205–14.

Cook, Richard I. *Bernard Mandeville.* Twayne's English Authors Series, 170. New York: Twayne, 1974.

Copley, Stephen. "Commerce, Conversation, and Politeness in the Early Eighteenth-Century Periodical." *British Journal for Eighteenth-Century Studies* 18 (spring 1995): 63–75.

Cotton, James. "The Harringtonian 'Party' (1659–1660) and Harrington's Political Thought." *History of Political Thought* 1 (1980): 51–67.

Cox, Virginia. *The Renaissance Dialogue: Literary Dialogue in Its Social and Political Contexts, Castiglione to Galileo.* Cambridge: Cambridge University Press, 1992.

Cranston, Maurice. "John Locke and John Aubrey." *Notes and Queries* 197 (1952): 383–84.

Crawford, Bartholow V. "The Prose Dialogue of the Commonwealth and the Restoration." *PMLA* 34 (1919): 601–9.

Cressy, David. *Literacy and the Social Order: Reading and Writing in Tudor and Stuart England.* Cambridge: Cambridge University Press, 1980.

Cropsey, Joseph. Introduction to *A Dialogue between a Philosopher and a Student of the Common Laws of England,* by Thomas Hobbes, edited by Joseph Cropsey. Chicago: University of Chicago Press, 1971.

Curtis, Mark H. *Oxford and Cambridge in Transition, 1588–1642.* Oxford: Clarendon, 1959.

Daniel, Stephen H. "Myth and Rationality in Mandeville." *Journal of the History of Ideas* 47 (1986): 595–609.

de Certeau, Michel. *The Writing of History.* Translated by Tom Conley. New York: Columbia University Press, 1988.

BIBLIOGRAPHY

Dickinson, H. T. Introduction to *The Mischiefs that Ought Justly to be Apprehended from a Whig-Government,* by Bernard Mandeville. Augustan Reprint Society, 174. Los Angeles: William Andrews Clark Memorial Library, 1975.

———. "Bernard Mandeville: An Independent Whig." *Studies on Voltaire and the Eighteenth Century* 152 (1976): 559–70.

———. "The Politics of Bernard Mandeville." In *Mandeville Studies: New Explorations in the Art and Thought of Dr. Bernard Mandeville,* edited by Irwin Primer, 80–97. The Hague: Martinus Nijhoff, 1975.

———. "Popular Politics in the Age of Walpole." In *Britain in the Age of Walpole,* edited by Jeremy Black, 45–68. London: Macmillan, 1984.

Douglas, Mary. "The Social Preconditions of Radical Scepticism." In *Power, Action, and Belief: A New Sociology of Knowledge,* edited by John Law, 68–87. Sociological Review Monograph, 32. London: Routledge & Kegan Paul, 1986.

Dowling, William C. *Jameson, Althusser, Marx: An Introduction to "The Political Unconscious."* Ithaca: Cornell University Press, 1984.

Eagleton, Terry. *The Function of Criticism: From "The Spectator" to Post-Structuralism.* London: Verso, 1984.

———. *The Ideology of the Aesthetic.* Oxford: Basil Blackwell, 1990.

Fink, Z. S. *The Classical Republicans: An Essay in the Recovery of a Pattern of Thought in Seventeenth-Century England.* Chicago: Northwestern University Press, 1945.

Fraser, Nancy. "Rethinking the Public Sphere: A Contribution to the Critique of Actually Existing Democracy." In *The Phantom Public Sphere,* edited by Bruce Robbins, 1–32. Minneapolis: University of Minnesota Press, 1993.

Fuller, Steven. "When Philosophers Are Forced to Be Literary." In *Literature as Philosophy / Philosophy as Literature,* edited by Donald G. Marshall, 24–39. Iowa City: University of Iowa Press, 1987.

Gadamer, Hans-Georg. *Truth and Method.* Translation revised by Joel Weinsheimer and Donald G. Marshall. 2nd rev. ed. New York: Crossroad, 1989.

Gaustad, Edwin S. *George Berkeley in America.* New Haven: Yale University Press, 1979.

Gay, Peter. *The Enlightenment: An Interpretation.* Vol. 1, *The Rise of Modern Paganism.* 1966. Reprint, New York: W. W. Norton, 1977.

Gerrard, Christine. *The Patriot Opposition to Walpole: Politics, Poetry, and National Myth, 1725–1742.* Oxford: Clarendon, 1994.

Goldgar, Bertrand A. *Walpole and the Wits: The Relation of Politics to Literature, 1722–1742.* Lincoln: University of Nebraska Press, 1976.

Goldsmith, M. M. *Private Vices, Public Benefits: Bernard Mandeville's Social and Political Thought.* Cambridge: Cambridge University Press, 1985.

BIBLIOGRAPHY

Gorak, Irene E. "The Satirist as Producer: Mandeville's *The Fable of the Bees Part Two.*" *Genre* 23 (spring 1990): 1–14.

Grean, Stanley. *Shaftesbury's Philosophy of Religion and Ethics: A Study in Enthusiasm.* Athens: Ohio University Press, 1967.

Gunn, J. A. W. *Beyond Liberty and Property.* Kingston: McGill-Queens University Press, 1983.

———. *Politics and the Public Interest in the Seventeenth Century.* London: Routledge & Kegan Paul, 1969.

Habermas, Jürgen. *Knowledge and Human Interests.* Translated by Jeremy J. Shapiro. Boston: Beacon, 1971.

———. *The Structural Transformation of the Public Sphere: An Inquiry into a Category of Bourgeois Society.* Translated by Thomas Burger with the assistance of Frederick Lawrence. Cambridge: MIT Press, 1989.

Hampton, Jean. *Hobbes and the Social Contract Tradition.* Cambridge: Cambridge University Press, 1986.

Harris, Michael. "Print and Politics in the Age of Walpole." In *Britain in the Age of Walpole,* edited by Jeremy Black, 189–210. London: Macmillan, 1984.

Harth, Phillip. *Contexts of Dryden's Thought.* Chicago: University of Chicago Press, 1968.

———. *Pen for a Party: Dryden's Tory Propaganda in Its Contexts.* Princeton: Princeton University Press, 1993.

———. "The Satiric Purpose of *The Fable of the Bees.*" *Eighteenth-Century Studies* 2 (summer 1969): 321–40.

Hayek, F. A. "Dr. Bernard Mandeville." *Proceedings of the British Academy* 52 (1967): 125–41.

Hill, Christopher. *The Century of Revolution, 1603–1714.* 2nd ed. New York: W. W. Norton, 1982.

Hirschman, Albert O. *The Passions and the Interests: Political Arguments for Capitalism before Its Triumph.* Princeton: Princeton University Press, 1977.

Hirzel, Rudolph. *Der Dialog: Ein Literarhistorischer Versuch.* 2 vols. 1895. Reprint, Hildescheim: Georg Olms Verlagsbuchhandlung, 1963.

Hohendahl, Peter Uwe. *The Institution of Criticism.* Ithaca: Cornell University Press, 1982.

Holdsworth, William. *A History of English Law.* 16 vols. 3rd ed. 1945. Reprint, London: Methuen, 1966.

Holmes, Stephen. Introduction to *Behemoth: Or, the Long Parliament,* by Thomas Hobbes, edited by Ferdinand Tönnies. 1889. Reprint, Chicago: University of Chicago Press, 1990.

Hopkins, Robert H. "The Cant of Social Compromise: Some Observations on Mandeville's Satire." In *Mandeville Studies: New Explorations in the Art and Thought of Dr. Bernard Mandeville*, edited by Irwin Primer, 168–92. The Hague: Martinus Nijhoff, 1975.

Horne, Thomas. "Politics in a Corrupt Society: William Arnall's Defense of Robert Walpole." *Journal of the History of Ideas* 41 (1980): 601–14.

Howell, Wilbur S. *Logic and Rhetoric in England, 1500–1700*. New York: Russell & Russell, 1961.

Hudson, Nicholas. "Dialogue and the Origins of Language: Linguistic and Social Evolution in Mandeville, Condillac, and Rousseau." In *Compendious Conversations: The Method of Dialogue in the Early Enlightenment*, edited by Kevin L. Cope, 3–14. Frankfurt: Peter Lang, 1992.

———. "Language, Abstract Thought, and Political Power in Vico, Mandeville, and Rousseau." *Studies on Voltaire and the Eighteenth Century* 303 (1992): 256–58.

Hundert, E. J. *The Enlightenment's "Fable": Bernard Mandeville and the Discovery of Society*. Cambridge: Cambridge University Press, 1994.

Hutton, Ronald. *The British Republic, 1649–1660*. New York: St. Martin's, 1990.

———. *The Restoration: A Political and Religious History of England and Wales, 1658–67*. Oxford: Clarendon, 1985.

Jack, Malcolm. *Corruption and Progress: The Eighteenth-Century Debate*. New York: AMS, 1989.

Jessop, T. E. Introduction to *Alciphron, or the Minute Philosopher*. In *The Works of George Berkeley*, edited by A. A. Luce and T. E. Jessop, 3:1–20. London: Thomas Nelson & Sons, 1950.

———. Introduction to *Three Dialogues between Hylas and Philonous*. In *The Works of George Berkeley*, edited by A. A. Luce and T. E. Jessop, 2:149–61. London: Thomas Nelson & Sons, 1949.

———. Introduction to *A Treatise concerning the Principles of Human Knowledge*. In *The Works of George Berkeley*, edited by A. A. Luce and T. E. Jessop, 2:3–17. London: Thomas Nelson & Sons, 1949.

Johnson, Laurie M. *Thucydides, Hobbes, and the Interpretation of Realism*. DeKalb: Northern Illinois University Press, 1993.

Johnston, David. *The Rhetoric of "Leviathan": Thomas Hobbes and the Politics of Cultural Transformation*. Princeton: Princeton University Press, 1986.

Jones, J. R. *The First Whigs: The Politics of the Exclusion Crisis, 1678–1683*. London: Oxford University Press, 1961.

Kahn, Victoria. "Habermas, Machiavelli, and the Humanist Critique of Ideology." *PMLA* 105 (May 1990): 464–76.

———. *Rhetoric, Prudence, and Skepticism in the Renaissance*. Ithaca: Cornell University Press, 1985.

Kantorowicz, Ernst H. *The King's Two Bodies: A Study in Mediaeval Political Theology*. Princeton: Princeton University Press, 1957.

BIBLIOGRAPHY

Kaye, F. B. Introduction to *The Fable of the Bees, or, Private Vices, Publick Benefits,* by Bernard Mandeville, edited by F. B. Kaye, 1:xvii–cxlvi. 1924. Reprint, Indianapolis: Liberty Classics, 1988.

Keeble, N. H. *The Literary Culture of Nonconformity in Later Seventeenth-Century England.* Athens: University of Georgia Press, 1987.

Kenyon, John. *The Popish Plot.* London: Heinemann, 1972.

Klein, Lawrence E. "Berkeley, Shaftesbury, and the Meaning of Politeness." In *Studies in Eighteenth-Century Culture,* vol. 16, edited by O. M. Brack Jr., 57–88. Madison: University of Wisconsin Press, 1988.

———. *Shaftesbury and the Culture of Politeness: Moral Discourse and Cultural Poetics in Early Eighteenth-Century England.* Cambridge: Cambridge University Press, 1994.

———. "The Third Earl of Shaftesbury and the Progress of Politeness." *Eighteenth-Century Studies* 18 (winter 1984–85): 186–214.

Knights, Mark. *Politics and Opinion in Crisis, 1678–81.* Cambridge: Cambridge University Press, 1994.

Knox, Ronald A. *Enthusiasm: A Chapter in the History of Religion with Special Reference to the Seventeenth and Eighteenth Centuries.* Oxford: Clarendon, 1951.

Koselleck, Reinhart. *Critique and Crisis: Enlightenment and the Pathogenesis of Modern Society.* Cambridge: MIT Press, 1988.

Kramnick, Isaac. *Bolingbroke and His Circle: The Politics of Nostalgia in the Age of Walpole.* Cambridge: Harvard University Press, 1968.

———. Introduction to *Historical Writings,* by Lord Bolingbroke (Henry St. John), edited by Isaac Kramnick. Chicago: University of Chicago Press, 1972.

Kramnick, Jonathan Brody. "'Unwilling to Be Short, or Plain, in Any Thing Concerning Gain': Bernard Mandeville and the Dialectic of Charity." *Eighteenth Century: Theory and Interpretation* 33 (summer 1992): 148–75.

Landau, Norma. "Country Matters: *The Growth of Political Stability* a Quarter-Century On." *Albion* 25 (summer 1993): 261–74.

Laslett, Peter. Introduction to *Two Treatises of Government,* by John Locke, edited by Peter Laslett. Cambridge: Cambridge University Press, 1960.

Lloyd, S. A. *Ideals as Interests in Hobbes's "Leviathan": The Power of Mind over Matter.* Cambridge: Cambridge University Press, 1992.

Macpherson, C. B. *The Political Theory of Possessive Individualism, Hobbes to Locke.* Oxford: Oxford University Press, 1962.

Markley, Robert. "Shaftesbury, Sterne, and the Theatrics of Virtue." In *The New Eighteenth Century: Theory, Politics, English Literature,* edited by Felicity Nussbaum and Laura Brown, 210–30. New York: Methuen, 1987.

———. "Style as Philosophical Structure: The Contexts of Shaftesbury's *Characteristicks.*" In *The Philosopher as Writer: The Eighteenth Century,* edited by Robert Ginsberg, 140–54. Selinsgrove, Pa.: Susquehanna University Press, 1987.

Maxwell, J. C. "Ethics and Politics in Mandeville." *Philosophy* 26 (July 1951): 242–52.

McKeon, Richard. *Freedom and History and Other Essays: An Introduction to the Thought of Richard McKeon.* Edited by Zahava K. McKeon. Chicago: University of Chicago Press, 1990.

Meier, Thomas Keith. *Defoe and the Defense of Commerce.* English Literary Studies, 38. Victoria, B.C.: University of Victoria, 1987.

Merrill, Elizabeth. *The Dialogue in English Literature.* Yale Studies in English 42. New York: Henry Holt, 1911.

Morrisroe, Michael, Jr. "Ciceronian, Platonic, and Neo-Classic Dialogues: Forms in Berkeley and Hume." *Enlightenment Essays* 3 (fall/winter 1973): 147–59.

Neel, Jasper. "The Degradation of Rhetoric; or, Dressing Like a Gentleman, Speaking Like a Scholar." In *Rhetoric, Sophistry, Pragmatism,* edited by Steven Mailloux, 61–81. Cambridge: Cambridge University Press, 1995.

Norton, David Fate. *Shaftesbury and Two Skepticisms.* Studi e Ricerche di Storia Della Filosofia, 96. Turin: Edizioni di Filosofia, 1968.

Okin, Susan Moller. "'The Soveraign and his Counsellours': Hobbes's Reevaluation of Parliament." *Political Theory* 10 (1982): 49–75.

Olscamp, Paul J. *The Moral Philosophy of George Berkeley.* The Hague: Martinus Nijhoff, 1970.

Pagden, Anthony, ed. *The Languages of Political Theory in Early-Modern Europe.* Cambridge: Cambridge University Press, 1987.

Peters, Richard. *Hobbes.* Harmondsworth: Penguin, 1956.

Pettit, Alexander. *Illusory Consensus: Bolingbroke and the Polemical Response to Walpole, 1730–1737.* Newark: University of Delaware Press, 1997.

Phillipson, Nicholas. "Politics and Politeness in the Reigns of Anne and the Early Hanoverians." In *The Varieties of British Political Thought, 1500–1800,* edited by J. G. A. Pocock with Gordon J. Schochet and Lois G. Schwoerer, 211–45. Cambridge: Cambridge University Press, 1993.

Pincus, Steven. "'Coffee Politicians Does Create': Coffeehouses and Restoration Political Culture." *Journal of Modern History* 67 (December 1995): 807–34.

Pitcher, George. *Berkeley.* London: Routledge & Kegan Paul, 1977.

Pitkin, Hanna Fenichel. *The Concept of Representation.* Berkeley: University of California Press, 1967.

Plumb, J. H. *The Growth of Political Stability in England, 1675–1725.* London: Macmillan, 1967.

Pocock, J. G. A. *The Ancient Constitution and the Feudal Law: A Study of English Historical Thought in the Seventeenth Century.* 1957. Cambridge: Cambridge University Press, 1987.

————. Historical introduction to *The Political Works of James Harrington*, edited by J. G. A. Pocock, 1–152. Cambridge: Cambridge University Press, 1977.

————. "James Harrington and the Good Old Cause." *Journal of British Studies* 10 (1970): 30–48.

————. *The Machiavellian Moment: Florentine Political Thought and the Atlantic Republican Tradition.* Princeton: Princeton University Press, 1975.

————. *Politics, Language, and Time: Essays on Political Thought and History.* 1971. Chicago: University of Chicago Press, 1989.

————. *Virtue, Commerce, and History: Essays on Political Thought and History, Chiefly in the Eighteenth Century.* Cambridge: Cambridge University Press, 1985.

Popkin, Richard H. *The High Road to Pyrrhonism.* Edited by Richard A. Watson and James E. Force. San Diego: Austin Hill, 1980.

Potkay, Adam. *The Fate of Eloquence in the Age of Hume.* Ithaca: Cornell University Press, 1994.

Price, Martin. *To the Palace of Wisdom: Studies in Order and Energy from Dryden to Blake.* Garden City, N.Y.: Doubleday, 1964.

Primer, Irwin. "Mandeville and Shaftesbury: Some Facts and Problems." In *Mandeville Studies: New Explorations in the Art and Thought of Dr. Bernard Mandeville,* edited by Irwin Primer, 126–41. The Hague: Martinus Nijhoff, 1975.

————, ed. *Mandeville Studies: New Explorations in the Art and Thought of Dr. Bernard Mandeville.* The Hague: Martinus Nijhoff, 1975.

Prince, Michael. *Philosophical Dialogue in the British Enlightenment: Theology, Aesthetics, and the Novel.* Cambridge: Cambridge University Press, 1996.

Prostko, Jack. "'Natural Conversation Set in View': Shaftesbury and Moral Speech." *Eighteenth-Century Studies* 23 (fall 1989): 42–61.

Purpus, Eugene R. "'The Plain, Easy, and Familiar Way': The Dialogue in English Literature, 1660–1725." *ELH* 17 (1950): 47–58.

Richetti, John J. *Philosophical Writing: Locke, Berkeley, Hume.* Cambridge: Harvard University Press, 1983.

Robbins, Caroline. *The Eighteenth-Century Commonwealthman: Studies in the Transmission, Development, and Circumstance of English Liberal Thought from the Restoration of Charles II until the War with the Thirteen Colonies.* Cambridge: Harvard University Press, 1961.

————, ed. *Two English Republican Tracts.* Cambridge: Cambridge University Press, 1969.

Roberts, Clayton. "The Growth of Political Stability Reconsidered." *Albion* 25 (summer 1993): 237–56.

Rogers, Pat. "Shaftesbury and the Aesthetics of Rhapsody." *British Journal of Aesthetics* 12 (summer 1972): 244–57.

Rogow, Arnold A. *Thomas Hobbes: Radical in the Service of Reaction.* New York: W. W. Norton, 1986.

Rosenberg, Nathan. "Mandeville and Laissez-Faire." *Journal of the History of Ideas* 24 (1963): 183–96.

Schwoerer, Lois G. "Liberty of the Press and Public Opinion: 1660–1695." In *Liberty Secured? Britain Before and After 1688,* edited by J. R. Jones, 199–230. Stanford: Stanford University Press, 1992.

Sekora, John. *Luxury: The Concept in Western Thought, Eden to Smollett.* Baltimore: Johns Hopkins University Press, 1977.

Shapiro, Gary. "Reading and Writing in the Text of Hobbes's *Leviathan.*" *Journal of the History of Philosophy* 18 (April 1980): 147–57.

Shields, David S. *Civil Tongues and Polite Letters.* Chapel Hill: University of North Carolina Press, 1997.

Silver, Victoria. "Hobbes on Rhetoric." In *The Cambridge Companion to Hobbes,* edited by Tom Sorell, 329–45. Cambridge: Cambridge University Press, 1996.

———. "A Matter of Interpretation." *Critical Inquiry* 20 (autumn 1993): 160–71.

Skinner, Quentin. *Rhetoric and Reason in the Philosophy of Hobbes.* Cambridge: Cambridge University Press, 1996.

Solkin, David H. *Painting for Money: The Visual Arts and the Public Sphere in Eighteenth-Century England.* New Haven: Yale University Press, 1993.

Sorell, Tom. "Hobbes's Persuasive Civil Science." *Philosophical Quarterly* 40 (1990): 342–51.

Stolnitz, Jerome. "On the Origins of 'Aesthetic Disinterestedness.'" *Journal of Aesthetics and Art Criticism* 20 (winter 1961): 131–43.

Stoner, James R., Jr. *Common Law and Liberal Theory: Coke, Hobbes, and the Origins of American Constitutionalism.* Lawrence: University Press of Kansas, 1992.

Strauss, Leo. *The Political Philosophy of Hobbes: Its Basis and Its Genesis.* Translated by Elsa M. Sinclair. 1936. Reprint, Chicago: University of Chicago Press, 1952.

Strong, Tracy B. "How to Write Scripture: Words, Authority, and Politics in Thomas Hobbes." *Critical Inquiry* 20 (autumn 1993): 128–59.

———. "When Is a Text Not a Pretext? A Rejoinder to Victoria Silver," *Critical Inquiry* 20 (autumn 1993): 172–78.

Struever, Nancy S. "The Conversable World: Eighteenth-Century Transformations of the Relation of Rhetoric and Truth." In *Rhetoric and the Pursuit of Truth: Language Change in the Seventeenth and Eighteenth Centuries,* 77–119. Los Angeles: William Andrews Clark Memorial Library, 1985.

Sullivan, Robert E. *John Toland and the Deist Controversy: A Study in Adaptations.* Cambridge: Harvard University Press, 1982.

Tuveson, Ernest Lee. *The Imagination as a Means of Grace: Locke and the Aesthetics of Romanticism.* 1960. Reprint, New York: Gordian Press, 1974.

BIBLIOGRAPHY

Uphaus, Robert W. "Satire, Verification, and *The Fable of the Bees.*" *Papers on Language and Literature* 12 (spring 1976): 142–49.

Vickers, Brian. "Territorial Disputes: Philosophy *versus* Rhetoric." In *Rhetoric Revalued.* Edited by Brian Vickers. Binghamton, N.Y.: Center for Medieval and Early Renaissance Studies, 1982.

Viner, Jacob. Introduction to *A Letter to Dion,* by Bernard Mandeville. Augustan Reprint Society, 41. Los Angeles: William Andrews Clark Memorial Library, 1953.

Voitle, Robert. *The Third Earl of Shaftesbury, 1671–1713.* Baton Rouge: Louisiana State University Press, 1984.

Von Maltzahn, Nicholas. "Henry Neville and the Art of the Possible: A Republican *Letter Sent to General Monk* (1660)." *Seventeenth Century* 7 (1992): 41–52.

Walmsley, Peter. *The Rhetoric of Berkeley's Philosophy.* Cambridge: Cambridge University Press, 1990.

Walzer, Michael. "A Critique of Philosophical Conversation." *Philosophical Forum* 21 (fall-winter 1989–90): 182–96.

Warnke, Georgia. *Gadamer: Hermeneutics, Tradition, and Reason.* New York: Polity, 1987.

Warnock, G. J. "On Passive Obedience." *History of European Ideas* 7 (1986): 555–62.

Weinsheimer, Joel. *Gadamer's Hermeneutics.* New Haven: Yale University Press, 1985.

Whelan, Frederick G. "Language and Its Abuses in Hobbes's Political Philosophy." *American Political Science Review* 75 (1981): 59–75.

Whitaker, S. F. "The First Edition of Shaftesbury's *Moralists.*" *Library,* 5th ser., 7 (1952): 235–41.

Wieseltier, Leon. "Total Quality Meaning." *New Republic,* 19 and 26 July 1993, 16–26.

Williams, Raymond. *Keywords: A Vocabulary of Culture and Society.* Rev. ed. New York: Oxford University Press, 1983.

Wilson, K. J. *Incomplete Fictions: The Formation of English Renaissance Dialogue.* Washington, D.C.: Catholic University of America Press, 1985.

Woodmansee, Martha. *The Author, Art, and the Market: Rereading the History of Aesthetics.* New York: Columbia University Press, 1994.

Zappen, James P. "Aristotelian and Ramist Rhetoric in Thomas Hobbes's *Leviathan:* Pathos versus Ethos and Logos." *Rhetorica* 1 (1983): 65–92.

Zwicker, Stephen N. "Lines of Authority: Politics and Literary Culture in the Restoration." In *Politics of Discourse: The Literature and History of Seventeenth-Century England,* edited by Kevin Sharpe and Stephen N. Zwicker, 230–70. Berkeley: University of California Press, 1987.

INDEX

INDEX

INDEX

L'Estrange, Roger, 5, 10, 117, 170; *Citt and Bumpkin*, 7; *The Intelligencer*, 10; *Toleration Discuss'd*, 5
Licensing Act, 4, 5, 162
Lloyd, S. A., 177 n. 8, 179 n. 27
Locke, John, 3, 13, 80, 114, 137–38, 143, 148, 152, 154, 163; *An Essay Concerning Human Understanding*, 136, 184 n. 17, 187 n. 18; *Two Treatises of Government*, 6, 174 n. 16
London Journal, 170
Long Parliament, 28, 46, 55
Luce, A. A., 136
Lucian, 12–13

Machiavelli, Niccolò, *The Prince*, 30
Macpherson, C. B., 182 n. 6
Mandeville, Bernard, 15–17, 132–33, 136–37, 152, 158; on audience, 129–30; on charity schools, 117, 192 n. 22; on class difference, 108–9, 111; on commerce, 105, 111; on dialogue, 118–20, 191 n. 12; on the discursive nature of the social bond, 105–6, 110; on disinterestedness, 116, 122, 128; on dissimulation, 105; on diversity, 111–12; on dueling, 119–20; economic theory of, 190 n. 2, 191 n. 14, 194 n. 2; on emulation, 108–9; on enlightenment, 121, 123–24, 126, 129–30, 197 n. 32; irony of, 120, 123, 192 n. 18; on liberty, 165–66; on moral reform, 116–17; on the origin of society, 107–10, 191 n. 9; on polite conversation, 115–18; on politics, 191 n. 16; politics of, 165–66, 190 n. 4; public sphere of, 130–31, 193 n. 32; as satirist, 190 n. 5; skepticism of, 190 n. 3; on "skilful Politicians," 105, 107–8, 127, 167–68, 193 n. 28; on sociability, 110–11; on speculation, 167–68; on virtue, 109, 115, 118, 123–24, 129–30, 193 n. 30; on women, 193 n. 33. Works: *An Enquiry into the Origin of Honour*, 127, 191 n. 12; "An Enquiry into the Origin of Moral Virtue," 107–9; "An Essay on Charity, and Charity-Schools," 117–18, 129; *The Fable of the Bees*, 15, 16, 105–31, 167, 169; *Free Thoughts on Religion, the Church,*

and National Happiness, 120, 190 n. 3; "The Grumbling Hive," 107, 116–17; *A Letter to Dion*, 165; *The Mischiefs that Ought Justly to be Apprehended from a Whig-Government*, 190 n. 4, 191 n. 12; "A Search into the Nature of Society," 109, 115–16, 190 n. 6; *A Treatise on the Hypochondriack and Hysterick Passions*, 191 n. 12; *The Virgin Unmask'd*, 191 n. 12
Marcet, Jane, 199 n. 5
Markley, Robert, 188 nn. 24, 27
Marx, Karl, 192 n. 20
Maxwell, J. C, 190 n. 3
McKeon, Richard, 8, 174 n. 25
Meier, Thomas Keith, 192 n. 23
Merrill, Elizabeth, 174 n. 24
Milton, John: *Areopagetica*, 9; *The Readie and Easie Way to Establish a Free Commonwealth*, 75
Modest Attempt for Healing the Present Animosities in England, A, 18–19
monarchy, 62. *See also* absolutism; Hobbes, Thomas: on sovereignty
Monck, George, 61–62, 185 n. 33
More, Thomas, *Utopia*, 9
Morrice, Bezaleel, *The Present Corruption of Britons*, 163
Morrisroe, Michael, Jr., 196 n. 19
Moyle, Walter, 165, 184–85 n. 28

natural law, Hobbes's definition of, 177 n. 6
Neel, Jasper, 189 n. 31
Neville, Henry, 14, 52, 56, 60, 72, 74–76, 84–85, 169, 183 n. 17, 184 n. 22, n. 24; on democracy, 182–83 n. 8; parliamentary career of, 56, 65, 183 n. 15; *The Parliament of Ladies*, 55; *Plato Redivivus*, 14, 52–54, 56–60, 65–71, 73, 75–76, 85; view of audience, 65, 74
Newton, Isaac, 197 n. 38
Norton, David Fate, 80, 186 n. 4
Norton, Thomas, 196 n. 22
Nowell, Alexander, 196 n. 22

Okin, Susan Moller, 181 n. 46
Olscamp, Paul J., 195 n. 8, n. 10
Onslow, Richard, *A Dialogue between the Pope and a Phanatick, Concerning Affairs in England*, 7